Scott Foresman
Reading
Off We Go!

Grade K, Unit 5

Off We Go!

scottforesman.com

Editorial Offices: Glenview, Illinois • Parsippany, New Jersey • New York, New York
Sales Offices: Parsippany, New Jersey • Duluth, Georgia, • Glenview, Illinois
Carrollton, Texas • Ontario, California

About the Cover Artist

While Lyn Martin was growing up in Tennessee, her father let her work in his paint store, where
she learned all about colors and how to mix them. Since she also loved to draw and read, painting
pictures for stories is the perfect job for her.

ISBN 0-328-01826-0

12345678910V0631009080706050403 0201

Program Authors

Peter Afflerbach, Ph.D.

Professor, Department of Curriculum and Instruction, Director of The Reading Center, University of Maryland at College Park; Member of the Board of Directors of the National Reading Conference; Advisor to the National Assessment of Educational Progress and the Voluntary National Test of Reading
Research Contributions: Assessment, Reading Comprehension, Strategic Reading

James W. Beers, Ph.D.

Professor, School of Education, College of William & Mary, Williamsburg, Virginia; Director of the Eastern Virginia Writing Project of the National Writing Project; Author of Scott Foresman-Addison Wesley's *Everyday Spelling*
Research Contributions: Intervention Strategies, Phonics and Spelling in Literacy Development, Writing for Critical Thinking

Camille L. Z. Blachowicz, Ph.D.

Professor of Education, Codirector of The Reading Leadership Institute, National College of Education, National–Louis University, Evanston, Illinois
Research Contributions: Comprehension Development, Vocabulary Instruction, Staff Development

Candy Dawson Boyd, Ph.D.

Professor, School of Education, Saint Mary's College, Moraga, California; Founder and Director of the Masters and Specialist Credential and Certificate Programs in Reading/Language Arts; Award-Winning Children's Author
Research Contributions: Cultural Diversity, Early Literacy, Intervention Strategies, Multicultural Literature

Wendy Cheyney, Ed.D.

Professor of Special Education, Department of Educational Psychology and Special Education, Associate Dean for Academic Affairs, College of Education, Florida International University, University Park Campus, Miami
Research Contributions: Phonological and Phonemic Awareness, Early Literacy

Deborah Diffily, Ph.D.

Assistant Professor, Early Childhood Education, Southern Methodist University, Dallas, Texas

Dolores Gaunty-Porter, Ph.D.

Professor of Literacy, Language, and Learning, School of Education, Chapman University, Orange County, California
Research Contributions: English as a Second Language, Inclusion, Staff Development

Connie Juel, Ph.D.

Professor of Education, Director of the Jeanne Chall Reading Lab, Graduate School of Education, Harvard University, Cambridge, Massachusetts
Research Contributions: Literacy Development, Word Recognition Instruction, Reading Difficulties

Donald J. Leu, Ph.D.

John and Maria Neag Endowed Chair in Literacy and Technology, Neag School of Education, University of Connecticut, Storrs-Mansfield; Member of the Board of Directors for the National Reading Conference; Member of the Research Committee for the International Reading Association
Research Contributions: Reading Comprehension, Technology in the Classroom

Jeanne R. Paratore, Ed.D.

Associate Professor of Education, Department of Developmental Studies, Boston University; Founder of the Intergenerational Literacy Project; Member of the Board of Directors of the International Reading Association
Research Contributions: Intervention Strategies, Grouping Practices, School-Home Partnerships

Sam L. Sebesta, Ed.D.

Professor Emeritus, College of Education, University of Washington, Seattle
Research Contributions: Children's Literature, Decoding in Linguistic Development, Oral Reading Fluency, Reader Response

Karen Kring Wixson, Ph.D.

Dean of the School of Education and Professor of Education, University of Michigan, Ann Arbor; Advisor to the National Research Council; Co-Director of the Michigan English Language Arts Framework Project
Research Contributions: Alignment of Reading Curriculum and Assessment, Instruction for Reading and Writing Disabilities, Development of Thematic Units

Consultants and Reviewers

Consultants

Consulting Authors

Carol Berkin, Ph.D Professor of History
Baruch College, City University of New York:
Reading in the Content Areas

Anna Uhl Chamot, Ph.D Associate Professor of ESL
George Washington University, Washington, D.C.:
English as a Second Language

Jim Cummins, Ph.D Professor
Modern Language Centre and Curriculum Department
Ontario Institute for Studies in Education, Toronto, Canada:
English as a Second Language

Karen Erickson, Ph.D Assistant Professor
Department of Education, University of New Hampshire,
Durham: *Intervention Strategies, Learning Styles*

George González, Ph.D Professor (Retired)
School of Education, University of Texas Pan-American,
Edinburg: *Bilingual Education, English as a Second Language*

Lily Wong Fillmore, Ph.D Professor
Graduate School of Education, University of California, Berkeley:
English as a Second Language

Priscilla Griffith, Ph.D Professor and Department Head
Curriculum and Instruction, College of Education and Health
Professions, University of Arkansas at Fayetteville:
Phonemic Awareness, Phonics Instruction, Writing

Carolyn Kessler, Ph.D Professor Emerita of ESL
University of Texas, San Antonio: *English as a Second Language*

Jackson Lee, Jr., Ed.D Professor of Education
Francis Marion University, Florence, South Carolina:
Reading in the Content Areas

Senior Consultants

Margaret Gritsavich, C.A.S. Faculty Associate
Arizona State University, Tempe: *Writing, Assessment*

Nancy Reeves Radcliffe, Ph.D.
Houston Baptist University, Houston, Texas: *Gifted and Talented*

Reviewers

Student Edition

Connie Barnhart Second and Third Grade Teacher
Gilder Elementary School, Bellevue, Nebraska

Cheryl Borovitcky Second Grade Teacher and President
Mahoni Valley Council, Ohio Council IRA, Poland City Schools
Youngstown, Ohio

Gail F. Brown Reading Specialist
Perrymont Elementary School, Lynchburg, Virginia

Julia M. Chaney Reading Specialist
Taylor Elementary School, Hobbs, New Mexico

Ynette Colyer Third Grade Teacher
Bel Air Elementary, Albuquerque, New Mexico

Barbara Giese Fourth Grade Teacher
Rocky Run Elementary Schools, Fredericksburg, Virginia

Lloyd Hardesty CCIRA President 2002–2003
Colorado Springs, Colorado

Jeannene A. Henry Reading Methods Instructor
Prescott SD, Prescott, Arizona

Karen R. Jackson Third Grade Teacher
Joseph Leidy Elementary School, Philadelphia, Pennsylvania

Laura Kaiser Literacy Staff Developer
PS 222, Brooklyn, New York

Collette M. Martin Reading Specialist
Mary Carr Creer Elementary, Charlottesville, Virginia

Louise McGinnis First Grade Teacher
Golden Grove Elementary School, West Palm Beach, Florida

Sherri Moss First Grade Teacher
Bethune Elementary School, Hollywood, Florida

Catherine M. Radu Reading and Language Arts
Consultant, Traverse City Schools, Traverse City, Michigan

Tamara Jo Rhomberg
Rockwood School District, Eureka, Missouri

Amy D. Taylor First Grade Teacher
Twinbrook Elementary School, Rockville, Maryland

Sharon B. Webber Fifth Grade Teacher

Teacher's Edition

Robin Atwood First Grade Teacher
Taylorsville Elementary School, Taylorsville, Mississippi

Mari Carlson Reading Coordinator
Waukegan School District, Waukegan, Illinois

Paul A. Coleman Assistant Principal
Montview Elementary School, Aurora, Colorado

Catherine Fox
Englishtown, New Jersey

Judith W. Gillette Title One Director
Standish Elementary School, Bay City, Michigan

Charlotte Hall Teacher on Assignment
Grinnett County Curriculum Center, Lawrenceville, Georgia

Linda Hinton First Grade Teacher
Soldier Creek Elementary, Midwest, Oklahoma

Carol Ann Hulton Reading Coordinator
Talmadge School, Springfield, Massachusetts

Nicki Johnson First Grade Teacher
Wildewood Elementary School, Ralston, Nebraska

Kim King Sixth Grade Teacher
Soldier Creek Elementary, Midwest, Oklahoma

Catherine Kuhns First Grade Teacher
Country Hill School, Coral Springs, Florida

Pamela J. McAtee First Grade Teacher
Target Range Elementary School, Missoula, Montana

Dr. Janet Perrin
Thomas J. Lahey Elementary, Greenlawn, New York

Tamara Jo Rhomberg
Rockwood School District, Eureka, Missouri

Dr. Mae S. Sheftall Title I Coordinator
Bibb County Public School, Macon, Georgia

Dr. Maureen Siera Professor of Education
St. Martins College, Kent, Washington

Linda Squires Reading Specialist
Southern Heights Elementary, Hobbs, New Mexico

Scheneithia Stickler First Grade Teacher
Signal Hills Elementary School, Manassas, Virginia

Dr. Margaret Timmons Language Arts Supervisor
Paterson Public Schools, Paterson, New Jersey

Janet Titensor deHoyos Second Grade Teacher
Joaquin Elementary School, Provo, Utah

Anita R. Turner District Reading Specialist
Carver Educational Center, Gambrills, Maryland

Joetta Whiteley First Grade Teacher
Crosby Park Elementary, Lawton, Oklahoma

Kindergarten

Ellen M. Christie Kindergarten Teacher
Holland Elementary School, Satellite Beach, Florida

Leslie Coburn Kindergarten Teacher
Middleburg Elementary School, Middleburg, Virginia

Sandra Connolly Kindergarten Teacher
Ralph Blevins Elementary, Eureka, Missouri

Trisha Evans Kindergarten Teacher
Madison Elementary School, Ocala, Florida

Debra R. Friedman Kindergarten and First Grade Teacher
Welleby Elementary School Sunrise, Florida

Cynthia Giovo Kindergarten Teacher
Millard Hawk Primary School, Central Square, New York

Gwen Mora Kindergarten Teacher
Hillsborough County, Temple Terrace, Florida

Rebecca Pickard Kindergarten Teacher
Arrowhead Elementary School, Glendale, Arizona

Robin Robb Kindergarten Teacher
Indialantic Elementary School, Indialantic, Florida

Marilyn Russell Kindergarten Teacher
Southside Estates Elementary, Jacksonville, Florida

Dr. Mae S. Sheftall Title I Coordinator
Bibb County Public School, Macon, Georgia

Linda Sholar Kindergarten Teacher
Sangre Ridge Elementary, Stillwater, Oklahoma

Dot Solenski Kindergarten Teacher
Riverglades Elementary School, Parkland, Florida

Every child will succeed.

Every child will be a successful reader

who is prepared for both state and national tests.

This is the goal of Scott Foresman Reading.

And because we are so committed to this goal,

we put accountability at the heart of our story.

We are accountable, just like you,

for the development of kindergartners

who are ready and eager for first grade.

Scott Foresman
Reading

*E*very child is like no other child in the world.

With Scott Foresman Reading, every child succeeds because accountability is built into every part of the program.

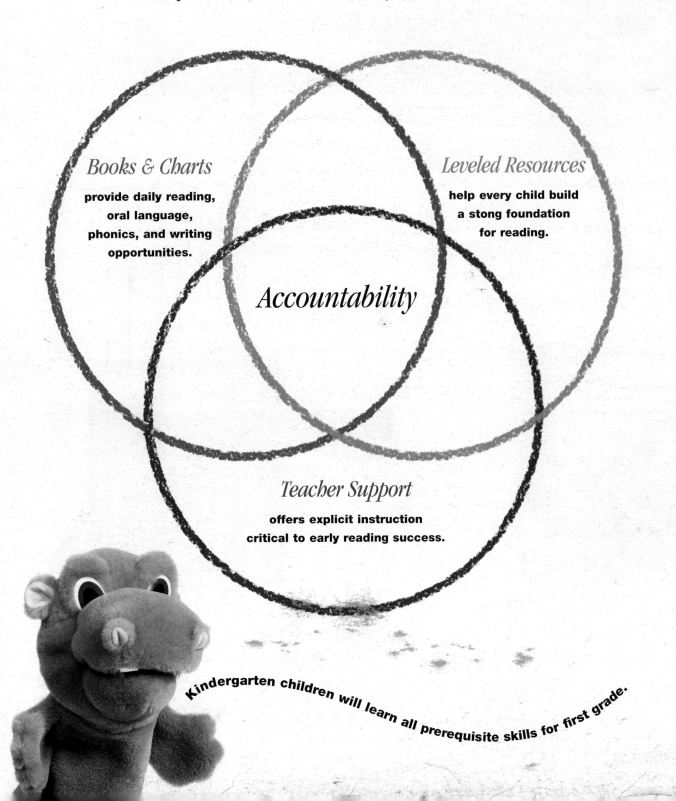

Books & Charts
provide daily reading,
oral language,
phonics, and writing
opportunities.

Leveled Resources
help every child build
a stong foundation
for reading.

Accountability

Teacher Support
offers explicit instruction
critical to early reading success.

Kindergarten children will learn all prerequisite skills for first grade.

Books & Charts: For Daily Instruction

Build reading and language skills every day.

Begin with Daily Reading

- 22 Big Books or 15 Trade Books, one per week
- Targets a comprehension skill each week
- Provides opportunities for guided reading and language development throughout the week
- Introduces all letters and their sounds, and 36 sight words

Follow with Daily Oral Language

- Oral Language Flip Chart, 36 charts, one per week
- Classic and contemporary poems for reading aloud
- Develops the target oral language skill of the week
- Provides activities for speaking, listening, and building vocabulary

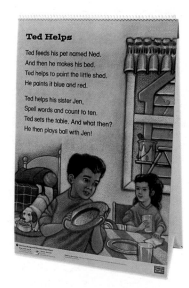

Continue with Daily Phonics

- Phonics Songs and Rhymes Flip Chart, 36 charts, one per week
- Provides engaging songs and predictable rhymes
- Develops the target phonics skill of the week
- Builds phonemic awareness, connects sound to letters, and reinforces phonological awareness

Finish with Daily Writing

- Introduces various types of writing each week
- Shared Writing on Day 1 and Day 5
- Modeled Writing and Guided Writing on Day 2 and Day 3
- Interactive Writing on Day 4
- Independent Writing on Day 5

Additional practice every day.

Full-Day Options

- Provide daily extension activities for full-day kindergarten classrooms
- Apply and practice reading, oral language, phonics, writing, and handwriting skills
- Ensure mastery of target skills

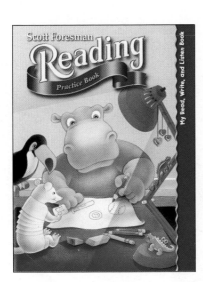

My Read, Write, and Listen Practice Book

- Provides additional phonics, reading, and writing practice for each weekly selection
- Helps you assess children's understanding of concepts
- Includes "Family Times" books for at-home practice each week
- Includes "My Little Book" take-home books for each unit

Every child deserves the very best.

Leveled Resources: For Every Child

Leveled books and practice for each week.

Wordless Story

- For oral language development
- Builds story concepts through pictures
- Invites children to identify objects with the same sound as the target phonics skill of the week
- 36 titles, one per week
- Reproducible take-home version available

Kindergarten Reader

- For children developing skills at grade level
- Additional practice for each week's target phonics skill
- Reinforces assessed high-frequency words
- Lesson plan to model writing in the Teacher's Edition
- 36 titles, one per week
- Reproducible take-home version available

the mug

Independent Reader

- For children who are reading on their own
- Additional practice for the week's target comprehension skill
- Reinforces assessed high-frequency words
- 36 titles, one per week
- Lesson plans in the Independent Reader Resource Guide

s a fish.

My fish can swim.

For hands-on learners.

Effective tools for active skills development

Children enter kindergarten with vastly different backgrounds and experiences. Scott Foresman Reading provides a variety of multisensory materials to make learning active and rewarding for each child at his or her particular level.

- **Alphabet Picture Cards** for developing children's understanding of the alphabetic principle

- **Alphapotamus Puppet** that motivates children and helps introduce the letters of the alphabet

- **Magnetic Word-Building Cards** with letters, phonograms, and high-frequency words

- **Student Phonics and Word-Building Board** to build words and sentences with the Magnetic Word-Building Cards

- **Teacher Phonics and Word-Building Board** for group demonstrations using the Magnetic Word-Building Cards

- **Phonics Activity Mats** to help children practice phonics elements and develop phonemic awareness

- **Picture/Word Cards** for phonics instruction and practice

- **Word-Building Wall and Cards** to practice letter recognition, letter-sound correspondences, and high-frequency words

Every child shines like a little star.

Teacher Support: For Reading Success

Direct, explicit instruction every day of the week.

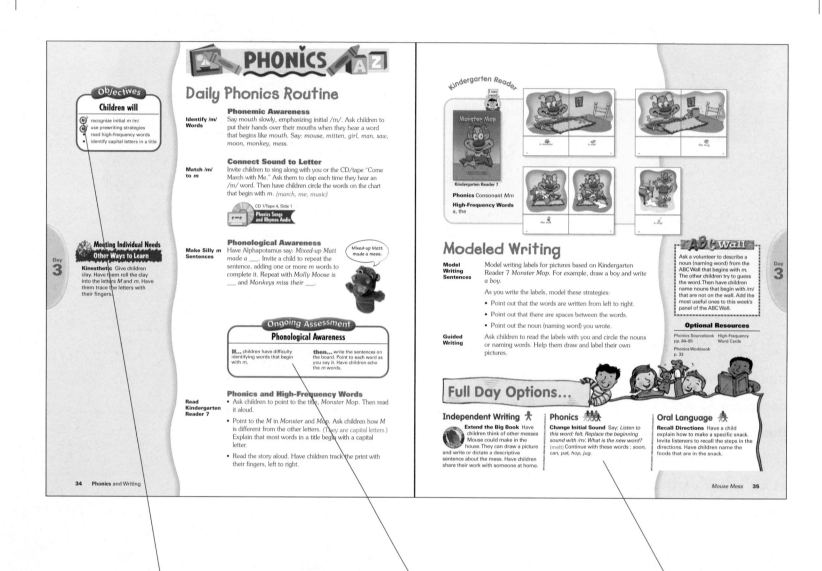

Teach

Each week targets a reading, phonics, oral language, and writing skill to ensure success for beginning readers.

Assess

Ongoing Assessment allows you to assess children's understanding of concepts and intervene when necessary.

Manage

Management tools help you address individual needs, flexible grouping, learning centers, and guided reading.

Built-in teacher support.

Preparing children for first grade

Scott Foresman Reading helps you teach all prerequisite skills children will need for first grade. The carefully designed lesson plan balances explicit instruction with strategies for managing an effective learning environment.

- **Content Connections** at point of use to extend learning across the curriculum

- **Cross-Curricular Work Stations** to support weekly learning centers in your classroom

- **Daily Explicit Instruction** for reading, oral language, phonics, and writing

- **5-Day Planner** for easy lesson planning

- **Full-Day Options** with extension activities for full-day kindergarten classrooms

- **Guiding the Reading** suggestions at point of use to develop critical thinking skills

- **Language Development** strategies at point of use to build reading-related skills

- **Meeting Individual Needs** strategies to support diverse learning styles and needs every day

- **Message Board** for daily warm-up activities that reinforce the week's target skills

- **Phonics and Phonemic Awareness Literacy Activities** to extend weekly phonics instruction

- **Reaching Every Student** unit guide to ensure that every child is successful

- **Reader Response** with oral language/vocabulary and comprehension activities after each main selection

- **Welcome to Kindergarten** guide for establishing effective classroom routines

Every child needs a hand to hold.

Program Organization

Kindergarten

**22 Big Books
(Including an
Alphabet Big Book)**

**15 Read Aloud
Trade Books**

Oral Language Chart

**Phonics Songs and
Rhymes Chart**

**6 Teacher's Editions
(1 per unit)**

Grade 1

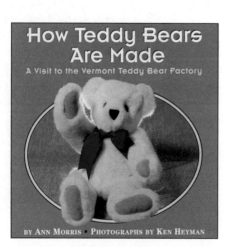

**Kindergarten
Review**

13 Big Books

5 Student Books

**6 Teacher's Editions
(1 per unit)**

Grades 2–3

2 Student Books

**6 Teacher's Editions
(1 per unit)**

Grades 4–6

**6 Teacher's Editions
(1 per unit)**

1 Student Book

*Every child
matters most
of all.*

Program Components

Assessment

Assessment Handbook contains information about conference records, self-assessment, portfolio analysis, reading progress summaries, and running records.

Benchmark Assessment and Skill Development checklists in the Kindergarten and Grade 1 (Unit 1) Teacher's Edition track skill development over the course of the year.

Individual Reading Inventory and Running Record provides diagnostic information about individual students and helps with instructional and placement decisions.

Kindergarten Skills Assessment collects information about a child's reading, writing, and language skills development.

Placement Tests identify instructional needs and establish a baseline for each student.

Running Record and Miscue Analysis guidelines are included in each Teacher's Edition.

Selection Tests help you assess student abilities and monitor progress.

"Test Talk" Transparencies contain additional short response, extended response, and multiple-choice questions with answers.

Unit and End-of-Year Benchmark Tests help assess students' progress at the end of each unit and at the end of the school year.

Unit and End-of-Year Skills Tests measure students' ability to apply unit skills in a standardized test format.

Leveled Resources

Wordless Story develops phonemic awareness, oral language skills, and key story concepts for kindergartners.

Kindergarten Reader provides targeted practice of phonics skills and high-frequency words for on-level readers.

Independent Reader reinforces early reading behaviors and allows children to practice skills and strategies independently.

Independent Reader Resource Guide contains lesson plans for every Independent Reader, management ideas, ways to extend the reading, and an assessment chart.

Collection for Readers (Very Easy Reader) may be used for intervention with students reading two levels below grade level.

Easy Reader (A) provides additional direct instruction for each week's target comprehension skill and tested vocabulary and is written one to one-and-a-half years below grade level.

On-Level Reader (B) provides additional direct instruction for each week's target comprehension skill and tested vocabulary and is written on grade level to one-half year below grade level.

Challenge Reader (C) is a collection of thematically related articles, stories, and projects for each unit that can be used with students reading at or above grade level.

Leveled Reader Resource Guide A and B provides lesson plans for Leveled Readers A and B, guided reading, activity sheets, and comprehension and vocabulary support.

Leveled Reader Resource Guide C contains lesson plans for Leveled Readers C, pacing guides, research projects, comprehension support, and scoring guides.

Leveled Practice and Test Link provides leveled practice in test format for each main selection, practice tests, and test-taking strategies.

Adding English/ESL is a companion program that provides parallel ESL lessons, strategies, full-color vocabulary posters, comprehension strategy posters, and blackline masters.

Ten Important Sentences is a booklet of blackline masters, strategies, and activities that build comprehension skills for each selection.

Trade Book Library for self-selected reading features a thematically related On-Level and Challenge book for each unit.

Phonics

Decodable Readers provide decodable text for blending practice, application of sound-spelling patterns, and cumulative review.

Decodable Readers Teaching Guide contains lessons for each Decodable Reader, blending practice, spelling connections, and activities to apply decoding skills.

Phonemic Awareness and Phonics Manipulatives Kit helps you teach phonics with a variety of hands-on, word-building resources and multisensory phonics games.

Phonemic Awareness Audiocassette presents standard pronunciations of all target sounds plus blending and segmenting of sounds.

Phonics and Word-Building Board (Student) helps students build words and sentences using the magnetic word-building cards.

Phonics and Word-Building Board (Teacher) can be used with magnetic word-building cards for modeling or group work in building words and sentences.

Phonics Handbook details current research and best practices in teaching phonics and phonemic awareness.

Phonics Readers reinforce each week's target phonics skills and high-frequency words.

Phonics Songs and Rhymes Audiocassettes/CDs provide recordings of all songs and rhymes in the program plus instrumental tracks.

Phonics Songs and Rhymes Flip Chart develops phonemic awareness and phonics skills with songs and rhymes set to familiar tunes.

Phonics Songs and Rhymes Posters build phonemic awareness and help review kindergarten skills at the beginning of first grade.

Phonics Sourcebook consists of reproducible blackline master game boards, cards, and words and letters from the Phonemic Awareness and Phonics Manipulatives Kit.

Phonics Take-Home Readers are reproducible blackline versions of the Phonics Readers that students can share with their families.

Phonics Workbook contains additional paper-and-pencil practice to reinforce weekly phonics target skills.

Phonics Workbook Blackline Masters and Answer Key provides all Phonics Workbook pages in a reproducible format.

Small Group Manipulative Package provides magnetic letters, phonograms, and high-frequency word cards for working with small groups of students.

Word Wall Cards help children practice high-frequency words and can be displayed on the magnetic Word-Building Wall using magnetic clips.

Word-Building Wall is a large magnetic board you can use to make your own word wall.

Program Components

Program Components

Teacher Support

Daily Word Routines Flip Chart provides a quick, daily review of phonics/word study, vocabulary, and language skills.

Family Reading Activities Calendar is a daily activity calendar with literacy activities for students and their families.

Family Reading Guide explains key reading terms and provides effective activities to develop reading skills at home.

Grammar Practice Book provides extra practice in grammar, usage, and mechanics each week to help children apply the skills they are learning.

Graphic Organizer Flip Chart has a write-on, wipe-off surface to demonstrate reading comprehension techniques.

Graphic Organizer Transparencies model higher-level thinking skills and organize information to build comprehension.

My Read, Write, and Listen Practice Book is a full-color workbook to help kindergartners and first graders practice phonics, reading, writing, and vocabulary skills.

Oral Language Flip Chart features traditional rhymes to enhance students' oral language skills and activate prior knowledge each week.

Practice Book provides weekly practice to reinforce target skills along with tests for each main reading selection.

Spelling Workbook contains a weekly spelling pretest along with three practice worksheets that apply the spelling generalization taught each week.

Teacher's Resource Book contains blackline masters of all Practice Book pages, Selection Tests, and family activities.

Topic/Theme Posters can introduce unit themes, build background, and assess prior knowledge as well as develop students' vocabulary and phonics skills.

Vocabulary Flip Chart displays selection vocabulary in context sentences for practice and review.

Writing Transparencies model steps of the writing process for practice and discussion and include papers as models for weekly writing.

Technology

AstroWord CD-ROM reinforces phonics, vocabulary, and word study skills using an exciting intergalactic theme.

Background-Building Audiocassettes/CDs support concept development for every main selection.

BookBuilder CD-ROM motivates students to practice target comprehension skills as they create their own books.

Computer Assessment Management System lets teachers and administrators monitor, evaluate, and plan instruction based on criterion-referenced materials.

Internet Guide unlocks the power of the Web with clear explanations, projects, troubleshooting tips, and more.

The Know Zone™ provides test preparation practice online. Also available on CD-ROM for Grades K–1.

Multimedia Studio CD-ROM helps students create dynamic multimedia presentations with illustrations, photos, video clips, sound effects, and Web connections.

Reading Road Show contains skill-building videos, audio cassettes, hand puppets, and activities from Children's Television Workshop, the creators of Sesame Street.

Reading Together: The School-Home Connection Video demonstrates techniques parents can use at home to support their child's literacy development.

Scott Foresman Reading Web Site provides instant access to information, activities, and projects for students, teachers, and parents.

Selection Audiocassettes/CDs allow students to listen to each selection and follow along word for word.

Staff Development Videos (5) highlight the latest research and demonstrate best practices of master teachers.

Teacher's Resource Planner CD-ROM is a scheduling and planning tool that can print worksheets and correlate curriculum to specific objectives.

Teacher's Technology Companion CD-ROM offers an easy tutorial for integrating technology into your curriculum.

TestWorks CD-ROM can create personalized, multiple-choice tests, free-response tests, and practice worksheets.

Components by Grade Level

	K	1	2	3	4	5	6
Student Editions		●	●	●	●	●	●
Teacher's Editions	●	●	●	●	●	●	●
Big Books	●	●	●	●			
Read Aloud Trade Books	●						
Assessment							
Assessment Handbook	●	●	●	●	●	●	●
Kindergarten Skills Assessment	●						
Placement Tests	●	●	●	●	●	●	●
Selection Tests		●	●	●	●	●	●
"Test Talk" Transparencies		●	●	●	●	●	●
Unit and End-of-Year Benchmark Tests		●	●	●	●	●	●
Unit and End-of-Year Skills Test		●	●	●	●	●	●
Leveled Resources							
Wordless Story	●						
Kindergarten Reader	●						
Independent Reader	●						
Collection for Readers (Very Easy Reader)				●	●	●	●
Leveled Readers (A, B, and C)		●	●	●	●	●	●
Leveled Reader Resource Guides		●	●	●	●	●	●
Leveled Practice and Test Link	●	●	●	●	●	●	●
Adding English/ESL		●	●	●	●	●	●
Ten Important Sentences		●	●	●	●	●	●
Phonics							
Phonemic Awareness and Phonics Manipulatives Kit	●	●	●				
Phonics and Word-Building Boards	●	●	●	●	●	●	●
Phonics Readers		●	●	●			
Phonics Songs and Rhymes Audiocassettes/CDs	●	●	●	●			
Phonics Songs and Rhymes Flip Chart	●	●	●	●			
Phonics Workbook	●	●	●	●	●	●	●
Teacher Support							
Daily Word Routines Flip Chart				●	●	●	●
Grammar Practice Book		●	●	●	●	●	●
Oral Language Flip Chart	●						
Practice Book	●	●	●	●	●	●	●
Spelling Workbook				●	●	●	●
Teacher's Resource Book	●	●	●	●	●	●	●
Writing Transparencies		●	●	●	●	●	●
Technology							
Background-Building Audiocassettes/CDs	●	●	●	●	●	●	●
BookBuilder CD-ROM	●	●	●	●			
The Know Zone™	●	●	●	●	●	●	●
Selection Audiocassettes/CDs	●	●	●	●	●	●	●
Scott Foresman Reading Web Site	●	●	●	●	●	●	●
TestWorks CD-ROM	●	●	●	●	●	●	●

Contents

Off We Go!

Unit 4
Every Day Is Special

Additional Resources......AR1–AR62

Unit 5
Off We Go!

Additional Resources......AR1–AR62

Unit 6
Open the Doors

Off We Go!

Let's Explore
How do we get from here to there?

Make a Wish
How do dreams keep us going?

Unit 5 Skills Overview

		Week 1	Week 2	Week 3
Reading		Jump into the Jungle	Listen Buddy	Five Little Ducks
🎯	**Comprehension Target Skills**	🎯 Classifying 27, 32–33, 36, 40	✔ 🎯 Drawing Conclusions 65, 70–71, 74, 78	🎯 Sequence 101, 106–107, 110, 114
Comprehension Review **Vocabulary**		*Review* Predicting, 44–45 High-Frequency Words, 29	*Review* Classifying, 82–83 High-Frequency Words, 67	✔ *Review* Drawing Conclusions, 118–119 High-Frequency Words, 103
Phonics/Word Study				
🎯	**Phonics Target Skills**	✔ 🎯 Consonant *j* /j/ 28, 30, 34, 38, 42	✔ 🎯 Consonant *v* /v/ 66, 68, 72, 76, 80	✔ 🎯 Consonant *qu* /kw/ 102, 104, 108, 112, 116
Phonics Review		*Review* Consonant *w* /w/, 38	✔ *Review* Consonant *j* /j/, 76	✔ *Review* Consonant *v* /v/, 112
Oral Language **Speaking** **Listening** **Viewing**		Listen to a Poem, 19 Listen to a Big Book, 20 Build Vocabulary: Movement Words, 26, 32 Retell a Message, 32, 36, 40–41 *Review* Make Introductions, 44–45	Listen to a Poem, 55 Listen to a Trade Book, 56 Build Vocabulary: Head Words, 64, 70 Listen for Rhyming Words, 70, 74, 78–79 *Review* Retell a Message, 82–83	Listen to a Poem, 93 Listen to a Big Book, 94 Build Vocabulary: Number Words, 100, 106 Choral Reading, 106, 110, 114–116 *Review* Listen for Rhyming Words, 118–119
Writing **Grammar, Usage, and Mechanics**		Action Words, 31, 39, 43 Modeled/Guided Writing, 31, 35 Shared Writing, 29, 43 Interactive Writing, 39 Independent Writing, 43 *Review* Nouns, 39 Handwriting *Jj*, 31	Verbs Ending in -*s*, 69, 77, 81 Modeled/Guided Writing, 69, 73 Shared Writing, 67, 81 Interactive Writing, 77 Independent Writing, 81 ✔ *Review* Using Capital Letters and Periods, 77 Handwriting *Ww*, 69	✔ Complete Sentences, 105, 113, 117 Modeled/Guided Writing, 105, 109 Shared Writing, 103, 117 Interactive Writing, 113 Independent Writing, 117 *Review* Verbs Ending in -*s*, 113 Handwriting *Qq*, 105

🎯 Target Skill   *Review* Review Skill

Also in Unit 5

Projects
Ways to Go Mural, 9
Things We Wish for Game Board, 121

Storytelling
Create an Adventure Story, 230–232

Self-Selected Reading
For suggestions on Self-Selected Reading, see pages 11, 47, 85, 123, 159, and 195.

D.E.A.R.
Drop Everything And Read

Week 4	Week 5	Week 6
Corduroy	**I Need a Lunch Box**	**Franklin Plays the Game**
✔ ⟳ **Drawing Conclusions** 139, 144–145, 148, 152	⟳ **Author's Purpose** 175, 180–181, 184, 188	⟳ **Character** 211, 216–217, 220, 224
(Review) Sequence, 156–157 High-Frequency Words, 141	✔ (Review) Drawing Conclusions, 192–193 High-Frequency Words, 177	(Review) Author's Purpose, 228–229 High-Frequency Words, 213
✔ ⟳ **Short e** 140, 142, 146, 150, 154	✔ ⟳ **Consonant x /ks/** 176, 178, 182, 186, 190	✔ ⟳ **Consonant y /y/** 212, 214, 218, 222, 226
✔ (Review) Consonant qu /kw/, 150	✔ (Review) Short e, 186	✔ (Review) Consonant x /ks/, 222
Listen to a Poem, 131 Listen to a Trade Book, 132 Build Vocabulary: Furniture Words, 138, 144 ✔ Speak with Proper Grammar, 144, 148, 152–153 (Review) Choral Reading, 156–157	Listen to a Poem, 167 Listen to a Big Book, 168 Build Vocabulary: Food Words, 174, 180 Speak Well, 180, 184, 188–189 ✔ (Review) Speak with Proper Grammar, 192–193	Listen to a Poem, 203 Listen to a Trade Book, 204 Build Vocabulary: Soccer Words, 210, 216 Listen for Main Idea, 216, 220, 224–225 (Review) Speak Well, 228–229
✔ Complete Sentences, 143, 151, 155 Modeled/Guided Writing, 143, 147 Shared Writing, 141, 155 Interactive Writing, 151 Independent Writing, 155 (Review) Action Words, 151 Handwriting Ee, 143	Past Tense, 179, 187, 191 Modeled/Guided Writing, 179, 183 Shared Writing, 177, 191 Interactive Writing, 187 Independent Writing, 191 (Review) More Than One (Plural Nouns), 187 Handwriting Xx, 179	Types of Sentences, 215, 223, 227 Modeled/Guided Writing, 215, 219 Shared Writing, 213, 227 Interactive Writing, 223 Independent Writing, 227 ✔ (Review) Complete Sentences, 223 Handwriting Yy, 215

✔ Skills assessed on the Unit 5 Skills Assessment

Skills Overview 3

Reaching Every Student

Target Skills	Teach			Assess
	Teacher's Edition Comprehension and Phonics Skills	**Big Books/Trade Books** Comprehension and Phonics Skills	**Leveled Books**	**Ongoing Assessment**
⌖ **Classifying** Consonant *j*	**Lesson 1** Classifying: 27 Consonant *j* /j/: 28	**Lesson 1** *Jump into the Jungle*	**Easy** *Jelly and Jam* (25) **On-Level** *The Museum* (25) **Challenge** *In the Jungle* (25)	Teacher's Edition: 26, 28, 30, 33, 34, 36, 39, 40, 41, 42, 44
⌖ **Drawing Conclusions** Consonant *v*	**Lesson 2** Drawing Conclusions: 65 Consonant *v* /v/: 66	**Lesson 2** *Listen Buddy*	**Easy** *The Van* (26) **On-Level** *Val and Vin* (26) **Challenge** *The Dog Took It* (26)	Teacher's Edition: 65, 66, 68, 70, 71, 72, 74, 77, 78, 79, 80, 82
⌖ **Sequence** Consonant *q*	**Lesson 3** Sequence: 101 Consonant *qu* /kw/: 102	**Lesson 3** *Five Little Ducks*	**Easy** *The Queen and the Quilt* (27) **On-Level** *One, Two, Three* (27) **Challenge** *A Good Day* (27)	Teacher's Edition: 100, 102, 107, 108, 110, 112, 113, 114, 115, 116, 118
⌖ **Drawing Conclusions** Short *e*	**Lesson 4** Drawing Conclusions: 139 Short *e*: 140	**Lesson 4** *Corduroy*	**Easy** *Em, Ed, and Jet* (28) **On-Level** *Sick in Bed* (28) **Challenge** *Party at the Pond* (28)	Teacher's Edition: 138, 140, 145, 146, 148, 151, 152, 153, 154, 156
⌖ **Author's Purpose** Consonant *x*	**Lesson 5** Author's Purpose: 175 Consonant *x* /ks/: 176	**Lesson 5** *I Need a Lunch Box*	**Easy** *Six Monkeys* (29) **On-Level** *A Big Blue Box* (29) **Challenge** *My Big Yellow Hat* (29)	Teacher's Edition: 174, 176, 181, 184, 187, 188, 189, 190, 192
⌖ **Character** Consonant *y*	**Lesson 6** Character: 211 Consonant *y* /y/: 212	**Lesson 6** *Franklin Plays the Game*	**Easy** *Yoki and Yum Yum* (30) **On-Level** *Yes! We Get Wet!* (30) **Challenge** *Red and Blue Play Soccer* (30)	Teacher's Edition: 210, 212, 216, 218, 220, 222, 223, 224, 225, 226, 228

Assess		Review
Benchmark Assessment	**Skills Assessment**	**Review Skills** Comprehension and Phonics Skills
Teacher's Edition: AR1–AR3	Unit 5 Skills Assessment	Teacher's Edition: Predicting: 44 Consonant *w* /w/: 38
Teacher's Edition: AR1–AR3	Unit 5 Skills Assessment	Teacher's Edition: Classifying: 82 Consonant *j* /j/: 76
Teacher's Edition: AR1–AR3	Unit 5 Skills Assessment	Teacher's Edition: Drawing Conclusions: 118 Consonant *v* /v/: 112
Teacher's Edition: AR1–AR3	Unit 5 Skills Assessment	Teacher's Edition: Sequence: 156 Consonant *qu* /kw/: 150
Teacher's Edition: AR1–AR3	Unit 5 Skills Assessment	Teacher's Edition: Drawing Conclusions: 192 Short *e:* 186
Teacher's Edition: AR1–AR3	Unit 5 Skills Assessment	Teacher's Edition: Author's Purpose: 228 Consonant *x* /ks/: 222

- **Big Books**
- **Trade Books**
- **Leveled Stories**

More Assessment Resources

Assessment Handbook contains information about conference records, self-assessment, portfolio analysis, reading progress summaries, and running records.

Technology

TestWorks can create personalized multiple-choice tests, free-response tests, and practice worksheets.

Teacher's Resource Planner CD-ROM is a scheduling and planning tool that can print worksheets and correlate curriculum to specific objectives.

National Computer Systems (NCS) provides management software, training, staff development, and communication tools for the school and home. NCS also provides standards-based assessments and resources to support achievement gaps.

Assessment Overview

Diagnostic Assessment

Unit 5 Kindergarten Skills Assessment

Skills Assessment Teacher's Manual

Assessment Handbook
Assessment tools

Ongoing Assessment

"If . . . then . . ." statements throughout the lessons guide the instruction.

Ongoing Assessment

Phonics

If... children have difficulty identifying words with/F/,

then... have them put their teeth on their lower lip and blow air to make the initial sound in *fun*.

Informal Assessment

End-of-Unit Observable Behaviors
By the end of this unit, most of your children should be able to demonstrate that they can:

Listening and Speaking
- Listen for rhyming words and main idea
- Speak well and with proper grammar and speak to retell a message; read chorally

Word Identification and Word Knowledge
- Identify sound-symbol relationships for *j, v, qu, x, y*
- Identify words with short *e* and the phonograms *-en, -et*
- Recognize high-frequency words: *do, not, what, one, two, three, red, yellow, blue*

Variety of Texts and Genres
- Participate in listening to and discussing classic and contemporary selections

Reader Response
- Respond to a selection by drawing conclusions

Writing and Grammar Skills
- Write labels or sentences using developing writing skills
- Distinguish between telling sentences and asking sentences

See page AR30 of this Teacher's Edition for complete grade-level benchmarks.

National Test Correlation

Tested Skills	ITBS Form M	CTBS 5th Ed.	CAT 5th Ed.	SAT 9th Ed.	MAT 7th Ed.	Your Test
Comprehension						
Classifying	●		●	●	●	
Drawing Conclusions	●	●	●	●	●	
Sequence	●	●	●	●	●	
Author's Purpose						
Character			●	●		
Phonics and Word Study						
Initial Consonants *j, v, qu, x, y*	●	●	●	●	●	
Final Consonant *x*						
Short Vowel *e (-en, -et)*						
Rhyming Words	●		●	●	●	
Grammar, Usage, and Mechanics Skills						
Past and Present Tense Verbs						
Complete Sentences						
Types of Sentences						

Key

ITBS Iowa Test of Basic Skills
CTBS Comprehensive Test of Basic Skills (TerraNova)
CAT California Achievement Test

SAT Stanford Achievement Test
MAT Metropolitan Achievement Test

Theme Launch
Let's Explore

Value of the Theme

Let's Explore refers to why we want to go places and how we get there. Children at this age are curious and eager to explore—from places in their own community to planets in outer space. They are also fascinated by all forms of transportation—from bicycles and skates to space shuttles.

Discuss the Theme Question

How do we get from here to there?

Read the theme question to children. Brainstorm with them a list of places to go in your community and ways to get to those places. Encourage children to discuss

- **how animals get from place to place**
- **how children get where they want to go**
- **places children have explored**

Setting Up the Classroom

The theme *Let's Explore* can be supported by placing books about animal migration, transportation, and travel in a classroom library. Display toy cars, trains, airplanes, and spacecraft. Create an "I Want to Explore" bulletin board. Have children draw and post pictures of places they would like to visit.

Launch the Theme

Explain to children that they will be reading stories and doing projects about going to new places and ways to get there. Ask children:

- **How do you get to school?**
- **When you visit relatives or friends, how do you get there?**
- **Have you ever ridden on a train or plane? Tell what it was like.**

Discuss children's favorite way to get around. Then introduce "Choo-Choo Train" by telling children that they are going to do a finger play about a train going down a track.

Finger Play: Choo-Choo Train

This is a choo-choo train

Puffing down the track.
(Rotate forearms in rhythm.)

Now it's going forward,

Now it's going back.
(Pull arms forward and back; continue rotating motion.)

Now the bell is ringing,
(Pull bell cord with closed fist.)

Now the whistle blows.
(Hold fist near mouth and blow.)

What a lot of noise it makes

Everywhere it goes.
(Cover ears with hands.)

Crossing Cultures

 Use the following selections to help children learn about their own and other cultures.

Jump into the Jungle Explain to children that a jungle is also called a tropical rainforest. Use a world map or globe to show children where tropical rainforests are located—South America, Africa, and Southeast Asia.

Five Little Ducks Point out that this is a very old counting rhyme. Ask children who are familiar with other cultures to offer counting rhymes used in those cultures.

Poster Activities

Topic Activities

Use the poster to build background on the weekly topics.

Activity 1 Tell children that the boy with the map just came from school. Have a volunteer find his school on the poster.

Activity 2 Tell children that the boy wants to go to the park. Have volunteers show how the boy can get to the park.

Activity 3 Ask children to point out and name as many different places on the poster as they can.

Language Arts Connection

Verbs Ending in -s Ask volunteers to point to one of the people on the poster and say a sentence about what the person is doing, using a verb that ends in -s. For example, *The boy looks at the map. The man sells a hot dog. The police officer rides a horse.*

Project

Draw a background on mural paper that shows a cityscape with roads, bike paths, the sky, and so on. Ask children to draw and cut out pictures of different kinds of transportation. They can add people biking, walking, and running, as well as animals on the move, to the mural. Ask:

Why do people move from place to place?

What kinds of animals would you expect to see moving around?

Lesson Overview

Big Book

Jump into the Jungle

Genre
Nonfiction

Phonemic Awareness/Phonics
Consonant *j* /j/

Comprehension
Classifying

High-Frequency Words
do   not   what

About the Author

Theresa Volpe
began her professional writing career at the age of 15 when she was hired as a weekly reporter for her neighborhood newspaper. For the past six years, she has written educational children's books and has developed several Parent's Choice award-winning edu-tainment products for children. She developed *The Time Twister Chronicles*, an interactive adventure book series for children.

Leveled Books

Easy	On-Level	Challenge

Wordless Story 25	**Kindergarten Reader 25**	**Independent Reader 25**

Trade Books for Self-Selected Reading and Read Aloud

Crocodile Beat
by Gail Jorgensen

Giraffe
by Mary Ling

Junglewalk
by Nancy Tafuri

Little Gorilla
by Ruth Bornstein

My Friend Gorilla
by Atsuko Morozumi

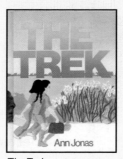

The Trek
by Ann Jonas

Theme Let's Explore   **Lesson Topic** A Place to Discover

5-Day Planner

Customize your week with the Teacher's Resource Planner CD-ROM!

Reading

Comprehension

Vocabulary

Phonics

Phonemic Awareness

Day 1

Activate Prior Knowledge p. 19
Poem "Eletelephony"

Reading pp. 20–27
Shared Reading
Jump into the Jungle
Reader Response:
Act Out Favorite
Animals
  Comprehension:
Classifying
Group Animals to
Understand Classifying

Phonics pp. 28–29
✓ Consonant *j* /j/
Phonemic Awareness:
Listen to a Song
• Phonics Songs and
Rhymes Chart 25
**Connect Sound to
Letter:** Match /j/ to *j*
Phonological Awareness:
Delete Phonemes
✓ **High-Frequency Words**

| do | not | what |

Day 2

Phonics pp. 30–31
✓ Consonant *j* /j/
Phonemic Awareness:
Identify Words with /j/
• Phonics Songs and
Rhymes Chart 25
Find Pictures Whose
Names Begin with /j/
• Wordless Story 25
Jelly and Jam
Connect Sound to Letter:
Match /j/ to *j*
Phonological Awareness:
Substitute /j/ for Other Sounds
✓ **High-Frequency Words:**
Use *do, not,* and *what* in
sentences

Reading pp. 32–33
 Comprehension: Classifying
Recall Information
from the Big Book
Use Vocabulary in
Sentences
Classify Animals

Oral Language

**Speaking, Listening,
and Viewing**

Oral Language pp. 26–27
Introduce Vocabulary:
Moving Words
crawl creep slide stretch swing
Use Vocabulary Words to Answer
Questions

Oral Language pp. 32–33
 Speaking: Retell
a Message
Retell a Message
• Oral Language Chart 25

Writing

**Grammar, Usage,
and Mechanics**

Writing pp. 28–29
 Shared Writing:
Write Sentences Together

Writing pp. 30–31
 Modeled Writing: Write About
Places to Explore
Guided Writing
Handwriting: Practice Writing *Jj*

Self-Selected Reading
Read Aloud

Self-Selected Reading p. 27
Have children select books to
read. They might like to read
other books about jungle
animals. See page 11 for
suggestions.

Self-Selected Reading p. 33
From the collection of books you
have assembled for self-
selected reading, ask children to
choose a book. Some children might
enjoy *Crocodile Beat* by Gail Jorgensen.

 Target Skill   (Review) **Review Skill**

Target Skills of the Week

Reading	Classifying
Phonics	Consonant *j* /j/
Oral Language	Retell a Message
Writing	Action Words (Verbs)

Day 3

Phonics pp. 34–35

 Consonant *j* /j/

Phonemic Awareness: Identify Pictures Whose Names Begin with /j/

Connect Sound to Letter: Identify Words That Begin with *j*/j/
• Phonics Songs and Rhymes Chart 25

Phonological Awareness: Listen for Rhymes

Read Kindergarten Reader 25: *The Museum*

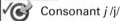

Reading pp. 36–37

Comprehension: Classifying

Sort Words

Reader Response: Relate Story to Own Life

Model Writing Captions

Oral Language pp. 36–37

Speaking: Retell a Message

Practice Retelling a Message

Writing pp. 34–35

 **Modeled Writing:** Model How to Write Sentences

Guided Writing

Self-Selected Reading p. 37

From your self-selected reading collection, have children choose books to read. You might suggest *Junglewalk* by Nancy Tafuri.

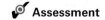

Day 4

Phonics pp. 38–39

Review Consonant *w* /w/

 Consonant *j* /j/

Phonemic Awareness:

Consonant *w* /w/

Discriminate Words with /j/ and /w/

Connect Sound to Letter: Match /j/ to *j*

Phonological Awareness: Answer Riddles with /j/ Words

✔ **High-Frequency Words:** Use Words in Sentences

Challenge: Independent Reader 25

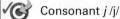

Reading pp. 40–41

Comprehension: Classifying

Activate Prior Knowledge

 Assess Classifying

Oral Language pp. 40–41

Speaking: Retell a Message
• Read Aloud *"If You Should Meet a Crocodile"*

 Assess Retell a Message

Writing pp. 38–39

Review **Interactive Writing:** Nouns

Use Nouns

Self-Selected Reading p. 41

Children who like animals may enjoy reading about the friendship between a boy and a gorilla in *My Friend Gorilla* by Atsuko Morozumi.

Day 5

Phonics pp. 42–43

 Consonant *j* /j/

Phonemic Awareness: Prepare to Assess

 Connect Sound to Letter: Assess *j* /j/

Phonological Awareness: Blend Words with /j/

 High-Frequency Words: Assess

Reading pp. 44–45

Review **Comprehension:** Predicting
• Read Aloud "The Lion and the Mouse"

Dramatize Characters' Actions

Oral Language pp. 44–45

Review **Speaking:** Make Introductions

Practice Making Introductions

Writing pp. 42–43

 Independent Writing: Assess Writing Development

Shared Writing: Add to the Class Diary

Self-Selected Reading p. 45

Children may enjoy reading *The Trek* by Ann Jonas, in which a little girl and her friend meet imaginary animals on the way to school.

 Assessment   ✔ **Benchmark Assessment of Target Skills and Skills Assessment**

Cross-Curricular Work Stations

Community Link

Ideas for bringing the school and community together

Field Experiences
zoo
park
nature preserve

Guest Speakers
zoologist
meteorologist
someone who has
    traveled to a tropical
    rain forest

Letters and Sounds

Jump for J 10 minutes

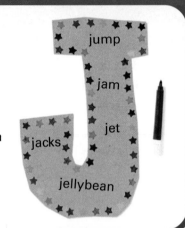

Materials: tape recorder, cassette tape

Learning Styles Kinesthetic, Auditory, Social

On a cassette tape, record a list of words children are familiar with. Many of the words should begin with /j/. Children listen to the tape and jump whenever they hear a word that begins with /j/.

Challenge Children cut a large letter *J* out of construction paper and write a list of words that begin with /j/.

Social Studies

Celebrate in Different Ways 10 minutes

Materials: paper, crayons, markers

Learning Styles Individual, Kinesthetic

 Have children draw pictures showing celebrations they are familiar with. Encourage them to include celebrations that come from other countries or cultures. Display the pictures on a world map.

Media

Follow the Weather 10 minutes

Materials: teacher-prepared checklist, pencil, TV or newspaper weather report

Learning Styles Individual, Kinesthetic, Visual

Prepare a checklist of the weather symbols used on TV and in newspaper weather reports. Discuss the symbols, such as a sun, clouds, snowflakes, and rain, with children. Have each child draw his or her own weather symbols. Tell children they can place one on their desk each day to tell the weather.

Challenge Have children prepare a weather report for a typical day in the jungle. Suggest that they look for weather clues in the story and use the TV or newspaper weather report as a model.

⚠️ **INTERNET SAFETY** Establish guidelines for your students' safe and responsible use of the Internet. See the Scott Foresman Internet Guide for tips.

Technology

AstroWord   10 minutes

Learning Styles Visual, Auditory

AstroWord reinforces children's understanding of phonemic awareness. Children can work individually or collaboratively.

Web Site  two days for 10 minutes

Learning Styles Individual, Visual

Visit the Scott Foresman web site (sfreading.com) for current hyperlinks to sites that can be used by children for an Internet Workshop investigation of places to explore. Also see the Scott Foresman Internet Guide for additional information on the Internet Workshop method.

sfreading.com

Drama

Act Out the Story 10 minutes

Materials: name cards for each animal in the big book *Jump into the Jungle*

Learning Styles Kinesthetic, Spatial, Social

Have children choose an animal to act out from the story. Groups of children can act out the story if desired. Encourage children to move and make sounds like their animal does in the story.

tarsier

insect

Math

Who Is First? 10 minutes

Learning Styles Social, Kinesthetic, Spatial, Logical

Have children draw a picture of their favorite animal, either from the story or elsewhere. Have children lay the pictures out in alphabetical order. Tell groups to name which animal is first, second, third, and last.

ESL Children can tell the order of the animals aloud using ordinal numbers. For examples: *The bear is first. The ladybug is second.* Or, ask questions such as *Which animal is fourth?* which children can answer in complete sentences.

Introduce the Reading Road Show Activity Stations to reinforce this week's skills.

Phonemic Awareness & Phonics
Literacy Activities

Use these activities during the week to reinforce skills.

Phonemic Awareness

Jumping Jacks 10 minutes

Learning Styles Kinesthetic, Auditory

Show children how to do the jumping jack exercise by clapping their hands over their heads as their feet jump apart. Then tell children you will say a word. If the word begins like *jumping jack*, they are to jump once like a jumping jack. Say words such as *jar, jelly, sun, jam, juggle, joke, moon, jeep, jug, hammer, just,* and *jewel*.

The activity can be varied by having children suggest other body movement to go with other letter sounds such as hopping for /h/, tapping for /t/, wiggling for /w/, and marching for /m/. Children can take turns being the "leader" and saying the words while the others move.

jelly   jar   jam

Working with Letters

Letter Write 15 minutes

Materials: paper, letter cards

Learning Styles Visual, Kinesthetic, Spatial

Divide children into small groups. Have children fold a paper to make eight boxes. Place a set of letter cards in a pile for each group. Have one child in the group take a letter card and name the letter. Then children write the capital and lowercase forms of that letter in the first box. The child with the card displays the card so that everyone can check to see that he or she wrote the correct letters. Continue until all the boxes are filled. Have children fold a new sheet of paper to begin a new game.

The game can be extended by having the child say a word that begins with the letter rather than naming the letter.

Working with Words

Match the Word   15 minutes

Materials: two sets of lowercase letter cards

Learning Styles Visual, Kinesthetic, Logical

Write the following words on the board: *cat, jet, big, mop, fun.* Give the following letter cards to each child: *a, e, i, o, u, c, t, j, b, g, m, p, f* and *n.* Have children use his or her letters to make one of the words on the board. Continue until several or all words are made.

ABC Wall

ABC Wall   10 minutes

Materials: set of lowercase letter cards

Learning Styles Visual, Auditory, Verbal

Give a set of letter cards to a volunteer. Have the child take a card, name the letter, and give a category—animals. The rest of the group looks at the ABC Wall to find a word that fits the beginning letter and the category. The child who finds a word says the word and writes it on the board. Continue with other letters and words for the category. After several rounds, have the child who chooses a letter give a new category for words.

(ESL) Children may benefit from closing their eyes while someone gives a more detailed description of the word and trying to "see it in their mind." An example would be *I'm thinking of a large animal with four legs, brown fur, and a big hump on its back.*

Daily Warm-Up

Message Board

Day One

Today we will read about the jungle and the animals that live there.

> Discuss with children what they know about jungles and jungle animals.

> Ask children: "Do you know someone whose name begins with *J/j*?"

Day Two

We will look and listen for words with Jj.

Day Three

We will learn the words *do, not,* and *what.*

> Ask children: "*What* are some things you *do not do* on the playground?"

> Discuss with children times when they have had messages to give to someone.

Day Four

Today we will retell a message.

Day Five

Today we will write a list of animals.

> Ask children: "What are some animals that live in the jungle?"

Getting Ready for the Week

Day One
children's magazines, envelopes (Full Day)
tape recorder, tape recording of sounds (Auditory)
calendar (Full Day)

Day Two
jacket (Full Day)

Day Three
large index cards, tape recorder, blank audiotape
small boxes, colored buttons, paper clips, and counters (Full Day)

Day Four
box, index cards (Kinesthetic)

Day Five
sheet of paper with eight numbered squares

Family Times

Send home the newsletter with fun instructional activities to reinforce this week's target skills.

Practice Book, pp. 159–160
Teacher's Resource Book, pp. 159–160

Activate Prior Knowledge

Take an Imaginary Jungle Trip

Tell children that this week's story is about a trip through a jungle. Ask them what a jungle is. Then have children pretend to be in a jungle filled with animals and plants. Lead the group around the room creeping quietly and pointing out the various sights. Ask children to tell what they know about the jungle:

- **What are some things you see?**

- **Is it warm or cold in the jungle?**

Objectives

Children will

- discuss jungle plants and animals
- listen and respond to a poem

Build Background

Choose one or more of these activities to build background for concepts presented in this week's selection, *Jump into the Jungle.*

Read Aloud a Poem

Share this poem. Then ask children what the elephant in the poem was trying to do. Encourage them to repeat some of the nonsense words.

Eletelephony
by Laura Richards

Once there was an elephant,
Who tried to use the telephant—
No! no! I mean an elephone
Who tried to use the telephone—
(Dear me! I am not certain quite
That even now I've got it right.)
Howe'er it was, he got his trunk
Entangled in the telephunk;
The more he tried to get it free,
The louder buzzed the telephee—
(I fear I'd better drop the song
Of elephop and telephong!)

Use Illustrations to Develop Oral Language

Tell children that this animal is called a tarsier (TAR see uhr). Point out the size of its eyes. Ask children to imagine what it might be looking at. Invite them to tell a story about the tarsier and what it is looking at.

Use Audio to Develop Story Concepts

Have children talk about jungles. Ask:

- **Do most jungles have lots of plants or only a few? Why do you think so?**

- **Do many animals or only a few live in a jungle? Why do you think so?**

Share the Background-Building CD/tape which features many sounds heard in the jungle.

CD 5/Tape 13, Side 1
Background-Building Audio

Day 1

Concepts of Print

Print Conveys Meaning

Display *Jump into the Jungle*. Point to the title and ask:

- **What is this called?** (the title)
- **What do these words tell us?** (the name of the book)

Point to and read the author's name. Ask:

What does an author do? (writes stories and books)

Words and Spaces

Sweep your hand under the title from left to right. Ask:

- **How many words are in this title?** (four)
- **What do you see between words?** (spaces)

Model Reading Behaviors

Picture Walk and Predict

Preview the story by having children look at the photographs. Ask:

- **What animals do you see?** (possible answers: lion, frog, cheetah, parrot, sloth, tarsier, hippopotamus, otter, lizard, monkeys, elephant, crocodile, jaguar)
- **Where does the story take place?** (a jungle)
- **Do you think the animals in the story are real or make-believe? Why do you think so? Let's read to find out.**

Shared Reading Routine

Read Aloud the Story

Day 1

- Read the story through for enjoyment.
- To practice the reading strategy predicting, use the stopping point on TE page 23.

Day 2

- Reread the story, using the activities found in the margins on pages 22–25.

Days 3–5

- Reread the entire big book or portions of it each day, using the activities suggested in the lessons.

Jump into
the Jungle

Written by Theresa Volpe

Big Book

Guiding the Reading

Critical Thinking

What sounds might you hear in a jungle? Can you make the sounds?
Possible answers: An elephant might trumpet. Monkeys might chatter. Birds might squawk or chirp.

Language Development

Parrots flap and stretch their wings.

What does *stretch* mean in that sentence? How do you know? How can you use other words and the photographs to figure out what *stretch* means?

stretch

average

Content Connection: Science

- A rainforest, or jungle, is made up of layers. The canopy is the top layer. Most animals live there.
- The understory is where ferns and shrubs grow.
- Large mammals such as the jaguar live on the forest floor.

Jump into the jungle.
Come explore.
2

Hear insects buzz
and lions roar.
3

pages 2–3 Lion

Leap into the jungle.
What a sight!
4

Frogs bump and jump
all day and night.
5

pages 4–5 Red-Eyed Tree Frog

Churr, churr, churr,
the cheetah sings.
6

Parrots flap and
stretch their wings.
7

pages 6–7 Cheetah; Scarlet Macaw

8 Big raindrops fall on open flowers.

The jungle stirs throughout the hours. 9

pages 8–9 Rafflesia Flower; Three-Toed Sloth

10 Look in the darkest, deepest places.

What you see are funny faces. 11

pages 10–11 Coppery Brushtail Possum; Philippine Tarsier

12 See wiggling ears and blinking eyes.

a muddy hippo in disguise. 13

pages 12–13 Hippopotamus

Guiding the Reading

Critical Thinking

Do you think there is a lot of rain or only a little rain in a jungle? Possible answer: There are many plants in a jungle. Plants need water to grow. So a jungle must have a lot of rain.

Day
1

Language Development

Share with children the meaning of *disguise*.

The hippo covered itself with mud so no one could tell what it was. The mud was the hippo's disguise.

disguise

challenge

Stopping Point

Predict On the first reading, you may want to stop at the bottom of page 13 and ask children to predict what else they might see and hear in the jungle.

pages 14–15 Giant Otter

Guiding the Reading

Critical Thinking

Why do insects scatter when a lizard flicks its tongue?
Possible answer: Lizards use their tongues to catch insects and then eat them. The insects did not want to be caught.

Content Connection: Science

- About 50 percent of all plant and animal species are found in the rain forest.
- About half of the total global rain forest is found in the Amazon River basin.
- Most rain forests have more than 80 inches of rain a year.

pages 16–17 Chameleon

pages 18–19 Gray Langur

A thirsty elephant
takes a sip.

20

Slip and slide—
it's time for a dip.

21

pages 20–21 Elephant; Crocodile

Watch the jaguar
crawl and creep.

22

The busy jungle
does not sleep.

23

pages 22–23 Jaguar

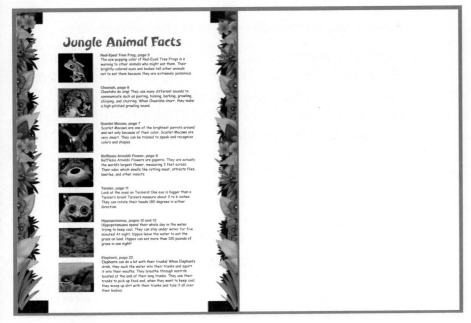

Jungle Animal Facts

Red-Eyed Tree Frog, page 5
The eye-popping color of Red-Eyed Tree Frogs is a warning for other animals who might eat them. Their brightly-colored eyes and bodies tell other animals not to eat them because they are extremely poisonous.

Cheetah, page 6
Cheetahs do sing! They use many different sounds to communicate such as purring, hissing, barking, growling, chirping, and churring. When Cheetahs churr, they make a high-pitched growling sound.

Scarlet Macaw, page 7
Scarlet Macaws are one of the brightest parrots around and not only because of their color. Scarlet Macaws are very smart. They can be trained to speak and recognize colors and shapes.

Rafflesia Arnoldii Flower, page 8
Rafflesia Arnoldii Flowers are gigantic. They are actually the world's largest flower, measuring 3 feet across. Their odor, which smells like rotting meat, attracts flies, beetles, and other insects.

Tarsier, page 11
Look at the eyes on Tarsiers! One eye is bigger than a Tarsier's brain! Tarsiers measure about 3 to 6 inches. They can rotate their heads 180 degrees in either direction.

Hippopotamus, pages 12 and 13
Hippopotamuses spend their whole day in the water trying to keep cool. They can stay under water for five minutes! At night, hippos leave the water to eat the grass on land. Hippos can eat more than 100 pounds of grass in one night!

Elephant, page 22
Elephants can do a lot with their trunks! When Elephants drink, they suck the water into their trunks and squirt it into their mouths. They breathe through nostrils located at the end of their long trunks. They use their trunks to pick up food and, when they want to keep cool, they scoop up dirt with their trunks and toss it all over their bodies.

pages 24

Share with children the meaning of the word *dip*.

The crocodile decided to take a swim. It was a nice day to take a dip in the warm water.

dip

average

Guiding the Reading

Critical Thinking

Why does the jungle not sleep? What in the book lets you know this?
Possible answer: Some animals are up and busy during the day, and some animals are up and busy during the night.

Content Connection: Science

- The jaguar lives in Central and South America. It is the largest and most powerful cat.
- Jaguars can be yellow or red with black spots. Black jaguars are in fact dark brown with black spots.

Children will

- classify animals
- identify and use movement words
- give personal responses to a story

Day 1

Reader Response

Act Out Favorite Animals

Ask: *What was your favorite animal? Why did you like that animal best? Show me how that animal moves and what sounds it makes.*

Let children answer these questions by dramatizing.

- **What are some things the monkeys do?** (chatter, swing, jump, do flip-flops)

- **How does a cheetah prowl through the jungle and what sound does it make?** (Cheetahs move as cats move; they sing "churr.")

Oral Language/Vocabulary

Use Vocabulary Words to Answer Questions

The vocabulary words are related to ways of moving. Let children act out the words as they answer the questions.

 crawl   creep   slide   stretch   swing

- **What might a tired parrot do with its wings?** (stretch them out)

- **How can monkeys get from tree to tree?** (swing)

- **What two words tell how a jaguar moves through the jungle?** (crawl and creep)

- **How does a crocodile get into the water?** (slide)

Encourage children to use the vocabulary words in sentences of their own. Then say: *The crocodile goes into the water. The crocodile slides into the water. Which of those sentences is more interesting and helps you picture what the alligator is doing? Why?*

Skills Trace

 Classify

Introduce	TE: K.4 136–137
Practice	PB: 142, 144, 162, 164, 212, 214, 224, 226
Reteach/ Review	TE: K.4 143, 146, 150, 190, AR19 K.5 **26–27**, 33, 36, 40, 82, AR16 K.6 100–101, 107, 110, 114, 156, 176–177, 183, 186, 190, 234, AR20
Skills Assessment	Skills Assessment Unit 6 TE: K.4 AR1–AR3 K.5 AR1–AR3 K.6 AR1–AR3

Ongoing Assessment

Vocabulary

If... children cannot answer questions with the words *crawl, creep, slide, stretch,* and *swing,*

then... ask a volunteer to act out the word as you read the appropriate part of the story.

Comprehension

Group Animals to Understand Classifying

Write *Pets* and *Wild Animals* as two headings on the board. Read the headings. Then show picture cards for *alligator, cat, dog, elephant, fish, hippo, kangaroo,* and *rabbit,* one at a time. Ask:

- **What is this animal?**

- **Is it a pet? Is it a wild animal?**

Have a volunteer put the card under the appropriate heading. When all the cards are sorted, review the animals in each group. Talk about why the animals in the group belong together. Note that *fish* and *rabbit* could be listed in both categories.

Remind children that when things are alike in some way, they can be put into groups, or categories.

Day
1

Meeting Individual Needs
Other Ways to Learn

Auditory Tape record household sounds, such as a doorbell chiming, a phone ringing, a radio playing, and a clock ticking. Tape or imitate the sounds animals make. Let children listen to the tape and identify the sounds as those heard around the house or those made by animals.

Self-Selected Reading

D.E.A.R. Drop Everything And Read

Have children select books to read. They might like to read other books about jungle animals. See page 11 for suggestions.

Optional Resources

Phonics Sourcebook pp. 1–78

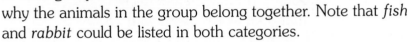

Full Day Options...

Classifying

Sort Pictures Give each group some children's magazines and two envelopes. Ask children to find and cut out pictures of animals to put in one envelope. Have each group choose another category, such as people or toys, and find pictures to put in the second envelope.

Classifying

Group Animals Help children fold a sheet of paper in half. Write *Wild Animals* and *Pets* on the board. Have children copy each heading on one half of the paper and then draw at least two animals that belong in each group.

Oral Language

Describe Animals Let children take turns using as many words as they can to describe an animal pictured in *Jump into the Jungle.*

Vocabulary

Act Out Words Whisper one of these words to a child: *crawl, creep, slide, stretch,* or *swing.* Ask the child to pantomime the word and have classmates guess it.

Objectives

Children will

- recognize initial /j/
- recognize the letters *Jj*
- delete phonemes to make new words
- participate in a shared writing activity

Day 1

Meeting Individual Needs

Intervention

Have children sort picture cards by putting those whose names begin with /j/ in one pile and those whose names begin with other sounds in another pile. Use the picture cards for *jacket, jacks, jam, jar, jet, jug, bell, car, dog, pickle,* and *monkey.*

Skills Trace

Consonant *Jj*

Introduce	TE: K.5 28
Practice	PB: 161, 163
Reteach/ Review	TE: K.3 30, 34–35, 38, 42, 76, AR4
Skills Assessment	Skills Assessment Unit 5 TE: K.5 AR1–AR3

Daily Phonics Routine

Phonemic Awareness

Listen to a Song

Play the CD/tape of "A Journey." Ask children to listen for and name words that begin with /j/ as in *journey.* (journey, join, jet, jolly, January, June, July, jumbo, jog, jungle, Jan, jackal, jack rabbit, jump, jeep)

CD 2/Tape 13, Side 1
Phonics Songs and Rhymes Audio

A Journey

Join us on a journey in a jet.
We'll have a jolly time. Ready, get set.

We'll go in January, June, or July.
We'll take a jumbo jet in the sky.

We'll go on a jog to a jungle or two.
We'll take our friend Jan and her puppy too.

We'll see a jackal or jack rabbit jump.
We'll take a jeep that goes bumpety-bump.

Phonics Songs and Rhymes Chart 25

Identify /j/ Picture Cards

Display picture cards for *jam* and *jet.* Have children identify each picture by name. Elicit that both words begin with /j/.

Ongoing Assessment

Phonemic Awareness

If... children are having difficulty hearing the /j/ sound,	**then...** say an alliterative sentence, such as *Jolly jugglers juggled juice jars,* emphasizing the /j/ sounds. Have children repeat the sentence.

Connect Sound to Letter

Match /j/ to j

Have Alphapotamus show the alphabet card for *Jj.* Say *jump rope* slowly, emphasizing the /j/. Then explain that the /j/ sound in *jump* is written with the letter *j* or *J.* Point to the letters on the alphabet card. Then write *jump.* Circle the letter *j* and have children say /j/ several times. Then have them blend the word: /j/ *ump.*

Alphabet Cards

Phonological Awareness

Delete Phonemes

Say the word *jam.* Ask children what word they would make by taking away the beginning sound: *Jam without /j/ is _____.* (am) Continue with *Jill, Jan, win, kit, wink.*

High-Frequency Words

Use *do, not,* and *what* in Sentences

Say the word *do* and ask a volunteer to find the word on the ABC Wall. Then have several children use the word in a sentence. Repeat with the words *not* and *what.*

Choose a word from the ABC Wall that begins with *Jj.* Make up a sentence, using the word. Then repeat the sentence, omitting the word. Let a volunteer say the word and point to it.

Modeled Writing

Write About Places to Explore

Discuss with children new places they would like to explore. Invite them to imagine they are exploring one of these places and they want to write a note to a friend back home. Write: *I ride in a jeep.* Say:

- **Action words, or verbs, tell about things people do.**
- **My sentence has one action word, or verb:** *ride.*

Guided Writing

Say: *Write a note about something you might do while exploring a new place.* Help children use action words (verbs) in writing their notes. Some may need to dictate or draw.

Handwriting

Practice Writing *Jj*

Distribute lined writing paper and have children practice writing *j* and *J.* Children who are proficient writing these letters can write these phrases: *jam in a jar, Jan and Jim.*

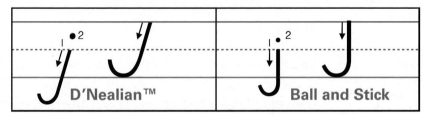

D'Nealian™	Ball and Stick

Meeting Individual Needs
Challenge

Ask children to write or dictate a message they might give to a friend over the telephone. Have them circle any action words (verbs) they used in the message.

Optional Resources

Phonics Sourcebook pp. 30–33, 84–85

High-Frequency Word Cards

Phonics Workbook p. 122

Day **2**

Full Day Options...

Independent Writing 🚶

Write a Note Let children write or dictate sentences for one of these:

- a note to a friend about where to meet
- a note to a parent about bringing something to school

Phonics 👫👫

Listen for /j/ Place a jacket on a table. Show the picture cards for *jacks, jam, jar, jet, jug, king, ten, hat, raccoon,* and *doll.* Let volunteers put the picture cards with names that begin with /j/ next to the jacket.

Handwriting 🚶

Practice Have children choose one.

- Write the rhyming words *jar, car,* and *far.*
- Write this sentence: *Jan got a jar of jam.* Draw a picture to show where Jan got the jam.

Objectives

Children will

 retell a message

 classify story information

● use vocabulary words in oral sentences

Day **2**

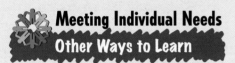

Meeting Individual Needs
Other Ways to Learn

Kinesthetic Have children put themselves into groups. Use categories such as boys and girls, colors of clothing, hair colors, or colors of socks. For example, have children with white socks stand at the front of the room, children with red socks at the back, and children with socks of other colors near the windows.

Oral Language

Retell a Message

Read "I Know an Old Woman Who Swallowed a Fly." Point out to children that this is a silly poem meant to entertain. Invite them to join in as you reread the poem.

Explain to children that a message is information one person says or writes to another person or group. Have children think of a message they would send to the woman who swallowed the fly, such as "Do not swallow any more flies!" Have one child give the message and another child act as the old woman who repeats the message to show she understands it.

I Know an Old Woman Who Swallowed a Fly
Anonymous

There was an old woman
Who swallowed a fly
I don't know why, she
Swallowed a fly—
Perhaps she'll die!

There was an old woman
Who swallowed a spider
That wiggled and wiggled
And jiggled inside her.

She swallowed the spider
To catch the fly.
I don't know why
She swallowed a fly—
Perhaps she'll die!

Oral Language Chart 25

Comprehension

Recall Information from Big Book

Hold up *Jump into the Jungle* and ask children to recall some of the animals they read about on their journey through the jungle. Have children pantomime the animals in action.

Use Vocabulary in Sentences

Use the words *crawl, creep, slide, stretch,* and *swing* in questions, such as *When might you crawl? Where might you slide?* Ask children to answer the questions with complete sentences, using the vocabulary words.

Listen to Big Book for Information

Ask children to listen as you reread *Jump into the Jungle.* Explain that as they listen to the words and look at the pictures, you want them to think about where they would see the jungle animals—on land, in the water, or in the air.

While reading, you may wish to use the ideas in the *Guiding the Reading* and *Language Development* boxes on pages 22–25 of this Teacher's Edition.

Shared Reading

Big Book

Classify Animals

Make a three-column chart or use Graphic Organizer 9. Label the columns *Walk on Land*, *Swim in Water*, and *Fly Through Air*. Ask children to classify the animals from the book by naming an animal and telling the column in which it should be listed.

Walk On Land	Swim In Water	Fly Through Air
lion	hippo	insects
cheetah	giant otter	parrots
lizard		
monkey		
elephant		

Self-Selected Reading

From the collection of books you have assembled for self-selected reading, ask children to choose a book. Some children might enjoy *Crocodile Beat* by Gail Jorgensen.

Optional Resources

Graphic Organizer 9 (Three-Column Chart)

Day 2

Ongoing Assessment

Classifying

If... children have difficulty classifying the animals,

then... review the photographs in the book and ask questions such as: *Is the animal on land? in the air? in the water?*

Full Day Options...

Oral Language

Retell a Message Together, reread "I Know an Old Woman Who Swallowed a Fly." Discuss what happens in the poem. Then suggest that children give a message about the poem to a family member. Let them practice giving the message to a partner. Encourage them to retell the message at home.

Modeled Writing

Write Action Words Brainstorm a list of action words (verbs) for animals. Then write this sentence model on the board: *An otter swims.* Let children write a sentence of their own, using an animal name and an appropriate action word (verb).

An otter swims.

Classifying

Group Animal Pictures Make a three-column chart or use Graphic Organizer 9 labeled *Walk on Land*, *Swim in Water*, and *Fly Through Air*. Ask children to classify these picture cards: *alligator, ant, bear, butterfly, cow, duck, fish, octopus, rabbit.*

Reader Response

What Did You Learn? Share the animal facts found on page 24 of *Jump into the Jungle.* Then ask children to choose one of the animals and tell something they learned about it.

Objectives

Children will

- recognize initial /j/
- match pictures with words that begin with *j*
- identify rhyming words

Meeting Individual Needs
ESL

Day 3

Using Alphapotamus, say: *Listen and tell me what word I am saying.* Have Alphapotamus segment the sounds in the following words and have children blend the sounds to make the words: /j/ /e/ /t/, /j/ /a/ /m/, /j/ /o/ /b/, /j/ /u/ /st/.

Daily Phonics Routine

Phonemic Awareness

Identify Pictures Whose Names Begin with /j/

Gather the picture cards for *jacket, jacks, jam, jar, jet, jug, bed, fan, sock,* and *turkey.* Let volunteers select a card and name the picture. If the word begins with /j/, the child says, "Everybody jiggle like jelly." If the word begins with another sound, the child says, "Nobody move."

Connect Sound to Letter

Identify Words That Begin with *j*/j/

Ask children to sing along as you play the CD/tape of "A Journey." Then ask a volunteer to jog up to the chart and point to something in the picture whose name begins with *j* /j/. Have the volunteer say the word and draw a line from the object in the picture to the word in the rhyme. Ask the child to circle the letter that stands for /j/ and to name the letter.

Phonics Songs and Rhymes Chart 25

CD 2/Tape 13, Side 1
Phonics Songs and Rhymes Audio

Phonological Awareness

Listen for Rhymes

Explain that you will say two words. If they rhyme, children are to jump. If there is no rhyme, children are to shake their heads. Say: *jump/bump, jar/car, just/hand, joy/boy, joke/hat, jet/get.* Repeat the pairs that rhyme. Have volunteers tell which word begins with /j/.

Phonics and High-Frequency Words

Read Kindergarten Reader 25

- Point to the title and track the print as you read it.

- Ask children what a museum is and have them predict what the characters might see there.

- Read the book together. Have children track the print and show how to sweep back to the left for the next line.

The Museum

Written by Marge Dalton
Illustrated by Joy Dunn Keenan

Kindergarten Reader 25

Phonics Consonant *Jj*

High-Frequency Words
do, not, what

We like the museum.
We see a lot.
2

Look! What is it?
Jan can see it.
3

It is a jaw.
Do not jog!
4

Look! What is it?
Jim can see it.
5

It is a bear.
Do not pat it!
6

Look! What is it?
Jill can see it.
7

Do not sit on top!
We like the museum.
8

Modeled Writing

Model How to Write Sentences

Model writing using sentences based on *The Museum*. For example, write *I see a bear*.

As you write, model these strategies:

- Begin each sentence with a capital letter.
- Use verbs, or action words.
- Include spaces between the words.

Guided Writing

Have children read the sentences with you. Help them write their own sentences based on *The Museum*.

ABC Wall

Ask children to name action words (verbs). Write the words on index cards and add them to the ABC Wall.

Optional Resources

Phonics Sourcebook pp. 1–78, 84–85

High-Frequency Word Cards

Phonics Workbook p. 123

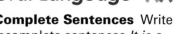

Full Day Options...

Independent Writing 🧍

Write Questions Help children write riddle questions about jungle animals, for example, *What is small and green?* On the back of the paper, the child can draw and label the answer.

Phonics 🧍

Make Pictures for *Jj* Help children write *J* and *j* on construction paper with glue and press strands of yarn onto the glue. Have children decorate the page with pictures of things whose names begin with /j/j/.

Oral Language 🧍🧍

Complete Sentences Write the incomplete sentences *It is a ___* and *Do not ___*. Ask one partner to complete the first sentence with something he or she would like to see in a museum. Have the other partner give a warning about what not to do.

Objectives

Children will

- ⟳ practice retelling a message
- ⟳ classify information in a story
- • use action words (verbs) in captions

Day
3

❄ Meeting Individual Needs
Intervention

Say three words that belong in the same category, such as *circle, square,* and *triangle.* Ask children why the three words go together. (They are all shapes.) Have children name another word that could go in the group. (rectangle) Use other categories such as sizes, numbers, and colors.

Classifying
Practice Book, p. 162
Teacher's Resource Book, p. 162

Oral Language

Retell a Message

Ask children to recall the message they told the woman who swallowed the fly. Have them suggest things a speaker should remember when retelling messages. Write children's suggestions on the board or chart paper to post for the rest of the week.

> A speaker should:
> Speak clearly.
> Keep the message short.

Practice Retelling a Message

Hold up *Jump into the Jungle.* Say: *Imagine you are on a jungle adventure and you call to tell a friend about your trip. Your friend isn't home and you have to leave a message. What message might you leave on the answering machine about your jungle adventure?* Let children practice giving messages. Then have them say their messages into a tape recorder. Play back the messages. Let volunteers retell the messages as if they were giving someone else telephone messages.

Shared Reading

Big Book

Ongoing Assessment
Retell a Message

If... children have difficulty retelling a message,

then... let them listen to the tape more than once. Have them add to their retelling as they remember more information.

Comprehension

Sort Words

Display Graphic Organizer 11 or draw two boxes on the board. Write *Animals* near one box and *Actions* near the other. Reread *Jump into the Jungle.* Stop after every two pages and ask children to name words for animals and words for actions that they heard. Have them tell you in which box to write each word.

Reader Response

Relate Story to Own Life

Ask children what they would do if they could "jump into a jungle." Encourage a variety of responses.

Model Writing Captions

Show children pages 11–12 in *Jump into the Jungle*. Ask them to think of one way to describe the picture of the hippo. Say: *A caption tells about a picture. If I want to write a caption for this picture, it might be "The hippo wiggles its ears."*

As you write the caption, model these strategies:

• Leave spaces between words.

• Use action words, or verbs.

Day 3

Full Day Options...

Oral Language

Play "Telephone" Remind children that it is important to listen carefully to a message so they can retell it correctly. Have children sit in a circle. Whisper a message to a child. Have him or her whisper it to the next child and so on. Have the last child repeat the message. Discuss the results.

Classifying

Sort Objects Give each group a box of small objects such as different colored buttons, paper clips, crayons, and counters. Ask children to work together to come up with two ways to sort the objects. Later let the groups explain how they sorted the objects.

Independent Writing

Write a Caption Ask children to draw a picture of a jungle animal and to write or dictate a caption. Remind them that a caption tells about a picture.

Handwriting

Write *Jj* Words Ask children to write silly combinations of words with /j/, such as *jungle juice, jogging jaguars, jiggling jam*.

Objectives

Children will

- recognize initial /j/
- discriminate between the sounds of /j/ and /w/
- identify nouns and use them in sentences

Meeting Individual Needs
Other Ways to Learn

Kinesthetic Together create a "Junk Box." Decorate a box with the letters *Jj*. Have children write *Jj* on one side of an index card and draw a picture of something that begins with /j/ on the back. Put the cards in the box. Children can choose a card and name the picture.

Day 4

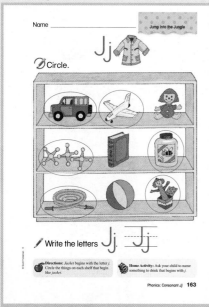

Consonant *Jj*
Practice Book, p. 163
Teacher's Resource Book, p. 163

Daily Phonics Routine

"I want to go for a walk."

Phonemic Awareness

Review
Consonant *w* /w/

Using Alphapotamus, say: *I want to go for a walk.* Tell children that if Alphapotamus says a word that begins with /w/ like *walk*, they should wave their hands at the puppet. Have Alphapotamus say: *winter, wagon, hall, wing, farm, window, wolf, water.*

Discriminate Words with /j/ and /w/

Divide the class into two groups: the *j*'s and the *w*'s. If you say a word beginning with /j/, children in the *j* group say /j/. If you say a word beginning with /w/, children in the *w* group say /w/. Say these words: *jump, water, jet, jeep, wall, window, winter, jeans, jaguar, wet.*

Connect Sound to Letter

Match /j/ to *j*

Place the picture cards for *jacket, jacks, jam, jar, jet, jug, moon, bell, ring, wagon, worm,* and *turtle* face up on a table. Show the alphabet card for *Jj*. Have children say *jump rope* and identify the beginning sound as /j/. Give the alphabet card to a volunteer who should choose a picture whose name begins with /j/. Have the child name the picture, turn it face down, and hand the alphabet card to another child.

Phonological Awareness

Answer Riddles with /j/ Words

Ask children to answer these riddles with a word that begins with /j/:

- **I come in a jar. You can put me on toast.** (jam or jelly)
- **I am something you fly in.** (jet)
- **I am a short coat you wear when it is cool outside.** (jacket)
- **I am something made from an orange. You can drink me.** (juice)

High-Frequency Words

Use Words in Sentences

Display word cards for *do, not,* and *what.* Have children ask safety questions using the word *What* and answer the questions using the words *do* and *do not.* For example, *What should you do when you cross a street? Do look both ways. Do not run into the street.* Other questions might relate to bike safety or playground safety.

Interactive Writing

Nouns

Remind children that words that name people, places, things, or animals are called naming words, or nouns. Write *People, Places, Things,* and *Animals* as headings on the board. Ask children to suggest words that begin with /j/ for each category: *Jane, Jeff, janitor; jungle, jail; jacket, jar, jaguar, jackal.*

Use Nouns

Write *I do like ___. I do not like ___.* Then ask children to choose one naming word (noun) from the list and another of their own choosing to complete each sentence.

I do like jam.
I do not like bugs.

Invite children to help you write the words. Have them circle each word with *j.* Read the sentences with children. (Add the word *a* before a singular noun, or use a plural form of the word.)

Ongoing Assessment

Writing

| **If...** children have trouble identifying naming words, | **then...** ask questions such as *Is jar a naming word? Does it name a person? a place? a thing? an animal?* |

Day 4

Full Day Options...

Independent Writing 🧍

Write Your Opinion Have children write about one of these:

- Tell what your favorite place is and why.
- Tell what your favorite thing is and why.

Phonics 👥

Revisit Kindergarten Reader 25, *The Museum* To provide practice with high-frequency words, have children reread *The Museum.* Let partners take turns reading the pages.

Kindergarten Reader 25

Phonics 👨‍👩‍👧‍👦

Shared Poetry Reread "A Journey" together. Review *g*/g/ and *r*/r/. Ask children to find words that begin with these letters and sounds. (get, go, goes; ready, rabbit)

Phonics Songs and Rhymes Chart 25

READING

Objectives

Children will

- classify information found in a story
- practice retelling a message
- listen to a poem

Meeting Individual Needs
Intervention

Display an assortment of crayons, markers, and colored pencils. Ask questions such as: *How are all these things alike? How are they different?* When children identify the differences, have them sort the objects into the categories they identified.

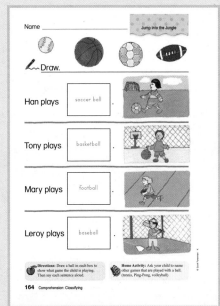

Classifying
Practice Book, p. 164
Teacher's Resource Book, p. 164

Day 4

Comprehension

Shared Reading

HONK! HONK! A STORY OF MIGRATION

Big Book

Activate Prior Knowledge

Display *Honk! Honk! A Story of Migration* from Unit 4. Ask:

What do you remember about this book?

Reread the big book. Then ask:

What do the little girl and the goose see on their trip? (city lights, railroads, highways, lakes, fields, flocks of geese, hunters, hawks, mountains, rivers, wolves, nesting grounds)

Assess Classifying

To assess children's ability to classify, write these headings: *Animals* and *Places*. Ask children to name animals from the story and write the words in the first column. (geese, foxes, hawks, wolves) Then have children name places and list these words in the second column. (cities, lakes, fields, mountains, rivers, nesting grounds)

Ongoing Assessment
Classifying

If... children are having difficulty classifying,

then... use the Classifying reteach lesson on page AR11 of this Teacher's Edition.

Oral Language

Establish a Purpose for Speaking

Ask children to listen carefully to the poem "If You Should Meet a Crocodile." Tell them the speaker in the poem has a message and that you want them to retell it.

Read Aloud

If You Should Meet a Crocodile

If you should meet a crocodile,
Don't take a stick and poke him;
Ignore the welcome in his smile,
Be careful not to stroke him.
For as he sleeps upon the Nile,
He gets thinner and thinner;
So when you meet the crocodile,
He's ready for his dinner.

Assess Retell a Message To check children's understanding of what they heard, ask:

- **What should you do if you meet a crocodile?** (don't poke him, ignore his smile, do not stroke him)

- **Why should you be careful when meeting a crocodile?** (He's ready for his dinner.)

Reread the poem. Have partners retell the story in the poem as if it were a message they were telling someone. Encourage them to use gestures if they wish and to make eye contact while talking. Then have partners switch roles.

Self-Selected Reading

D.E.A.R. Drop Everything And Read

Have children choose books to read independently. Children who like animals may enjoy reading about the friendship between a boy and a gorilla in *My Friend Gorilla* by Atsuko Morozumi.

Optional Resources

Assessment Handbook

Full Day Options...

Classifying 🚶

Sort Clothes Remind children that when they go on a trip, they need to take clothes. Point out that some clothes are kept in drawers and some are kept in closets. Help children divide a sheet of paper in half and label it *Drawer* and *Closet.* Let children draw pictures of clothes to show where they would find each item.

Independent Writing 🚶

Write About Journeys Ask children to choose one.

- Dictate or write about where you would like to go on a journey. Explain how you would get there.
- Dictate or write about a make-believe place you would like to go. Explain how you would get there.

Oral Language

Retell a Message Ask children to think of some news or something interesting they would like the class to know; for example, *I talked to Grandma on the phone last night.* Have each child tell a friend. Let the friend retell the message to the class.

Vocabulary

Create Oral Sentences Say the words *crawl, creep, slide, stretch,* and *swing.* Let children select two words and create a sentence using them.

Day **4**

PHONICS A Z

Objectives

Children will

- ☉ recognize initial /j/
- ☉ recognize and use verbs
- • use high-frequency words
- • write a list

Meeting Individual Needs
ESL

Brainstorm with children a list of words that begin with *j*/j/. Then work together to create tongue twisters or silly sentences using /j/ words; for example, *Jaguars jump in jungles.*

Day 5

Daily Phonics Routine

Prepare to Assess

Phonemic Awareness

Have children stand and do the activities you name—but only if the action word (verb) begins with /j/. Offer exercises such as: *Jump up and down. Run around your desk. Jog in place. Hop on one foot. Jiggle like jelly.*

Assess j /j/

Connect Sound to Letter

Give each child a sheet of paper with eight numbered squares. Hold up picture cards for: *jacket, jam, turkey, jar, fork, jet, bus, jacks.* Ask a volunteer to name the picture as you hold it up. Ask children to write *j* in the square if the name of the picture begins with /j/ and to put a big X in the square if it does not.

Ongoing Assessment
Phonics

If... children cannot correctly identify initial *j*/j/,	**then...** use the Consonant *Jj* reteaching activities on page AR10 of this Teacher's Edition.

Blend Words with /j/

Phonological Awareness

Have Alphapotamus say: *I need help figuring out some words. Can you help me? Listen: /j/ et. Blend the letters and tell me the word.* (jet) Repeat using these words: /j/ *ump*, /j/ *ungle*, /j/ *une*, /j/ *eans*, /j/ *umbo.*

/j/ et

High-Frequency Words

Assess

Write *What I Do* and *What I Do Not Do* on the board. Read the words and ask children to suggest things they do and do not do at school. Give each child two sheets of paper. Have them write or dictate words and draw pictures to describe on one sheet of paper what they do, and on the second sheet of paper what they do not do. Invite children to write a label on each paper: *What I Do* and *What I Do Not Do.* When children are finished, let them share their papers with the class.

Independent Writing

Assess Writing Development

Recall with children that in *Jump into the Jungle* they read about many different animals. Tell children you want to make a list of animals and their actions.

Think ALOUD

I will begin my list by writing an animal and an action word, or verb.
1. lions roar
2. monkeys swing

Display the illustrations in *Jump into the Jungle.* Have children write their own list of animals. Remind them to write an action word, or verb, with each animal. Encourage children to use transitional spelling. You may wish to assess each piece of work using the scoring guide.

Shared Writing

Add to the Class Diary

Help children recall activities from the past week. Encourage children to use good speaking skills when they make their suggestions.

Invite children to help you write a sentence for each activity. Then add the pages to the class diary.

Optional Resources

Phonics Sourcebook pp. 1–78

Assessment Handbook

Phonics Workbook p. 125

Full Day Options...

Phonics

Shared Poetry Copy the first two stanzas of "A Journey" on blank paper. Make a copy for each child. Invite children to decorate their papers with jets or jeeps.

Independent Writing

Make a List Ask partners to look through books for pictures of animals. Have partners make a list of five animals they see. Let children help each other write the animal names and draw pictures of them.

Reading

Read Aloud Invite children who have beginning reading skills to read *In the Jungle* aloud to you. Listen to determine what words they know and what strategies they use to decode unfamiliar words.

Independent Reader 25

Day 5

Comprehension

Review
Predicting

Introduce the fable "The Lion and the Mouse" by reading the title. Have children make predictions about the story by asking:

Read Aloud

- **Who do you think the characters in this story will be?**

- **Do you think the story will be about things that could really happen, or do you think it will be make-believe? Why do you think so?**

TE Volume 5, p. AR4

After reading the story, verify the predictions children made earlier by asking:

- **Who are the characters in the story?** (a lion, a mouse)

- **Are they real or make-believe animals? Why do you think so?** (make-believe because animals cannot talk)

- **Who made predictions that were correct? What were they?**

Ongoing Assessment

Predicting

| **If...** children cannot make predictions from a title, | **then...** show several books. Read the titles. Ask children to predict who will be in the story or what will happen. |

Dramatize Characters' Actions

Encourage children to use actions, facial expressions, and gestures to show some of the things the lion and the mouse did. Have them brainstorm ideas about what might be the next adventure for the lion and the mouse. Then invite them to act out their predictions.

Day 5

Oral Language

Review
Make Introductions

Remind children that when meeting someone for the first time, it is important to introduce yourself. Also remind children that when they are bringing someone home to meet a family member, it is polite to introduce the person. That way, each person knows the other person's name.

Practice Making Introductions

Review the procedure for making an introduction. Use two volunteers. Say: *[Name], this is [name]. He/she is a friend of mine from school.* Explain that after giving the names, it is helpful to give information about the person. Point out that after the introduction is made, the two people should say "Hello" to each other, and they may want to begin a conversation.

Jaguar, this is lion. I helped him escape.

Have groups of three children practice making introductions. Ask one child to be the lion, one child to be the mouse, and one child to be another animal. The lion can introduce the mouse to the other animal or the mouse can introduce the lion to the other animal.

Self-Selected Reading

D.E.A.R.
Drop Everything And Read

Help children search for books they can read independently. You might wish to suggest *The Trek* by Ann Jonas, in which a little girl and her friend meet imaginary animals on the way to school.

Full Day Options...

Reading

Reader Response: "The Lion and the Mouse"
Discuss the story by asking: *If you were the trapped lion, how would you have felt when you saw the mouse? Would you have thought she could help? Do you think the lion and the mouse will become friends? Why or why not?*

Read Aloud, p. AR10

Oral Language

DRAMA CONNECTION

Make Introductions Let groups of three choose story characters to introduce to a friend. For example, one person could be Goldilocks and one person Baby Bear. The third child makes the introduction by saying "Goldilocks, this is Baby Bear. You ate his porridge." The two characters can then say something to each other. Let children present their introductions to the class.

Independent Writing

Write About the Lion or the Mouse Have children choose the lion or the mouse. Ask them to draw a picture of the character and to write a sentence about the character.

Oral Language

Tell a Story Let children choose one of these prompts to tell a story:

• Tell about what happens when the mouse meets an elephant.
• Tell a story about how the lion helps a monkey.

Day 5

Lesson Overview

Trade Book

Listen Buddy

Selection Audio

Genre
Animal Fantasy

Phonemic Awareness/Phonics
Consonant *v* /v/

Comprehension
Drawing Conclusions

High-Frequency Words
do   not   what

About the Author and Illustrator

Helen Lester
grew up near Chicago, Illinois. She was a teacher for sixteen years before she started writing full-time. She continues to visit schools and lectures at teachers' conferences. She enjoys humorous stories that handle heavy concepts lightly.

Lynn Munsinger
was born in Massachusetts. She completed her education with an art history degree and a graduate degree in illustration. She has illustrated over forty books. In addition to illustrating books, she has also contributed to children's textbooks, greeting cards, and *Cricket* magazine.

Leveled Books

Easy	On-Level	Challenge
		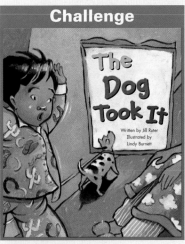
Wordless Story 26	Kindergarten Reader 26	Independent Reader 26

Trade Books for Self-Selected Reading and Read Aloud

Henry and Mudge in the Green Time
by Cynthia Rylant

One Hot Summer Day
by Nina Crews

Princess Penelope's Parrot
by Helen Lester

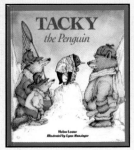

Tacky the Penguin
by Helen Lester

The Listening Walk
by Paul Showers

Whispering in the Park
by Fred Burstein

Theme Let's Explore   **Lesson Topic** A Path to Somewhere

5-Day Planner

 Customize your week with the Teacher's Resource Planner CD-ROM!

Reading
Comprehension
Vocabulary

Phonics
Phonemic Awareness

Day 1

Activate Prior Knowledge p. 55
Poem "The Swing"

Reading pp. 56–65
Read Aloud
Listen Buddy

Reader Response:
Pretend to Be Buddy

 Comprehension:
Drawing Conclusions

Play "I Spy" to Understand
Drawing Conclusions

Phonics pp. 66–67
 Consonant *v* /v/

Phonemic Awareness:
Identify /v/ Words
• Phonics Songs and
  Rhymes Chart 26

Connect Sound to Letter:
Match /v/ to *v*

Phonological Awareness:
Echo /v/ Words

✔ **High-Frequency Words**

| do | not | what |

Day 2

Phonics pp. 68–69
 Consonant *v* /v/

Phonemic Awareness:
Identify /v/ Words
• Phonics Songs and
  Rhymes Chart 26

Find /v/ Pictures
• Wordless Story 26
  The Van

Connect Sound to Letter:
Match /v/ to *v*

Phonological Awareness:
Change a Phoneme

✔ **High-Frequency Words:**
Use *do, not* and *what*

Reading pp. 70–71
 Comprehension:
Drawing Conclusions

Recall Book's
Main Character

Describe Characters

Draw Conclusions

Oral Language
**Speaking, Listening,
and Viewing**

Oral Language pp. 64–65
Introduce Vocabulary:
Head Words

| nose | teeth | ears | hair |

Use Vocabulary Words to Answer
Questions

Oral Language pp. 70–71
 Listening: Listen for
Rhyming Words

Recognize Rhyming
Words
• Oral Language Chart 26

Writing
**Grammar, Usage,
and Mechanics**

Writing pp. 66–67
 Shared Writing:
Write Sentences Together

Writing pp. 68–69
 Modeled Writing: Write About
Traveling

Guided Writing

Handwriting: Practice Writing *Vv*

Self-Selected Reading
Read Aloud

Self-Selected Reading p. 65
Children might enjoy reading
other books about animals that
get in trouble, such as *Tacky in
Trouble* by Helen Lester. See page 47 for
other suggestions.

Self-Selected Reading p. 71
Suggest a humorous story such
as *Princess Penelope's Parrot* by
Helen Lester.

 Target Skill   Review Skill

Target Skills of the Week

Reading Drawing Conclusions
Phonics Consonant *v* /v/
Oral Language Listen for Rhyming Words
Writing Verbs Ending in *-s*

Day 3	Day 4	Day 5

Day 3

Phonics pp. 72–73

 Consonant *v* /v/

Phonemic Awareness:
Identify the /v/ Picture

Connect Sound to Letter:
Add *v* to Make Words
• Phonics Songs and
Rhymes Chart 26

Phonological Awareness:
Listen for /v/

Read Kindergarten Reader 26:
Val and Vin

Reading pp. 74–75

 Comprehension:
Drawing Conclusions

Apply Drawing
Conclusions
Through Pantomime

Reader Response:
Compare and Contrast Rabbits

Model Writing Notes

Oral Language pp. 74–75

Listening: Listen for
Rhyming Words

Listen for Rhyming Words

Match Rhyming Words

Writing pp. 72–73

Modeled Writing:
Demonstrate Writing Sentences

Guided Writing

Self-Selected Reading p. 75

Children might enjoy reading
Henry and Mudge in the Green Time by Cynthia Rylant.

Day 4

Phonics pp. 76–77

Review Consonant *j* /j/

 Consonant *v* /v/

Phonemic Awareness:
Consonant *j* /j/

Identify Initial /j/ and /v/

Connect Sound to Letter:
Paste *v* on /v/ Pictures

Phonological Awareness:
Identify Alliteration

✔ **High-Frequency Words:**
Build Words

Challenge:
Independent Reader 26

Reading pp. 78–79

 Comprehension:
Drawing Conclusions

Activate Prior Knowledge

 Assess Drawing
Conclusions

Oral Language pp. 78–79

Listening: Listen for
Rhyming Words
• Read Aloud "At the Zoo"

 Assess Listening for Rhyming
Words

Writing pp. 76–77

Review **Interactive Writing:**
Use Capital Letters and
Periods

 Write Correct Sentences

Self-Selected Reading p. 79

Have children choose books to
read. Children may enjoy
reading *Whispering in the Park*
by Fred Burstein.

Day 5

Phonics pp. 80–81

 Consonant *v* /v/

Phonemic Awareness:
Prepare to Assess

Connect Sound to Letter:
Assess *v* /v/

Phonological Awareness:
Count Syllables

High-Frequency Words:
Assess

Reading pp. 82–83

Review **Comprehension:** Classifying
• Read Aloud "The Tortoise and the
Hare."
Act Out How Animals Move

Oral Language pp. 82–83

Review **Speaking:** Retell a Message

Practice Retelling a Message

Writing pp. 80–81

Independent Writing: Assess
Writing Development

Shared Writing: Add to the
Class Diary

Self-Selected Reading p. 83

Help children look for books they
can read independently. You
might suggest *One Hot
Summer Day* by Nina Crews.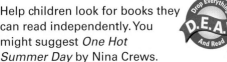

 Assessment   ✓ Benchmark Assessment of Target Skills and Skills Assessment

Cross-Curricular Work Stations

Community Link

Ideas for bringing the school and community together

Field Experiences
travel agency
library

Guest Speakers
librarian to discuss books about other places
travel agent
people who have traveled to other places

Letters and Sounds

Let's Volley 10 minutes

Materials: paper circles to represent volleyballs, magazine and catalog pictures of objects whose names begin with /v/ as well as other consonant sounds

Learning Styles Auditory, Visual, Kinesthetic, Individual

Attach pictures of objects to paper volleyballs. Children sort volleyballs into two groups: those with pictures that begin with /v/ and those with pictures that do not. Make a simple volleyball net. Children place the /v/ pictures on one side of the net and the pictures with other beginning consonant sounds on the other side.

Social Studies

Plan a Trip 10 minutes

Materials: simple map of the United States tacked to a bulletin board; map pins; books, brochures, and magazines about various states

Learning Styles Visual, Spatial, Individual

Invite children to look through materials about various states and decide which state they would visit if they were to plan a trip. Ask children to locate the state on a map and stick their name on it with a map pin.

 Provide children with books about different countries to look at and help them locate the countries on a world map or globe.

Media

Ha Ha Ha! two days for 10 minutes

Materials: TV cartoon, videos, drawing paper, crayons

Learning Styles Visual, Verbal

Invite children to recall a humorous cartoon or video they watched with the purpose of finding something that causes them to giggle. Have them draw a picture that represents what they thought was funny. During group time ask: *If you were the character in the story, would you still think that it was funny? Would you giggle if it happened to you?*

INTERNET SAFETY Establish guidelines for your students' safe and responsible use of the Internet. See the Scott Foresman Internet Guide for tips.

Technology

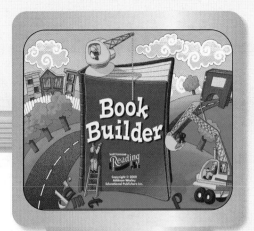

Book Builder Activity   10 minutes

Learning Styles Visual, Kinesthetic

Have children create their own book about an adventure. Children may need help locating some letters on the keyboard. If keyboarding proves too difficult, they can print their stories and write the words.

Web Site two days for 10 minutes

Learning Styles Individual, Visual

sfreading.com

Visit the Scott Foresman Web site (sfreading.com) for current hyperlinks to sites that can be used by children for an Internet Workshop investigation of journeys to other places. Also see the Scott Foresman Internet Guide for additional information on the Internet Workshop method.

Music

On the Road   10 minutes

Materials: recordings of songs with travel themes, masking tape to mark a two-foot-wide path on the floor

Learning Styles Auditory, Social, Spatial, Verbal

Discuss with children places they would like to visit. Play the music and have children walk in a line across the path. When the music stops, the child who is standing on the path is "on the road" and out of the game. Continue until one child is left.

Challenge Ask children to draw pictures or write sentences describing a favorite place.

I like my own backyard.

Science

Listen Buddy   10 minutes

Materials: paper clips, string, foam cups

Learning Styles Auditory, Social, Verbal

Punch a small hole in the bottom of two foam cups. Insert string into each cup, and tie a paper clip to each end to secure the string inside the cups. Ask partners to take turns talking into the cup and holding the cup to their ears to listen. Encourage children to discuss how sound travels from one cup to another.

Introduce the Reading Road Show Activity Stations to reinforce this week's skills.

Phonemic Awareness & Phonics
Literacy Activities

Use these activities during the week to reinforce skills.

Phonemic Awareness

Fill the Vase   20 minutes

Materials: paper flowers, vase

Learning Styles Kinesthetic, Verbal

Have children make flowers from construction paper. Display a vase. Tell children that they can "fill the vase" with flowers by following these directions. Have a volunteer come to the vase and name a word that begins like the word *vase*. If correct, the child places his or her flower in the vase and chooses someone to have the next turn. Continue until all children have placed their flowers in the vase.

You may choose to have children write or dictate their /v/ word on the flower.

ESL If children suggest a /v/ word from their first language, acknowledge their contribution and perhaps ask the child to teach the word to the rest of the group.

Working with Letters

Make a Basket   15 minutes

Materials: set of letter cards, wastebasket or box, beanbags

Learning Styles Visual, Spatial, Kinesthetic

Place a container such as a wastebasket or box at the front of the room. Have four children stand some distance away from the wastebasket. Give each player a beanbag. Hold up a letter card showing a capital or lowercase letter. The four children at the front of the room each try to be the first to name the letter. Whoever answers correctly tries to "make a basket" by throwing the beanbag into the wastebasket. After scoring a basket, he or she displays the next letter card. Continue until all children have had a turn.

Working with Words

Hidden Word   10 minutes

Learning Styles Visual, Kinesthetic, Logical

Explain that sometimes bigger words have smaller words in them. Write words on a chart or board such as *pencil, pants, forget,* and *kitten.* Have children look at the words closely and see if they can find any smaller words. Say each word slowly. You may wish to stress the "hidden" words as you say the larger word. Invite volunteers to circle the smaller words.

pencil

pants

kitten forget

ABC Wall

ABC Wall  20 minutes

Materials: paper

Learning Styles Visual, Social, Kinesthetic

Write the words *cap, car,* and *cat* on the board. Ask children to listen to the sentence and look for the word that best completes the sentence: *I drove a new _____.* (car) Have a child point to the word on the board. Continue with these sentences: *The kitten grew into a _____.* (cat) *I took off my _____.* (cap)

Divide the class into groups of three. Have the groups choose three words from the ABC Wall and think of or write a sentence using each word. Let the groups take turns writing the words on the board and saying their sentences.

I drove a new car.

cap
car
ca

Daily Warm-Up

Message Board

Day One

Today we will read about a rabbit named Buddy. He doesn't listen very well.

Discuss with children why it is important to listen carefully.

Ask: "Can you name something with a name that begins with *v*/v/?"

Day Two

We will look and listen for Vv.

Day Three

We will read the words *do, not,* and *what.*

Ask children: *"What do you not like to eat?"*

Discuss with children what makes two words rhyme.

Day Four

Today we will listen for rhyming words.

Day Five

Today we will write about a rabbit.

Ask children: "What do you know about rabbits?"

Getting Ready for the Week

Day One
photographs of animals
(Full Day)

Day Two
none

Day Three
string (Full Day)
large index cards
finger paints (Full Day)

Day Four
pipe cleaners
foil wrapping paper, small fuzzy craft balls
(Full Day)

Day Five
counters
grocery bags (Full Day)
fabric swatches, wallpaper
(Full Day)

Family Times

Send home the newsletter with fun instructional activities to reinforce this week's target skills.

Practice Book, pp. 165–166
Teacher's Resource Book, pp. 165–166

Activate Prior Knowledge

Play "Simon Says"

Talk with children about times when they didn't listen to someone as well as they should have. Ask:

- **Why do you think you weren't listening to the person talking to you?**

- **What happened because you didn't listen carefully enough?**

- **What can you do to be a better listener?**

Play "Simon Says" with children. Remind them to listen carefully to what you say and to be sure they hear "Simon says" before they follow the directions.

Build Background

Choose one or more of these activities to build background for concepts presented in this week's story, *Listen Buddy.*

Read Aloud a Poem

Share this poem with children. Then invite them to describe how they feel when they swing.

The Swing
by Robert Louis Stevenson

How do you like to go up in a swing,
    Up in the air so blue?
    Oh, I do think it the pleasantest
       thing
    Ever a child can do!

Up in the air and over the wall,
    Till I can see so wide,
Rivers and trees and cattle and all
    Over the countryside—

    Till I look down on the garden
       green,
    Down on the roof so brown—
Up in the air I go flying again,
    Up in the air and down!

Use Illustrations to Develop Oral Language

Hold up *Listen Buddy.* Have children look carefully at the cover illustration. Ask:

> **What do you notice most about the rabbit on the cover?** (his very large ears)

Have children make up a story about a rabbit and his very large ears.

Use Audio to Develop Story Concepts

Talk with children about a time when someone didn't listen to them. Ask:

- **Who had trouble listening to you?**

- **What happened when the person didn't listen?**

- **How did you feel when the person didn't listen to you?**

Share the Background-Building CD/tape, which presents a listening game in which children follow a set of directions.

CD 5/Tape 13, Side 2
Background-Building Audio

Concepts of Print

Read Left to Right, Top to Bottom

Display *Listen Buddy*. Point to the first word on the cover, *Helen,* and read it aloud. Ask:

Which word do I read next? Point to the next word I should read.

Children should point to *Lester*. Read the word aloud. Then ask:

Which word do I read now? Point to the next word I should read.

Children should point to *Listen*. Continue asking for help in reading the cover. After all the text is read, point to the words, going across and down, and say: *We read from left to right and from top to bottom.*

Model Reading Behaviors

Picture Walk and Predict

Preview the story and share the illustrations. Ask:

- **Who do you think the main character is?** (the rabbit)

- **What do you think Buddy's problem is?** (He doesn't listen.)

- **Do you think the story will be funny? Why or why not? Let's read to find out.**

Read Aloud Routine

Read Aloud the Story

Day 1

- Read the story through for enjoyment.

- Read expressively, conveying everyone's frustration with Buddy's poor listening skills.

- To practice the reading strategy predicting, use the stopping point on TE page 62.

Day 2

- Reread the entire story, using the activities found in the margins on pages 58–63.

Days 3–5

- Reread selected pages for specific purposes, as suggested in the lessons.

Read Aloud

HELEN LESTER
Listen
Buddy

Illustrated by
LYNN MUNSINGER

Trade Book

Buddy's father had a beautiful big nose.
He was a great sniffer.

page 3

Guiding the Reading

Critical Thinking

What is similar about the mistakes Buddy makes?
Possible answers: He brings items that rhyme with the items he is asked to bring.

Buddy's mother had beautiful big teeth.
She was a great chomper.

Buddy had beautiful big ears.

It didn't matter.

pages 4–5

Content Connection: Science

• Rabbits play from dusk to dawn. During the day they rest or sleep.

• Rabbits eat green leafy plants during the spring and summer.

• Rabbits eat bark, twigs, and fruit from trees and bushes during the winter.

When Buddy's parents sent him to the vegetable stand to get a basket of squash, he came home with a basket of wash.

When they asked him to buy fifteen tomatoes, he came home with fifty potatoes.

pages 6–7

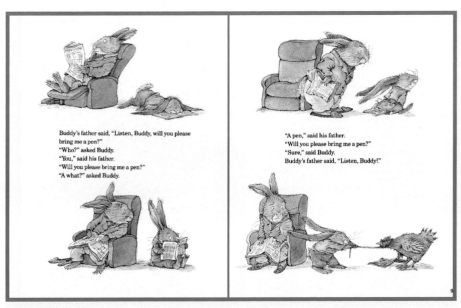

pages 8–9

pages 10–11

pages 12–13

Guiding the Reading

Critical Thinking

What would you tell Buddy to do to be a good listener?
Possible answers: Look at the speaker. Pay attention to what the speaker is saying.

Language Development

Share with children the meaning of *wandering.*

Buddy didn't hear what was said to him because his mind was wandering; he wasn't paying attention.

wandering

average

Guiding the Reading

Critical Thinking

Why might Buddy be confused when he hears the word *right*?
Possible answer: *Right* can mean two different things. It can mean a direction or it can mean *correct*. It also sounds like the word *write*.

Language Development

Point out to children that to look *scruffy* is to wear something that is dirty or very worn out, and a *varmint* is a troublesome or mean and crafty person or animal.

scruffy

varmint

challenge

pages 14–15

pages 16–17

pages 18–19

Buddy had forgotten his parents' warning about the Scruffy Varmint. He asked eagerly, "May I help?"

The Scruffy Varmint was not fond of having company, but with help he'd have his soup sooner, so he said, "Allllll right, Bunnyrabbit, come help me gather firewood."

"Who, what?" asked Buddy.

"You. Firewood."

Buddy eagerly hopped ahead of the Scruffy Varmint. Very gently he gathered a large prickly bundle, which he held out proudly.

Roughly the Varmint grabbed the bundle. "I said *firewood*, not *briarwood*," he yelped, plucking the sharp thorns from his paws.

pages 20–21

Later, when the pot was filled with water, the Scruffy Varmint lay against a rock, licking his paws and barking orders.

"Hustle, Bunnyrabbit. Get the flour."

"Yessir!" said Buddy.

"Five pinches of salt."

"Yessir!" said Buddy.

"Fifteen tomatoes."

"Yessir!" said Buddy.

pages 22–23

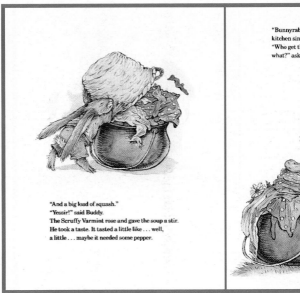

"And a big load of squash."

"Yessir!" said Buddy.

The Scruffy Varmint rose and gave the soup a stir. He took a taste. It tasted a little like . . . well, a little . . . maybe it needed some pepper.

"Bunnyrabbit, get the pepper from the left side of the kitchen sink," the Varmint growled.

"Who get the what from the where side of the where what?" asked Buddy.

pages 24–25

Guiding the Reading

Critical Thinking

Why do you think Buddy offers to help the Scruffy Varmint make his soup?

Possible answers: He wants to be helpful. He is curious about the Scruffy Varmint.

Language Development

Point out to children that *briarwood* is the wood from the root of the prickly briar bush. If children are familiar with Uncle Remus stories, remind them that the prickly briar patch is Brer Rabbit's home.

briarwood

challenge

Guiding the Reading

Critical Thinking

How could Buddy have known that the Scruffy Varmint was asking for cooking flour and not flowers that grow on a plant?

Possible answer: He should have known that flowers that grow on a plant wouldn't be used to make soup.

The Scuffy Varmint repeated, "WHO GET THE WHAT FROM THE WHERE SIDE OF THE WHERE WHAT? Never mind." He stalked into the kitchen and got the pepper himself and sprinkled it into the soup.

"There," he snarled. "Now, Bunnyrabbit, put the soup on the fire."

Buddy put the soup *in* the fire.

pages 26–27

Day 1

Stopping Point

Predict On the first reading, you may want to stop at the bottom of page 27 and ask children to predict what the Scruffy Varmint will do next.

Language Development

He stalked into the kitchen and got the pepper himself and sprinkled it into the soup.

What does *stalked* mean in that sentence? How do you know? How can you use other words and the pictures to figure out what *stalked* means?

stalked

average

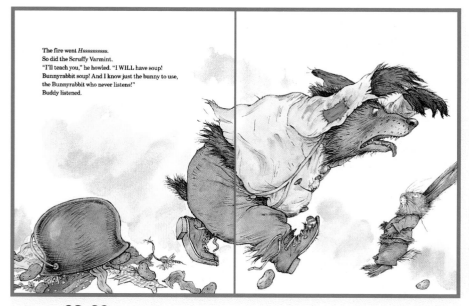

The fire went *Hsssssssss.*
So did the Scruffy Varmint.
"I'll teach you," he howled. "I WILL have soup! Bunnyrabbit soup! And I know just the bunny to use, the Bunnyrabbit who never listens!"
Buddy listened.

pages 28–29

Guiding the Reading

Critical Thinking

What do you think Buddy is going to do the next time he needs to listen to someone? Why do you think so? What in the story helped you decide this?
Possible answer: Next time Buddy will pay attention because he has learned his lesson.

He also hopped.
Veryveryvery fast.
Faster than he had ever hopped in his life.

He whizzed up the road past the vegetable stand and into the safety of his house.

pages 30–31

62 *Listen Buddy*

And a little later, when Buddy's parents asked him
to bring a pen and a slice of bread,
Buddy listened.

page 32

Critical Thinking

How do you think Buddy's parents feel about what happened to him?
Possible answers: They are relieved that he didn't get hurt. They feel happy that he has learned to listen.

Day
1

Listen Buddy **63**

Day
1

Objectives

Children will

 draw conclusions
- use life experiences to build vocabulary

Meeting Individual Needs
ESL

Children may have difficulty using the selection vocabulary in sentences. Point to your *nose*, *teeth*, *ears*, and *hair* and say a sentence about each. Have children repeat your actions and echo you.

Skills Trace

Drawing Conclusions

Introduce	TE: K.5 64–65
Practice	PB: 168, 170, 180, 182, 218, 220
Reteach/ Review	TE: K.5 71, 74, 78, 118, 138–139, 145, 148, 152, 192, AR13, AR17 K.6 138–139, 145, 148, 152, 194, AR17
Skills Assessment	Skills Assessment Unit 5 TE: K.5 AR1–AR3 K.6 AR1–AR3

Reader Response

Check Predictions

Ask: *Did you think this story was funny? Why or why not? Who was the funniest character? What did you think was the funniest part?*

Pretend to Be Buddy

Tell children that you are going to tell them to do something or to bring something to you. Have children pretend to be Buddy and do or bring the wrong thing because, like Buddy, they aren't listening properly. Remind them that the things Buddy brought or did for his parents rhymed with what they asked for. Say:

- **Go to the hall.** (Children might go to the wall.)

- **Bring me a fan.** (Children might bring you a can or a pan.)

- **Bring me some glue.** (Children might bring you a shoe or something blue.)

Oral Language/Vocabulary

Use Vocabulary Words to Answer Questions

The vocabulary words are things found on a person's head. Have children use these words to answer the questions.

 nose   teeth   ears   hair

- **What do you use to smell things?** (nose)

- **What do you use to chew food?** (teeth)

- **What do you hear with?** (ears)

- **What grows on top of your head?** (hair)

Encourage children to say sentences using the words *nose*, *teeth*, *ears*, and *hair*. For example, *I blow my* nose or *I braid my* hair.

Comprehension

Play "I Spy" to Understand Drawing Conclusions

Have children stand in a circle. Describe a child without naming him or her: *I spy someone wearing a red shirt and whose name begins with /v/.* After the group identifies the child, ask:

I spy someone wearing a red shirt.

- **How did you know who I was describing?** (by using the clues)

- **How did you know the child wasn't [another child's name]?** (He/she didn't match the clues.)

Continue describing other children for the group to identify.

Say: *When you used the clues to figure out who I described, you were using what you know to make up your mind. When you read or hear a story, you use what you know to decide what might happen to the characters. What did Buddy learn from his experience with the Scruffy Varmint?* (It is important to listen carefully). *How do we know that?* (Buddy was scared and that made him realize it was important to listen.)

Self-Selected Reading

D.E.A.R. Drop Everything And Read

Have children select books to read. They might enjoy reading other books about animals that get in trouble, such as *Tacky the Penguin* by Helen Lester. See page 47 for other suggestions.

Day 1

Full Day Options...

Drawing Conclusions 👫👫

Where Am I Going? Tell children you are going somewhere. Name things you will take with you. Have children draw conclusions about where you might be going. For example, *I am taking a tent, a flashlight, and a sleeping bag.* (camping)

Vocabulary 👫👫

Point to the Head Word Say the selection vocabulary and ask children to point to that part of their head as you say the word. Let children take turns calling out the words.

Oral Language 👫

Create a Face Have one child describe a creature's head for a partner to draw using the selection vocabulary. For example, *This creature has four eyes, a tiny green nose, two pointed ears, and purple hair.* Partners take turns describing a creature's head.

ART CONNECTION

run

Daily Phonics Routine

Children will

- recognize the letters *Vv*
- recognize initial /v/
- identify high-frequency words
- participate in a shared writing activity

Meeting Individual Needs
Challenge

If children are proficient at recognizing initial /v/, say more words, some of which have /v/ in other positions, such as *river, glove, every, gravy, have, move, heavy, even,* and *wave.* Have children echo the words and identify the position of /v/: *beginning, middle,* or *end.*

Skills Trace

Consonant *Vv*

Introduce	TE: K.5 66
Practice	PB: 219, 221
Reteach/ Review	TE: K.5 68, 72–73, 76, 80, 112, AR12
Skills Assessment	Skills Assessment Unit 5 TE: K.5 AR1–AR3

Phonemic Awareness

Identify /v/ Words

Recite "Vacation" or play the CD/tape. Ask children to name the words that begin with /v/. (vacation, video, volleyball, violin, very, van, veggies, vegetable, velvet, vest)

CD 2/Tape 13, Side 2

Phonics Songs and Rhymes Audio

Identify /v/ Picture Cards

Show picture cards for *valentine, van,* and *volcano.* Have children identify each picture card by name. Elicit that they all begin with /v/.

Vacation

Vacation, vacation is here today.
Let's rent a video and then we'll play.
Let's play volleyball all day long.
Let's play violin and sing a song.

Let's take a trip in a very big van.
Let's buy some veggies from the vegetable man.
Let's each wear a velvet vest.
Vacation, vacation is the best!

Phonics Songs and Rhymes Chart 26

Ongoing Assessment

Phonemic Awareness

If... children have difficulty hearing initial /v/,	**then...** have them repeat *van* several times, stressing the /v/, and let them feel the vibration of their lower lip against their top front teeth.

Connect Sound to Letter

Match /v/ to *v*

Show the alphabet card. Explain that /v/ can be written as *V* or *v.* Say *vegetables* slowly, emphasizing the initial /v/. Point to the letter *v* each time you say /v/. Write *van* on the board and then point to the *v* and to the ending *-an.* Have children say the sounds individually and then blend them together to say the word.

Alphabet Cards

Phonological Awareness

Echo /v/ Words

Have children identify the word that begins with /v/ in the following sentences.

I put the flowers in the vase.

She eats vegetables six times a day.

Vivian wants to play.

High-Frequency Words

Find *do, not,* and *what* on ABC Wall

Say the high-frequency word *do*. Have children point to the word on the ABC Wall and name the letters in the word. Continue with the words *not* and *what*.

  what

Ask children to say words that begin with /v/. Write the words on cards and add them to this week's panel of the ABC Wall.

Day
1

Optional Resources

Phonics Sourcebook pp. 68–70, 84–85

High-Frequency Word Cards

Phonics Workbook p. 126

Shared Writing

Write Sentences Together

Say: *We are going to write about going on vacation.* Ask children to think of things they would tell someone who was going on a vacation.

As children respond, they can

- Help you sound out the words as you write them
- Use high-frequency words
- Identify words with initial /v/

When you are finished, read the sentences together as a volunteer tracks the print.

Vacation Advice

Do what you want to do.

Do not pack too much.

Visit a new place.

Full Day Options...

Independent Writing

Write About Vacations Have children choose one.

- Write or dictate a sentence about a fun vacation.
- Draw and label pictures of people you like to visit on vacation.
- Draw and label a picture of an exciting way to travel.

Phonics

Load Vehicles Draw a large van and a dump truck on chart paper. Provide magazine pictures of items, including some with names that begin with /v/. Have children decide in which vehicle each picture should be placed. Pictures with names that begin with /v/ are pasted onto the van. All others are pasted onto the dump truck.

Oral Language

Describe Animals' Features
Provide children with books or magazines that have pictures of animals. Have children locate and describe each animal's nose, teeth, ears, and hair (or fur). Encourage them to use complete sentences, such as *The seal's ears are very small.*

Daily Phonics Routine

Objectives

Children will

- recognize the letters *Vv*
- identify singular action words (verbs)
  - recognize initial /v/
  - recite a rhyme

Day 2

Consonant *Vv*
Practice Book, p. 167
Teacher's Resource Book, p. 167

Skills Trace

Verbs Ending in *-s*

Introduce	TE: K.5 **69**
Reteach/ Review	TE: K.5 77, 81, 113
Skills Assessment	Skills Assessment Unit 5 TE: K.5 AR1–AR3

Phonemic Awareness

Identify /v/ Words

Play the CD/tape and encourage children to recite the rhyme "Vacation." Have them make a *v* with their fingers when they hear words that begin with /v/.

CD 2/Tape 13, Side 2
Phonics Songs and Rhymes Audio

Phonics Songs and Rhymes Chart 26

Find /v/ Pictures

Have children look through *The Van*. Ask them to look for pictures with names that begin with /v/. Children may wish to dictate or write a story in the take-home version.

Wordless Story 26

Connect Sound to Letter

Match /v/ to *v*

Have Alphapotamus show the alphabet card. Help children write a large *v* on construction paper. Have Alphapotamus hold up picture cards, some with names that begin with /v/ and some that do not. Tell children to hold up their *v* when Alphapotamus shows and names something that begins with /v/.

Alphabet Cards

Phonological Awareness

Change a Phoneme

Ask children to identify the word in the following sentences that doesn't make sense. Tell them to change the beginning sound of that word to /v/ and say the word that does make sense in the sentence.

Jenna wore her new *test*. (vest)

Monkeys swing on *mines*. (vines)

Mother drove the pan. (van)

Take the dog to the let. (vet)

High-Frequency Words

Use *do, not,* and *what* Model using *do, not,* and *what* in sentences. Have children find the words on the ABC Wall and use them in sentences of their own.

ABC Wall

Say words with initial /v/ that are on the ABC Wall. Help children find each word on the ABC Wall and say a sentence using the word.

Modeled Writing

Write About Traveling Discuss ways to travel with children. Write: *Three boys ride their bikes. The boy rides his bike.*

- **My first sentence is about three boys. My second sentence is about one boy.**
- **I used the verb *ride* to tell what three boys did.**
- **Because the second sentence tells about what one boy did, I add -s at the end of *ride* to make *rides*.**

Guided Writing Help children write a sentence about a boy or a girl traveling. Remind them to add *-s* to the end of the action word. Encourage children to use transitional spelling. Some may need to draw or dictate.

Handwriting

Practice Writing *Vv* Distribute writing paper and have children practice writing V and *v*. Have children who are already proficient writing V and *v* write *Vivian* and *violin*.

D'Nealian™	Ball and Stick

Meeting Individual Needs
Other Ways to Learn

Kinesthetic Ask children to make the letter *v* using many different objects in the classroom. For example, two pencils, two rulers, two crayons, two paper clips.

Day 2

Optional Resources

Phonics Sourcebook pp.68–70, 84–85

High-Frequency Word Cards

Phonics Workbook p. 127

Full Day Options...

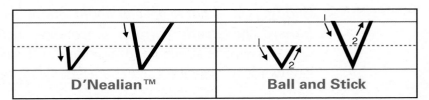

Phonics

Blend Sounds Have Alphapotamus say /v/ *et.* Have children blend the sounds and say the word aloud. (vet) Repeat with: *vine, vase, vest, van, vote.*

Handwriting

Practice Have children choose one.

- Write *van* and *varmint.* Draw a picture of a varmint in a van.
- Write words that rhyme with *van* by replacing *v* with another letter. (can, Dan, fan, man, Nan, pan, ran, tan)

Independent Writing

Write About a Vacation Have children write or dictate descriptive sentences about a vacation that leads to an exciting adventure.

Day
2

Objectives

Children will

- draw conclusions
- orally identify rhyming words
- listen to a rhyme
- listen for specific information

Meeting Individual Needs

Other Ways to Learn

Kinesthetic/Visual Ask children to work with partners to pantomime familiar activities. Encourage the rest of the group to observe the pantomime and use the visual clues to draw conclusions about what activities the partners pantomime.

Oral Language

Recognize Rhyming Words

Display "Little Bunny." Explain that the poem has rhyming words. Remind children that words rhyme when they have the same ending sounds. Offer *bunny* and *funny* as an example of rhyming words. Read the rhyme. Ask children to identify the rhyming words. (would, should, tree, me)

Little Bunny
Anonymous

There was a little bunny who
Lived in the wood,
He wiggled his ears
As a good bunny should.

He hopped by a squirrel,
He hopped by a tree.
He hopped by a duck,
And he hopped by me.

He stared at the squirrel.
He stared at the tree.
He stared at the duck.
But he made faces at me!

Oral Language Chart 26

Comprehension

Recall Book's Main Character

Hold up *Listen Buddy* and ask children to recall what Buddy doesn't do and why this causes problems. (He doesn't listen so he doesn't do what people ask him to.) Ask children to pantomime being Buddy when his parents are asking him to bring things. Ask: *What does he do instead of listening?*

Read Aloud

HELEN LESTER
Listen Buddy
Illustrated by
LYNN MUNSINGER

Trade Book

Describe Characters

Recall the other characters in *Listen Buddy.* Ask: *What is special about Buddy's mother? His father? The Scruffy Varmint?* Encourage children to answer with a complete sentence, using one of the selection vocabulary words to describe each character: *nose, teeth, ears,* or *hair.*

Listen to Trade Book for Information

Ask children to listen as you reread the trade book. Direct them to listen carefully for what Buddy's parents ask him to bring to them and what he brings instead.

While reading, you may wish to use the ideas in the *Guiding the Reading* and *Language Development* boxes on pages 58–63 of this Teacher's Edition.

Draw Conclusions

Ask the following questions that encourage children to draw conclusions.

- Display page 5. Ask: *What should Buddy be able to do with his beautiful big ears?* (hear or listen very well)

- Display the pictures on pages 10 and 12. Ask: *What can you tell by looking at the pictures?* (Buddy is not listening.)

- Show page 15 and ask: *How do Buddy's parents look?* (worried) *Why do you think they are feeling this way?* (They don't know if Buddy was listening, and they are worried he might go the wrong way.)

- Ask: *How would you describe Buddy at the end of the story?* (respectful, follows directions, behaves well)

Ongoing Assessment

Drawing Conclusions

If... children have difficulty drawing conclusions,

then... prompt them to choose one of two possible answers and have them explain why they chose that answer.

Day 2

Self-Selected Reading D.E.A.R. Drop Everything And Read

Have children choose their own books to read from your self-selected reading collection. Suggest a humorous story, such as *Princess Penelope's Parrot* by Helen Lester.

Full Day Options...

Drawing Conclusions 🧍

What Would Buddy Do? Remind children that because Buddy did not listen, he brought the wrong things to his parents. Ask children to draw what Buddy might bring if his mother said "Bring me a dish" and his father said "Get your hat." Ask children to explain why they drew those objects.

Oral Language 🧍

Make a Rhyme Book Give each child a sheet of paper. Brainstorm a list of rhyming words. Ask children to write or dictate and illustrate a sentence in which two words rhyme. Collect the pages and make them into a class book titled *Rhyming Words.*

Oral Language 👥

Find Rhyming Words Reread *"Little Bunny,"* leaving out the last word in each stanza. Ask children to replace the missing word with another word that rhymes. For example, *should* becomes *would* or *could; me* becomes *bee* or *flee.*

PHONICS

Objectives

Children will

- recognize the letters *Vv*
- distinguish between initial and final consonant sounds
- use prewriting strategies
- understand how print is organized and read

Day 3

❄ Meeting Individual Needs

ESL

Help children explore the sound similarities, particularly those communicated through the illustrations in *Listen Buddy,* for example, *squash/wash; fifteen tomatoes/fifty potatoes; pen/hen; bread/bed.*

Daily Phonics Routine

Phonemic Awareness

Identify the /v/ Picture

Display two picture cards. Ask children to choose the picture whose name begins with /v/. Repeat using other picture cards.

Picture Cards

Ongoing Assessment

Phonemic Awareness

If... children have difficulty choosing the correct picture,

then... have them reinforce the sound they are listening for by saying /v/ before naming each picture.

Connect Sound to Letter

Count *v* Words

Reread "Vacation" slowly. Have children write a *v* on their paper each time they hear a word that begins with /v/. When you are finished reading, count to find the total number of /v/ words in the poem.

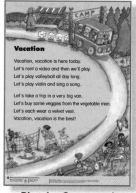

CD 2/Tape 13, Side 2

Phonics Songs and Rhymes Audio

Phonics Songs and Rhymes Chart 26

Phonological Awareness

Listen for /v/

Give children three-sound boxes and a marker. Tell children you will say a /v/ word. If /v/ is in the initial position, they should place the marker in the first sound box. If /v/ is in the final position, they should place the marker in the last box. Use the following words: *van, five, vine, vest, hive, vase, vote, give, Val.*

Phonics and High-Frequency Words

Read Kindergarten Reader 26

- Track the print as you read the title *Val and Vin.* Ask children which words begin with /v/.

- Have children use the title and illustrations to predict what the book will be about.

- Read the book aloud. When you get to the end of a sentence, ask children where you should read next.

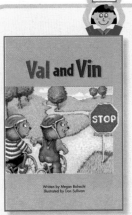

Kindergarten Reader 26

Phonics Consonant *Vv*

High-Frequency Words
do, not, what

Look Vin!
Do not ride!
What is it?
2

It is a mop Val.
We can look at it!
3

Look Vin!
Do not run!
What is it?
4

It is a rat, Val!
We can run.
5

Look Vin!
Do not hop!
What is it?
6

It is a van.
We can hop!
7

Look Val!
It is my house.
We can sit!
8

Modeled Writing

Demonstrate Writing Sentences

Model writing a sentence based on Kindergarten Reader 26 *Val and Vin.* For example, write *Do not run!*

As you write the sentence, model these strategies:

• Begin the sentence with a capital letter.

• Point out that words are written from left to right.

Guided Writing

Ask children to read the sentences with you. Help them write their own sentences based on *Val and Vin.*

ABC Wall

Point out a word beginning with *v* on the ABC Wall. Say the word and then have children spell it aloud. Repeat with other words that begin with *v.*

Optional Resources

Phonics Sourcebook
pp.1–78

Phonics Workbook
p. 128

Day 3

Full Day Options...

Phonics

/v/ Word Collages Have children make a collage of pictures with names that begin with /v/. They can use pictures they draw or cut out of magazines. Have children write *v* and *V* around the pictures.

Phonics

V-Word Vine Attach string along a wall at a height children can reach. Have them write words or draw pictures of things that begin with /v/ and attach them to the string to create a "V-Word Vine."

Independent Writing

Change the Story Remind children that in *Listen Buddy,* Buddy was supposed to go left on the path instead of right. Ask children to write about what they think would have happened if Buddy had gone left like he was supposed to.

Objectives

Children will

- ⟳ draw conclusions
- ⟳ listen for rhyming words
- • write notes about a topic

✹ Meeting Individual Needs
Challenge

Review the pictures on pages 22–24 that show what Buddy does because he does not listen carefully. Invite children to draw pictures to show other things Buddy might have done when he wasn't listening.

Drawing Conclusions
Practice Book, p. 168
Teacher's Resource Book, p. 168

Oral Language

Read Aloud
Trade Book

HELEN LESTER
Listen Buddy
Illustrated by
LYNN MUNSINGER

Listen for Rhyming Words

Reread pages 6–11 of *Listen Buddy*. Show the illustrations so that children can see what Buddy brought instead of what he was supposed to bring. Name the item Buddy was supposed to bring and have children say what Buddy brought instead. Repeat the two words and ask children if they rhyme.

Match Rhyming Words

Write rhyming CVC words, such as *cat/hat, pot/hot, van/man,* individually on large index cards. Make a simple drawing of the object at the bottom of the card. Distribute the cards to children. Have one volunteer read the word or name the picture on his or her card. The child with the rhyming word card should raise his or her hand and read the word or name the picture. Continue with other word pairs.

Comprehension

Apply Drawing Conclusions Through Pantomime

Briefly review the story events in *Listen Buddy* with children. Divide the class into groups of three or four. Have the groups take turns selecting and pantomiming an event from the story. The other groups should observe the pantomime and draw conclusions about what is happening and how the characters are feeling.

Ongoing Assessment
Drawing Conclusions

If... children have difficulty drawing conclusions from the pantomimes,

then... help them use the illustrations in the book to draw conclusions.

Day 3

Reader Response

Compare and Contrast Rabbits

Recall with children that the rabbits in *Listen Buddy* are make-believe rabbits. Let children look through books with photographs of real rabbits. Ask them to compare and contrast real and make-believe rabbits.

Model Writing Notes

Model writing notes using the information in the pictures: *Some rabbits dig holes. A rabbit eats green plants.* As you write the notes, model these strategies:

- Begin each sentence with a capital letter.

- Leave spaces between words.

- Point out any action words, or verbs, that have an *-s* at the end.

- Use correct end punctuation.

Self-Selected Reading

From your self-selected reading collection, have children choose their own books to read. Children might enjoy reading *Henry and Mudge in the Green Time* by Cynthia Rylant.

Day 3

Full Day Options...

Oral Language

Do the Words Rhyme? Have one child make up two silly sentences that rhyme, such as *A mouse ate my cheese. May I have more, please?* The partner listens for and identifies the rhyming words.

Handwriting

Finger Paint V and v Provide children with finger paints. Have them make a painting with *V* and *v* written in paint in all different sizes.

Independent Writing

Transportation Action Words Have children illustrate an action word related to transportation, such as *drive, travel, walk, fly, ride.* Children should draw one person or thing doing that action. Children write or dictate a sentence about their drawings using an action word that ends in *-s.* For example, *Mary rides her bike.*

Drawing Conclusions

What's the Question? Tell children you are going to say the answer to a question and they are to use your answer to draw conclusions about what the question could have been. Suggested answers: *No, thank you, I'm not hungry. I am 6 years old. I live in Centerville. She walks to school. It is in the refrigerator.*

Objectives

Children will

 recognize initial /v/
- use capital letters and periods
- identify the use of alliteration
- use high-frequency words

Meeting Individual Needs

Intervention

Write sentences using the high-frequency words and read them with children as you track the print. Have children circle the words *do, not,* and *what* in the sentences.

Day 4

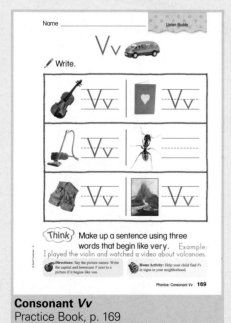

Consonant *Vv*
Practice Book, p. 169
Teacher's Resource Book, p. 169

Daily Phonics Routine

Review **Consonant /j/**

Phonemic Awareness

Tell children that you are going to say a word and they are to replace the beginning sound with /j/ to make a new word. For example, say *get.* Replace /g/ with /j/. Say the new word, *jet.* Continue with the following words: *ham* (jam), *racket* (jacket), *poke* (joke), *boy* (joy), *bob* (job), *sunk* (junk), *belly* (jelly).

Identify Initial /j/ and /v/

Ask children to listen to the beginning sounds in words and to jump if the word begins with /j/ or say "vvvroom" if the word begins with /v/. Use these words: *valentine, jacket, vase, vote, jump, vine, jam, jeans, van, junk.*

Connect Sound to Letter

Paste *v* on /v/ Pictures

Have each child make a *v* using a pipe cleaner. Display a collection of pictures pasted on poster board, some whose names begin with /v/ and some which do not. Ask children to find a picture whose name begins with /v/ and attach their letter v onto the picture.

Phonological Awareness

Identify Alliteration

Say a pair of sentences, such as *Betty Brown bounced her ball* and *Kittens drink pink milk.* Ask children to listen for the sentence in which most words begin with the same sound. When they hear such a sentence, ask children to repeat the sound and say the letter that stands for the repeated beginning sound.

High-Frequency Words

Build Words

Give each child the following letters on cards: *d, o, n, o, t, w, h, a,* and *t.* Also give them word cards for *do, not,* and *what.* Ask children to make the words *do, not,* and *what* by matching the letters to the word cards.

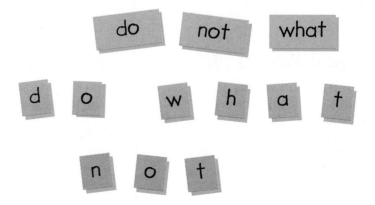

Interactive Writing

Review

Use Capital Letters and Periods

Remind children that a sentence always begins with a capital letter and ends with a punctuation mark, often a period. Write these sentences on the board: *the cave was very dark* and *my vest is too small,* omitting periods and capital letters. Ask: *What is wrong with these sentences?* Let children correct the sentences.

Write Correct Sentences

Write the incomplete sentence *we do not like _____.* Ask children to suggest a /v/ word to complete the sentence, such as *vans, violins,* or *vests.* Ask volunteers to write the word in the blank, and add a capital letter at the beginning and a period at the end.

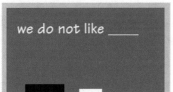

we do not like _____

Ongoing Assessment

Writing

If... children have trouble correcting sentences,

then... ask them to erase the first letter in the sentence and tell them what capital letter to write in its place. Ask them to find the last letter in the sentence and show them how to make a period after the letter.

Meeting Individual Needs

Challenge

Display *The Dog Took It* and identify the title, author, and illustrator. Encourage children to look for familiar words as you read the story together.

Independent Reader 26

Optional Resources

Phonics Sourcebook pp. 79–82, 84–85, 86–129

Phonics Workbook p.129

High-Frequency Word Cards

Phonics Kit

Day 4

Full Day Options...

Independent Writing 🤸

Write About Exploring Ask children to write descriptive text about exploring one of the following:

- their neighborhood
- another country
- another planet

Phonics 👥👥

Revisit Kindergarten Reader 26, *Val and Vin* For more practice in high-frequency word recognition, have children reread *Val and Vin.* Let them take turns reading aloud the pages.

Kindergarten Reader 26

Phonics 👥👥

Shared Poetry Write the poem, "Vacation," on paper for each child. Invite children to read the poem with you. Then ask them to circle the *v* words.

Phonics Songs and Rhymes Chart 26

READING A B C

Objectives

Children will

- draw conclusions
- orally identify rhyming words
- use illustrations to comprehend the text

Comprehension

Activate Prior Knowledge

Display *Looking for Crabs* from Unit 4. Ask:

- **What do you remember about this story?**
- **Where does the story take place?**

Reread the big book. Have children join in by reading the text with you.

Big Book

Assess Drawing Conclusions

To assess children's abilities to draw conclusions, display pages 16–17 of *Looking for Crabs*. Tell children to use the illustration to answer the questions:

- **Why couldn't the family find any crabs when Dad lifted up the rock?** (The crab was hiding on the bottom of the rock.)
- **Why did the family leave thinking there were no crabs at the beach?** (The crabs were hiding and the family never found any.)

Meeting Individual Needs

ESL

If children have difficulty verbalizing their conclusions, let them act them out. For example, they might hide behind a desk to act out their conclusion that the family didn't find any crabs because the crabs were hiding.

Ongoing Assessment

Drawing Conclusions

If... children have difficulty drawing conclusions,

then... use the Drawing Conclusions reteach lesson on page AR13 of this Teacher's Edition.

Day 4

Name _____ Listen Buddy

Children's drawings should include a silly response for Buddy's parents' request for a pan.

Directions: Draw a picture of what Buddy might bring if his parents asked for a pan. **Home Activity:** Talk with your child about things you will do this summer.

170 Comprehension: Drawing Conclusions

Drawing Conclusions
Practice Book, p. 170
Teacher's Resource Book, p. 170

Oral Language

Establish a Purpose for Listening

Ask children to listen for words that rhyme as you read aloud the poem "At the Zoo."

Read Aloud

At the Zoo

First I saw the white bear,
  Then I saw the black;
Then I saw the camel
With a hump upon
  his back;
Then I saw the gray wolf,
  With meat in his paw;

Then I saw a wombat
  Waddle in the straw;
Then I saw the elephant
  A-waving his trunk;
Then I saw
  the monkeys—
Wow, how they stunk!

Assess Listening for Rhyming Words

Point out that poems often have lines with words at the end that rhyme. Reread the poem. Stop after the lines ending with *back, straw,* and *stunk* and ask children to name rhyming words. (black, back; paw, straw; trunk, stunk) Have them explain why the words rhyme. (They have the same ending sounds.) Ask children to draw a picture illustrating one pair of the rhyming words.

Ongoing Assessment

Listening for Rhyming Words

| **If...** children have trouble identifying words that rhyme, | **then...** reread the poem and signal children to echo each of the rhyming words as you read it. |

Self-Selected Reading   D.E.A.R.

Have children choose books to read. Children may enjoy reading *Whispering in the Park* by Fred Burstein.

Optional Resources

Assessment Handbook

Day **4**

Full Day Options...

Drawing Conclusions

Draw Conclusions Provide pictures of situations, such as people cheering at a football game or someone falling in a puddle. Have children draw a face that shows how the people in those situations probably felt.

Phonics

Violets in Vases Provide children with construction paper with an outline of a vase on it, pipe cleaners, foil wrapping paper, and small fuzzy craft balls. Have children make violets with the materials and glue them to the vase.

Oral Language

Rhyming Word Tag One child is "it." This child says a simple word, such as *cat, let, pot, bake,* or *cut* and calls on a classmate to say a rhyming word. He or she continues calling on classmates to say other rhyming words. If a child can't name another word that rhymes, this child chooses someone else to become "it."

PHONICS

Objectives

Children will

↻ recognize initial /v/

↻ use singular action words (verbs)

- count syllables
- write a story

Daily Phonics Routine

very, really, much

Phonemic Awareness

Prepare to Assess

Have Alphapotamus say: *very, really,* and *much.* Have children repeat the word that begins with /v/ and make a *v* with their arms. Repeat with: *helicopter, windmill, volcano; feather, visit, monkey; rose, pony, violet.*

Connect Sound to Letter

Assess v /v/

Have children draw a van on a piece of construction paper. Tell children to write *V* or *v* on their van for each word you say that begins with /v/. Say: *vest, box, violin, hand, volcano, mitten, vegetable, football, valentine, necklace, vase.* Then check that children have written *V* or *v* on their van six times.

Ongoing Assessment

Phonics

If... children cannot correctly identify words with initial /v/,	**then...** use the Consonant *Vv* reteaching activities on pages AR12 of this Teacher's Edition.

Phonological Awareness

Count Syllables

Say *vacation* very slowly, emphasizing the syllables. Have children put down one counter for each syllable they hear. You may wish to have them clap the syllables first. Repeat with: *vest, volcano, visit, violin, vote, vegetable.*

High-Frequency Words

Assess

Invite children to make a *What Is It?* riddle book. Have them write the question *What Is It?* at the top of a sheet of paper. Then have them write or dictate a word and illustrate it to complete the sentence *It is not a* three times, for example, *It is not a cat. It is not a dog. It is not a fish.* Then, have children complete the sentence *It is a* by writing a word and drawing a picture. Collect the papers to make individual books. Invite children to take their book home and share it with a family member.

Day 5

Independent Writing

Assess Writing Development

Think ALOUD

Remind children that Buddy in *Listen Buddy* was a rabbit. Tell children they are going to write a story about a rabbit.

I am going to name my rabbit Vinnie. My rabbit hops very fast. I am going to write "Vinnie hops very fast."

Remind children that only one rabbit is hopping, so the verb, or action word, *hop* has -s at the end.

Have children write a story about a rabbit. Make sure they tell about things the rabbit does and include -s at the end of each action word. Encourage children to use transitional spelling. Make a class book titled *Rabbit Stories*. You may wish to assess each piece of work using the scoring guide.

Optional Resources

Phonics Workbook p.130

Assessment Handbook

Shared Writing

Add to the Class Diary

Ask children to recall things they have done during the week. Point out the action words they use in their sentences. Ask them to help you by writing letters, entire words, or phrases. Add the pages to the class diary.

Full Day Options...

Phonics 👫

Make a /v/ Word Vest Have partners make a vest from a grocery bag by cutting holes for their arms and head and cutting the bag open up the mid-dle. Have them decorate their vests with the letters *V* and *v* and words or pictures with names that begin with *v* /v/.

Independent Writing 🧍

Write About a Character's Actions Tell children to create a character and draw pictures of things their character likes to do. Have children label their pictures using action words to tell what the character is doing. For example, *He runs.*

Reading 🧍

Read Aloud Ask children who have beginning reading skills to read *The Dog Took It* aloud to you. Listen for evidence of sound blending and decoding strategies.

Independent Reader 26

Comprehension

Read Aloud

Review
Classifying

To introduce "The Tortoise and the Hare," ask children to tell what they know about the story. Ask them to think about what the characters are like as they listen to the story.

After reading, ask:

- **Who are the main characters?** (Tortoise and Hare)

- **How does Hare do things?** (very quickly)

- **How does Tortoise do things?** (very slowly)

TE Volume 5, p. AR5

When children note that Hare is always fast and Tortoise is always slow, write *Fast* and *Slow* as headings on the board. Ask: *What other animals are fast? Slow?* Write children's responses on the board in the appropriate column. If necessary, suggest animals to children and ask whether they are fast or slow.

Fast	Slow
cheetah	snail
lion	elephant
deer	koala

Ongoing Assessment

Classifying

If... children have difficulty classifying animals by their speed,

then... have them compare how fast the animal moves to how fast children walk or run and use the comparison to decide if the animal moves quickly or slowly.

Act Out How Animals Move

Reread each animal name on the chart aloud. Ask children to pantomime how the animal moves quickly, by imitating the hare running in the race, or slowly, by imitating the tortoise running in the race. Check the animal's name or erase it and write it in the appropriate column.

Summarize Main Points

Help children recall the story "The Tortoise and the Hare," by summarizing the main points and events. Encourage children to retell the story.

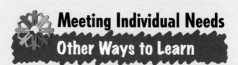
Meeting Individual Needs
Other Ways to Learn

Kinesthetic Invite children to act out the race in "The Tortoise and the Hare." Provide props or invite children to make props they need.

Day 5

Oral Language

Retell a Message

Remind children that a message is something that one person says or writes to another person or group. To retell a message accurately, the listener must pay attention to the speaker.

Practice Retelling a Message

Ask children what message they could send to the hare *before* the race to help him. Guide the discussion so that children recognize that they should warn the hare not to take a nap during the race. Together write a message to the hare. For example, write:

Hare, don't stop to take a nap. Keep running.

Then have pairs of children play the messenger and the hare, with the messenger giving the message orally and the hare responding. Have the hare repeat the message to make sure it is understood.

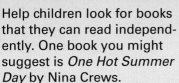

Self-Selected Reading

Help children look for books that they can read independently. One book you might suggest is *One Hot Summer Day* by Nina Crews.

Full Day Options...

Vocabulary

Make Funny Faces Have children cut *noses, teeth, ears,* and *hair* from construction paper, fabric swatches, or wallpaper and glue them on paper to make funny faces. Tell children to label each feature with its name.

Independent Writing 🚶

Write About Races Have children choose one.

- Write or dictate a sentence about how you would feel after winning a race.
- Write or dictate a sentence about a race you have been in or seen.

Reading

Reader Response: "The Tortoise and the Hare" Recall with children that, despite what others might have thought, the tortoise won the race against the hare. Ask: *Who do you think deserved to win the race? Why? What lesson do you think the hare learned from the race?*

TE Volume 5, p. AR5

Oral Language

Retell a Rhyme Reread the rhyming poem "At the Zoo." Help children recall the order of the things the author saw at the zoo by identifying the beginning, middle, and end of the poem. Then help children retell what happened at the zoo. Use puppets or pictures of the animals in the poem to prompt children through the poem.

Day
5

Lesson Overview

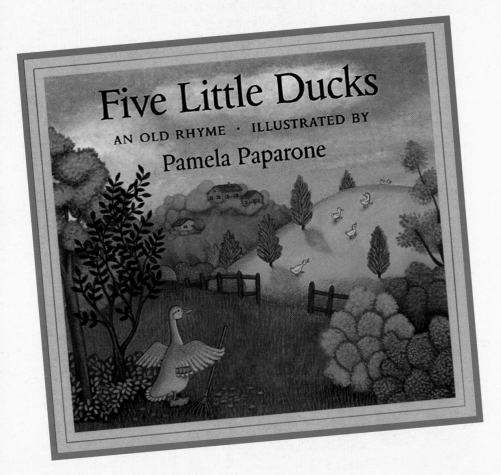

Five Little Ducks
AN OLD RHYME · ILLUSTRATED BY
Pamela Paparone

Big Book

Five Little Ducks

Selection Audio

Genre
Classic Poem

Phonemic Awareness/Phonics
Consonant *qu /kw/*

Comprehension
Sequence

High-Frequency Words
one   two   three

About the Illustrator

Pamela Paparone
moved many times as a child due to her father's military career. She lived in several states in the United States and even lived in Europe. Recently she has settled in Philadelphia, Pennsylvania, with her husband, where she writes and illustrates children's books.

Leveled Books

Easy

Wordless Story 27

On-Level

Kindergarten Reader 27

Challenge

Independent Reader 27

Trade Books for Self-Selected Reading and Read Aloud

Chicken Little
by Steven Kellog

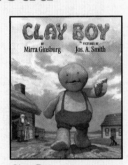

Clay Boy
by Mirra Ginsburg

Fin M'Coul: The Giant of Knockmany Hill
by Tomie de Paola

Lon Po Po: A Red-Riding Hood Story From China
by Ed Young

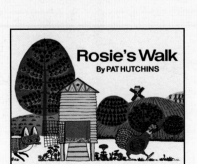

Rosie's Walk
by Pat Hutchins

The Enormous Turnip
by Kathy Parkinson

5-Day Planner

 Customize your week with the Teacher's Resource Planner CD-ROM!

Reading

Comprehension

Vocabulary

Phonics

Phonemic Awareness

Day 1

Activate Prior Knowledge p. 93

Poem "Quack, Quack!"

Reading pp. 94–101

Shared Reading
Five Little Ducks

Reader Response:
Check Predictions

Count How Many

Comprehension: Sequence

Sequence Events in the Day

Phonics pp. 102–103

✓ Consonant *qu* /kw/

Phonemic Awareness:
Listen to a Song
• Phonics Songs and
  Rhymes Chart 27

Identify /kw/ Picture Cards

Connect Sound to Letter:
Match /kw/ to *qu*

Phonological Awareness:
Substitute Initial Sounds

✔ **High-Frequency Words**

| one | two | three |

Day 2

Phonics pp. 104–105

✓ Consonant *qu* /kw/

Phonemic Awareness:
Sing a Song with /kw/ Words
• Phonics Songs and
  Rhymes Chart 27

Use Words That Begin
with /kw/
• Wordless Story 27
  *The Queen and
  the Quilt*

Connect Sound to Letter:
Match /kw/ to *qu*

Phonological Awareness:
Listen for /kw/ Words

✔ **High-Frequency Words:** Use
one, two and *three* in Sentences

Reading pp. 106–107

Comprehension: Sequence

Recall Actions of
Book's Characters

Use Vocabulary to
Tell How Many

Sequence Story
Actions

Oral Language

Speaking, Listening, and Viewing

Oral Language pp. 100–101

Introduce Vocabulary:
Number Words
one   two   three   four   five
Use Number Words

Oral Language pp. 106–107

Speaking: Choral Reading

Choral Read a Rhyme
• Oral Language Chart 27

Writing

Grammar, Usage, and Mechanics

Writing pp. 102–103

Shared Writing: Write
Sentences Together

Writing pp. 104–105

Modeled Writing: Write About
What's Over the Hills

Guided Writing

Handwriting: Practice Writing *Qq*

Self-Selected Reading
Read Aloud

Self-Selected Reading p. 101

Have children select books to
read. They might like to read
other traditional stories. See
page 85 for suggestions.

 D.E.A.R. Drop Everything And Read

Self-Selected Reading p. 107

Have children choose their own
books to read from your self-
selected reading collection.
Some children might be interested in
reading *Chicken Little* by Steven Kellog

 D.E.A.R. Drop Everything And Read

Target Skills of the Week

Reading Sequence

Phonics Consonant *qu* /kw/

Oral Language Choral Reading

Writing Complete Sentences

Day 3

Phonics pp. 108–109

 Consonant *qu* /kw/

Phonemic Awareness:
Choose the /kw/ Words

Connect Sound to Letter:
Find Words That Begin
with *Q* or *q*
• Phonics Songs and
Rhymes Chart 27

**Phonological
Awareness:**
Listen for Same
Ending Sound

**Read Kindergarten
Reader 27:**
One, Two, Three

Reading pp. 110–111

 Comprehension:
Sequence

Apply Sequence By Ordering
Events

Reader Response:
Recall the Story
Model Writing Questions

Oral Language pp. 110–111

 Speaking: Discuss
Choral Reading

Practice Choral
Reading

Writing pp. 108–109

 Modeled Writing:
Demonstrate Writing a Sentence

Guided Writing

Self-Selected Reading p. 111

From your self-selected reading
collection, have children choose
their own books to read. You
might suggest *The Enormous Turnip*
by Kathy Parkinson.

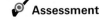

Day 4

Phonics pp. 112–113

Review Consonant *v* /v/

 Consonant qu /kw/

Phonemic Awareness:
Consonant *v* /v/
Identify Words with /kw/ and /v/

Connect Sound to Letter:
Make a /kw/ Quilt

Phonological Awareness:
Build Silly Sentences

✔ **High-Frequency Words:**
Make Number Cards

Challenge:
Independent Reader 27

Reading pp. 114–115

 Comprehension:
Sequence

Activate Prior
Knowledge

 Assess Sequence

Oral Language pp. 114–115

 Speaking: Choral Reading
• Read Aloud "Once I Saw a
Little Bird"

 Assess Choral Reading

Writing pp. 112–113

Review **Interactive Writing:** Verbs
Ending in -*s*
Use Verbs Ending in -*s*

Self-Selected Reading p. 115

Have children choose books to
read. They might like to read
Clay Boy by Mirra Ginsburg.

Day 5

Phonics pp. 116–117

 Consonant *qu* /kw/

Phonemic Awareness:
Prepare to Assess

 Connect Sound to Letter:
Assess *qu* /kw/

Phonological Awareness:
Count the Words

 High-Frequency Words:
Assess

Reading pp. 118–119

Review **Comprehension:**
Drawing Conclusions
• Read Aloud "Sunshine Stories"
Draw Conclusions
About the Swan

Oral Language pp. 118–119

Review **Listening:** Listen for
Rhyming Words

Practice Listening for Rhyming
Words

Writing pp. 116–117

 Independent Writing: Assess
Writing Development

Shared Writing: Add to the
Class Diary

Self-Selected Reading p. 119

Help children look for books they
can read independently. One
story you might suggest is
Rosie's Walk by Pat Hutchins.

Cross-Curricular Work Stations

Community Link

Ideas for bringing the school and community together

Field Experiences
library
petting zoo with ducks

Guest Speakers
drama group to act out a story
media specialist

Letters and Sounds

Say Quack!   10 minutes

Materials: rhyming cards

Learning Styles Kinesthetic, Auditory, Social

On index cards, draw a picture for several words, many of which begin with *qu*. Ask children to pretend they are ducks on a seesaw. Partners alternate standing on tiptoes and squatting down as they view the different words. When children see a word that begins with /kw/, both partners stand and say *quack* to balance the seesaw.

Social Studies

Compare Traditional Stories   10 minutes

Materials: traditional storybooks

Learning Styles Auditory, Individual, Verbal

Provide several versions of traditional storybooks that reflect different cultures. Children can look for similarities and differences in the stories, particularly in the illustrations. At group time, children can share what they have found.

Challenge Children make a storybook based on a traditional story. Encourage children to use themselves as well as family members as characters.

Science

Waterproof a Feather 10 minutes

Materials: feathers cut from brown paper bags, vegetable oil, containers of water

Learning Styles Kinesthetic, Auditory, Social, Verbal

Invite children to place a few drops of water on a feather and observe what happens to the water. Next ask children to place drops of water on a feather coated with vegetable oil and observe how the water rolls off the feather. Encourage children to discuss what happens to the oiled feather and how this might help a duck swim.

Challenge Provide books about birds. Ask children to draw feathers found on their favorite bird and label them with the bird's name. Children can cut out the feathers and make a feather scrapbook.

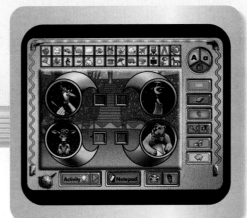

Technology

AstroWord   10 minutes

Learning Styles Visual, Auditory

AstroWord reinforces children's understanding of phonemic awareness. Children can work individually or collaboratively.

Web Site two days for 10 minutes

Learning Styles Individual, Visual

sfreading.com

www Visit the Scott Foresman web site (sfreading.com) for current hyperlinks to sites that can be used by children for an Internet Workshop investigation of traditional stories. Also see the Scott Foresman Internet Guide for additional information on the Internet Workshop method.

Math

Subtracting Ducks   10 minutes

Materials: blue yarn, five pictures of ducks, number cards 0–5

Learning Styles Auditory, Spatial, Social, Verbal

3

Have children arrange yarn in a circle to make a pond and place five ducks in the pond. Partners take turns turning over a number card and removing that many ducks from the pond. Have children tell how many ducks are left.

ESL Encourage children to use sentences to tell how many ducks are left in the pond.

Drama

Tell Stories Around a Campfire 10 minutes

Materials: logs, blankets

Learning Styles Auditory, Social, Verbal

 Discuss with children that many stories are passed down orally before they are written down and made into a book. Have children listen to a traditional story from another culture in the listening center. During group time, they can act out the story parts.

Introduce the Reading Road Show Activity Stations to reinforce this week's skills.

Phonemic Awareness & Phonics
Literacy Activities

Use these activities during the week to reinforce skills.

Phonemic Awareness

Quack, Quack 10 minutes

Learning Styles Verbal, Auditory, Kinesthetic, Social

Have children sit in a circle. Choose one child to be "it". The child walks around the circle and eventually taps a child and says "Quack, quack." The child tapped must say a word that has the same beginning sound as "Quack, quack." That child then walks around the circle. Continue until many children have had a turn.

The game can be varied to practice other initial consonant sounds by using other animal noises such as *moo* for /m/, *woof* for /w/, and *baa* for /b/.

Working with Letters

Treasure Hunt 15 minutes

Materials: letter cards or shapes

Learning Styles Visual, Kinesthetic, Spatial, Logical

Write the capital and lowercase letters of the alphabet on cards. (You may also use colored paper cut in a special shape such as leaves for fall, turkeys for Thanksgiving, snowflakes for winter, hearts for Valentine's Day, flowers for spring. Hide the cards or shapes around the room when children are not present.

Have children hunt for the cards. As soon as they find a card, they return to their desks. When all children are seated, have them take turns naming the letter on their card. Then have children look for the child with the matching capital or lowercase letter to finish the hunt.

Working with Words

Red Rover  15 minutes

Materials: word cards

Learning Styles Kinesthetic, Logical, Visual, Verbal

Make a set of high-frequency word cards. Have children stand in two lines. Place the word cards on a table between the two lines. Ask one line of children to begin and say the following, inserting the name of a player from the other line in the blank,

Red Rover,

Red Rover,

Send _____ over.

The child who is named comes to the table and takes a word card. If the child reads the high-frequency word correctly, the child returns to his or her line. If the child does not read the word correctly, he or she must join the team that called him or her over. Continue until many children have had turns to read words.

 Introduce children to the regular version of Red Rover and help them enjoy the rhythmic pattern of the verse.

ABC Wall

ABC Wall   20 minutes

Learning Styles Visual, Logical, Kinesthetic

Write the following words on the board: *am, can, dig, gas, hat, if, job, kit, mop, not, on, pot, quit, sit, up, van.* Give each child a blank word card and have them write one of the words on his or her card. Call on two children to come to the front of the room with their cards. Ask them to read the words on their cards (if they can) and to look at the first letter of their words. Have them check the ABC Wall and stand by the letter that begins their word. Continue until all the children are standing by the correct letter. Have them say their words in ABC order. Have children repeat the activity identifying the final sound of each word.

Daily Warm-Up

Message Board

Day One

Today we will read a story about five little ducks who go exploring.

Discuss with children where they might like to go exploring.

Ask children: "What does a duck say that begins like *queen*?"

Day Two

We will look and listen for Qq.

Day Three

We will use the words one, two, and three.

Ask children: "Do you want to listen to *one, two,* or *three* stories?"

Day Four

Today we will read together as a group.

Discuss with children why it is fun to read as a group.

Day Five

Today we will write a news story about the missing ducks.

Ask children: "How do you think a news story would begin?"

Getting Ready
for the Week

Day One
> pictures of daily events
> pictures of events in a sequence (Kinesthetic)

Day Two
> copies of paper with a six-box grid (Full Day)
> pictures of a sequence of daily events (Intervention)

Day Three
> pictures of one, two, and three objects (ESL)
> craft sticks (Kinesthetic)

Day Four
> copies of paper with a six-box grid

Day Five
> index cards
> buttons or other counters

Family Times

Send home the newsletter with fun instructional activities to reinforce this week's target skills.

Practice Book, pp. 171–172
Teacher's Resource Book, pp. 171–172

Activate Prior Knowledge

Recall an Adventure

Ask children to recall a favorite book. Invite them to tell about an adventure the main character had. Ask:

- **Where did the character go?**
- **Why did he (she) go there?**
- **What happened? Was it exciting? Scary?**

Tell children that this week's story is about five little ducks who go far away from home.

Build Background

Choose one or more of these activities to build background for concepts presented in this week's book, *Five Little Ducks*.

Read Aloud a Poem

Share this poem with children. Encourage them to imitate the sounds that ducks make. Some children may be willing to show how ducks walk.

Quack, Quack!
by Dr. Seuss

We have two ducks. One blue.
   One black.
And when our blue duck goes
   "Quack-quack"
our black duck quickly quack-quacks
   back.
The quacks Blue quacks make her
   quite a quacker
but Black is a quicker quacker-
   backer.

Use Illustrations to Develop Oral Language

Hold up *Five Little Ducks*. Ask children to describe what they see on the cover. Elicit that the big duck is watching five little ducks go over a hill. Have children create a story about where the five ducks are going.

Use Audio to Develop Story Concepts

Display *Five Little Ducks*. Ask:

- **What is the big duck holding on the cover?** (a rake)
- **Do real ducks use rakes?** (no)

Share the Background-Building Audio CD/tape, which provides a visit to a zoo to learn about real ducks. After listening, volunteers might enjoy identifying the points they found most interesting.

CD 5/Tape 14, Side 1
Background-Building Audio

Concepts of Print

Parts of a Book

Display *Five Little Ducks.* Point to the front cover. Ask:

- **What is this part of the book called?** (the cover)

- **What is usually on the cover of a book?** (the title, the author's name, the illustrator's name, a picture of something that happens in the book)

- **What is different about this cover?** (no author's name)

Point out that *Five Little Ducks* is a very old rhyme and no one knows who wrote it. Pamela Paparone took the rhyme and drew new pictures for it. Turn the book over to show children another illustration on the back cover.

Model Reading Behaviors

Picture Walk and Predict

Have children look at the illustrations. Ask:

- **Who else is in the story besides the five little ducks?** (a big duck)

- **Where do you think the little ducks are going? Let's read to find out.**

Big Book

Children will

- recognize a book's cover and the information it provides
- use illustrations to make predictions
- listen to a story

Day **1**

Shared Reading Routine

Day 1

- Read the story through for enjoyment, emphasizing the rhythm and rhyme.

- To practice the reading strategy predicting, use the stopping point on TE page 95.

Day 2

- Reread the entire story, using the activities found in the margins on pages 95–99.

Days 3–5

- Reread the entire big book or portions of it each day, using the activities as suggested in the lessons.

> Five little ducks went out one day,
> Over the hills and far away.

6 7

pages 6–7

Guiding the Reading

Critical Thinking

Why do you think the little ducks went out each day?
Possible answers: They went outside to play, they liked to explore, they went to a friend's house, they went to school.

Day
1

> Mother duck said,
> "Quack, quack, quack, quack."
> But only four little ducks came back.

8 9

pages 8–9

> Four little ducks went out one day,
> Over the hills and far away.

10 11

pages 10–11

 Stopping Point

Predict On the first reading, you may want to stop at the bottom of page 11 and ask children to predict what will happen next.

Guiding the Reading

Critical Thinking

What does mother duck do while the little ducks are away over the hills?
Possible answer: She does chores around the house, such as hanging out the laundry and ironing clothes.

Content Connection: Science

- Baby ducks are born with an urge to follow their mothers.
- They will follow the first slowly moving large thing they see.
- This is called imprinting.

Mother duck said,
"Quack, quack, quack, quack."
But only three little ducks came back.

pages 12–13

Three little ducks went out one day,
Over the hills and far away.

pages 14–15

Mother duck said,
"Quack, quack, quack, quack."
But only two little ducks came back.

pages 16–17

Two little ducks went out one day,
Over the hills and far away.

18 19

pages 18–19

Day
1

Guiding the Reading

Critical Thinking

Why does mother duck say, "Quack, quack, quack, quack"?
Possible answer: That is her way of calling her little ducks home.

As the two little ducks go off to play, what does mother duck do? Why?
Possible answers: She picks apples. She might want to give the little ducks apples as a snack. She might make apple sauce, apple juice, or an apple dessert.

Mother duck said,
"Quack, quack, quack, quack."
But only one little duck came back.

20 21

pages 20–21

One little duck went out one day,
Over the hills and far away.

22 23

pages 22–23

Guiding the Reading

Critical Thinking

How do you think mother duck feels when none of her children return home?
Possible answers: She may feel sad because her little ducks no longer need to be with her. She may be frightened that the little ducks may have been hurt.

Guiding the Reading

Critical Thinking

Why does mother duck go "over the hills and far away"? How do you know? What in the story tells you this?
Possible answers: She went out looking for the little ducks. She wanted to bring the little ducks home.

Content Connection: Science

- Ducks, geese, and swans are waterfowl. Waterfowl live on and near water.
- A duck's front toes are webbed. This helps it swim and dive.
- Baby ducks are called ducklings. Soon after they are born, ducklings can swim.

Mother duck said,
"Quack, quack, quack, quack."
But none of the little ducks came back.

24   25

pages 24–25

Sad mother duck went out one day,
Over the hills and far away.

26   27

pages 26–27

Mother duck said,
"Quack, quack, quack, quack."

28   29

pages 28–29

And all of her five little ducks came back!

30

31

pages 30–31

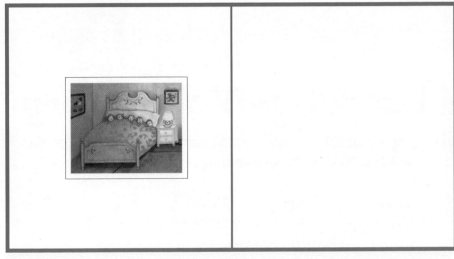

page 32

Guiding the Reading

Critical Thinking

Why do you think the five little ducks came back?
Possible answers: They were ready to come home. They were lost and their mother's call helped them find their way back.

How do you think mother duck felt when she saw her five little ducks?
Possible answers: She felt happy. She felt relieved.

Day
1

Objectives

Children will

- 🎯 sequence daily activities
- recognize numbers in sequence
- develop vocabulary by using number words

Day 1

❄ Meeting Individual Needs
ESL

Have children count from one to five in English. Provide groups of objects. Ask children to count them and tell how many in both English and their native languages.

Skills Trace

🎯 Sequence

Introduce	TE: K.2 178–179
Practice	PB: 72, 74, 174, 176, 200, 202
Reteach/ Review	TE: K.2 185, 188, 192, 232, AR19 K.5 **100–101**, 107, 110, 114, 154, AR15 K.6 28-29, 35, 38, 42, 82, AR11
Skills Assessment	TE: K.2 AR1–AR3 K.5 AR1–AR3 K.6 AR1–AR3

Reader Response

Check Predictions Ask: *Where did you think the little ducks were going before we started reading? Where did they go? Did you think the ducks would leave and come back?*

Count How Many Ask: *How many little ducks went out the first day? Hold up that number of fingers on one hand. How many came home?* Have children count off four fingers so that one finger remains. Ask: *How many ducks didn't come back?*

Oral Language/Vocabulary

Use Number Words The vocabulary words are numbers. Have children use the words to answer these questions.

 one   two   three   four   five

- **How many little ducks were in this story?** (five)
- **How many little ducks came home the first day?** (four)
- **How many little ducks came home the next day?** (three)
- **How many little ducks came home the third day?** (two)
- **How many ducks came home the fourth day?** (one)

Ongoing Assessment
Vocabulary

If... children can't correctly identify how many,

then... have them count groups of objects, such as crayons, pencils, or paper clips.

Comprehension

Sequence Events in the Day

Show pictures of daily events in children's lives, such as getting dressed, going to school, and going to bed. Discuss what is happening in each picture. Have children place the pictures in sequence and tell about what happens first, second, and so on, during their day.

Say: *During the day we do things in a certain order. Events in stories also happen in a certain order. In this week's story, five little ducks went out one day and only four came home. The next day four little ducks went out and only three came home. The story continues with the little ducks going out to play each day and one less duck coming home.*

Meeting Individual Needs
Other Ways to Learn

Visual Display three pictures that show a sequence of events. Explain that 1 tells what happens first, 2 what happens next, and 3 what happens last. Give children number cards for 1, 2, and 3 and have them place the cards on the pictures to show the sequence.

Day 1

Self-Selected Reading

Have children select books to read. They might like to read other traditional stories. See page 85 for suggestions.

Full Day Options...

Oral Language

Tell a Story Have children choose one.

- Make up another adventure story for the five little ducks.
- Tell a story about a family that lives in a house high up on a hill.

Vocabulary

Number Children Give five children each a card with a number and the corresponding number word *one, two, three, four,* or *five* on it. Have them stand in random order at the front of the room. Let classmates move them into the correct sequence. Have the class read the numbers left to right.

Sequence

Give Directions Have children tell how to make a peanut-butter-and-jelly sandwich. Encourage them to use the words *first, second, next,* and *last* in their directions.

Sequence

Alphabet Count Give each group five sequential letter cards and five cards numbered 1–5. Have children put the number cards in order and place the letters in order next to the numbers.

Objectives

Children will

- recognize initial *qu*/kw/
- recognize the letters *Qq*
- build new words by sound substitution
- identify high-frequency words

Day 1

Meeting Individual Needs
Intervention

Display the picture cards for *bowl, quilt,* and *mat.* Have children say each picture name, stressing the beginning sound. Ask them to choose the picture that begins with /kw/. Repeat with the picture cards for *king, house,* and *queen.*

Skills Trace

Consonant *Qq*

Introduce	TE: K.5 **102**
Practice	PB: 173, 175
Reteach/ Review	TE: K.5 104, 108–109, 112, 116, 150 AR14
Skills Assessment	Skills Assessment Unit 5 TE: K.5 AR1–AR3

Daily Phonics Routine

Phonemic Awareness

Listen to a Song

Sing "A Quilt" or play the CD/tape. Have children listen for and then name words that begin with /kw/. (queen, quilt, quickly, quail, quietly, quit)

CD 2/Tape 14, Side 1

Phonics Songs and Rhymes Audio

> ### A Quilt
>
> Queen will make a quilt today.
> She'll work quickly all the day.
>
> In the squares she'll stitch a Q
> And a little quail that's blue.
>
> She'll work quietly on this day.
> Then she'll quit and go to play.

Phonics Songs and Rhymes Chart 27

Identify /kw/ Picture Cards

Display picture cards for *quarter* and *queen.* Have children identify each picture by name. Ask: *Do quarter and queen begin with the same sound?* (yes)

Ongoing Assessment
Phonemic Awareness

If... children have trouble identifying the /kw/ sound,

then... have them say *quilt* while looking in a mirror and notice how their lips form /kw/.

Connect Sound to Letter

Match /kw/ to *qu*

Show children the alphabet card. Say *quilt,* then segment its sounds: /kw/ /i/ /l/ /t/. Write *quilt* on the board. Circle the *qu* and point out that /kw/ in *quilt* is written with two letters, *qu.* Have children say the word, emphasizing the /kw/. Write *Quilt* on the board and circle the *Qu.* Point out that /kw/ is also written *Qu.*

Qq

Alphabet Cards

Phonological Awareness

Substitute Initial Sounds

Have Alphapotamus say: *Help me replace the first sound in the word* pick *with /kw/. What is the new word?* (quick) Have Alphapotamus continue with: *sit* (quit), *back* (quack), *nail* (quail).

/kw/ ick

High-Frequency Words

Add *one*, *two*, and *three* to ABC Wall

Say the high-frequency words *one*, *two*, and *three*. Write them on index cards. Help children name the letters in each word. Have volunteers add the words to the ABC Wall.

one   two   three

ABC Wall

Invite children to think of the names of words in "A Quilt" that begin with /kw/. Add two or three to this week's panel of the ABC Wall.

Day 1

Optional Resources

Phonics Sourcebook pp. 54–55, 84–85

Phonics Workbook p. 131

High-Frequency Word Cards

Shared Writing

Write Sentences Together

Say: *We are going to write sentences about the queen.* Ask children to think about what the queen might do after she finishes her quilt.

As children respond, they can

- Help you sound out the words as you write them
- Use high-frequency words
- Tell you what mark goes at the end of the sentence

When you finish writing, have children read the sentences chorally as you track the print.

What the Queen Does

The queen buys one quail.

She bakes two pies.

The queen plays with three friends.

Full Day Options...

Phonics

Give /kw/ Riddles Tell children that the answer to each of these riddles is a word that begins with /kw/.

- **I'm thinking of a coin. What is it?** (quarter)
- **I'm thinking of a word that rhymes with *shake*. What is it?** (quake)
- **I'm thinking of the sound a duck makes. What is it?** (quack)

Independent Writing

Use a Writing Journal Have children choose one to write about in their journal.

- Write or dictate a sentence you might say to the queen.
- Write or dictate a sentence the queen might say to you.
- Write or dictate a sentence about something you could do to help the queen.

Sequence

Put Actions in Order Have children use the numbers *one*, *two*, and *three* to put the queen's actions in order:

- **She stitched a Q and a quail.** (two)
- **She went out to play.** (three)
- **She got out her quilt and needle and thread.** (one)

Objectives

Children will

 recognize initial *qu*/kw/

 write complete sentences
- write the letters *Qq*
- extend a story imaginatively

Day 2

Consonant *Qq*
Practice Book, p. 173
Teacher's Resource Book, p. 173

Skills Trace

 Complete Sentences

Introduce	TE: K.3 33
Reteach/ Review	TE: K.3 39, 43 K.5 **105**, 113, 117, 143, 151, 155, 227, K.6 189, 221, 229, 233
Skills Assessment	Skills Assessment Unit 3, Unit 5, Unit 6 TE: K.3 AR1–AR3 K.5 AR1–AR3 K.6 AR1–AR3

Daily Phonics Routine

Phonemic Awareness

Sing a Song with /kw/ Words

Have children sing along with the CD/tape "A Quilt." Ask them to quack when they hear a word that begins with /kw/.

CD 2/Tape 14, Side 1
Phonics Songs and Rhymes Audio

Phonics Songs and Rhymes Chart 27

Use Words That Begin with /kw/

Share *The Queen and the Quilt* with children. Have them tell the story using as many words as they can that begin with /kw/. Children can dictate or write their story in the take-home version.

Wordless Story 27

Connect Sound to Letter

Match /kw/ to *qu*

Show children the *Qq* alphabet card and say *quilt*, emphasizing the beginning sound. Display picture cards for *quarter, kitten, queen, fish,* and *quilt*. Hold the alphabet card above each picture card. Have children name the pictures and decide if the name begins with /kw/.

Alphabet Cards

Phonological Awareness

Listen for /kw/ Words

Have Alphapotamus say: *Raise your hand when you hear a word in my sentences that begins with /kw/.*

The queen played a drum.

Did you ask a question?

Kelly sat quietly in class.

The old king sat on a quilt.

The queen played a drum.

High-Frequency Words

Use *one*, *two*, and *three* in Sentences

Have children complete this sentence: *I have one ___.* (nose, mouth, head) Repeat with *two* and *three*.

ABC Wall

Ask children to find a word beginning with *qu* on the ABC Wall. Have them spell the word with you. Repeat with other *qu* words on the wall.

Optional Resources

Phonics Sourcebook pp. 54–55, 84–85

Phonics Workbook p. 182

High-Frequency Word Cards

Day 2

Modeled Writing

Write About What's Over the Hills

 Think ALOUD

Ask children to imagine what they might see on the other side of the hills. Write a sentence on the board: *We see a big lake.* Say:

- **I am writing a period at the end.**

- **A complete sentence always tells a complete thought. My sentence tells about someone—*We*—and what they did—*saw a big lake.* That is a complete thought.**

Guided Writing

Ask: *What do you think is on the other side of the hills?* Help children write a complete sentence. Some may need to dictate or draw.

Practice Writing *Qq*

Handwriting

Distribute writing paper and have children practice writing *q* and *Q*. You may wish to show children how to write the letter *u* at this time. Children who are already proficient writing *q* and *Q* can write *quack* and *quilt*.

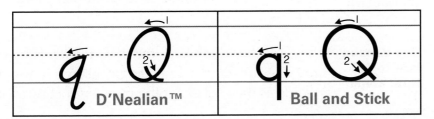

q Q	q Q
D'Nealian™	Ball and Stick

Full Day Options...

Phonics

Count Syllables Have Alphapotamus say: *Help me count the syllables in the word* quarter *by clapping. How many syllables do you hear?* (two) Write the word on the board with a 2 beside it. Repeat with: *quack, quality, question.*

Handwriting

Practice Have children choose one:

- Write *Quit quacking.* Make the words into a sign that is posted by a pond.
- Write this headline: *Duck Quacks Quite Quickly*

Independent Writing

Write About Birds Have children write a descriptive sentence about other water birds, such as swans or geese.

Objectives

Children will

- read a rhyme chorally
- listen to recall story actions and sequence story events
- use number words to tell how many
- recite repeated pattern in story

Day 2

Oral Language

Choral Read a Rhyme

Display "Quack! Quack! Quack!" Read the rhyme while children listen. Reread and invite children to join in. Continue until they feel comfortable with the rhyme.

Then explain that today children will read a rhyme together in small groups. A different group will read each line and then the class will read it all together. This is called *choral reading.*

Quack! Quack! Quack!
Anonymous

Five little ducks that I once knew,
Big ones, little ones, skinny ones too,
But the one little duck with the
Feather on his back,
All he could do was, "Quack, Quack, Quack."

Oral Language Chart 27

Assign lines to groups and have them practice so everyone knows the words and begins and ends at the same time. Then have the class do a choral reading.

Comprehension

Recall Actions of Book's Characters

Hold up *Five Little Ducks* and ask what the little ducks did each day. Have five children act out the little ducks leaving each day while another child pantomimes the mother duck's actions.

Use Vocabulary to Tell How Many

Say: *Mother duck had five little ducks. How many children are in your family?* Encourage children to use the vocabulary words as they tell about the number of children in their family.

Listen to Big Book for Information

Invite children to listen as you reread the story. Ask them to listen for what mother duck does when no little ducks come back.

While reading, you may wish to use the ideas in the *Guiding the Reading* and *Language Development* boxes on pages 95–99 of this Teacher's Edition.

Shared Reading

Big Book

Sequence Story Actions Explain that in a story, events happen in a certain order. Invite children to tell what happened first in *Five Little Ducks*. Then help them sequence other events in the story:

- **What happened after four little ducks went out?** (Only three came back.)

- **What happened the next day?** (Three little ducks went off, and two came back.)

- **What did mother duck do when no ducks came back?** (She quacked and all five little ducks came back.)

Ongoing Assessment

Sequence

If... children have difficulty sequencing story events,	**then...** reread the story, pausing to let children count the ducks leaving and coming home and summarize what happens each day.

Meeting Individual Needs
Intervention

Give a child who has trouble sequencing events number cards and pictures showing a sequence of daily events, such as breakfast, lunch, and dinner. Ask the child to put the pictures in order, left to right, and label them 1, 2, and 3.

Self-Selected Reading D.E.A.R. Drop Everything And Read

Have children choose their own books to read from your self-selected reading collection. Some children might be interested in reading *Chicken Little* by Steven Kellog.

Day **2**

Full Day Options...

Sequence

Order the Queen's Search Let groups review Wordless Story 27 *The Queen and the Quilt*. Invite them to tell where the queen and her maids looked for the quilt first, next, and last.

Phonics

Color a /kw/ Quilt Give each child a paper with a quilt pattern of six squares. Ask children to color a square when they hear a word that begins with /kw/. Say: *quarter, kitten, queen, quilt, hand, quit, kind, quack, wagon, quick.* Check to see that children colored all six squares.

Oral Language

Choral Reading Choose a previous Oral Language chart and have partners practice reading it chorally. Invite pairs to read their poem for the class.

Reader Response

Add to the Story Ask children to imagine what the little ducks did while they were gone. Have them draw a picture of one of the little ducks and write or dictate a sentence about what the duck is doing.

Objectives

Children will

↻ recognize *qu*/kw/
- identify words with the same ending sound
- work with high-frequency words
- match print to speech

✳ Meeting Individual Needs

ESL

Ask children who are learning English to match word cards for *one, two,* and *three* with pictures that have one, two, or three objects in them.

Daily Phonics Routine

Phonemic Awareness

Choose the /kw/ Words

Have Alphapotamus say: *nickel, dime, quarter.* Which word begins with /kw/? (quarter) Have Alphapotamus continue with: *pillow, quilt, bed; quiet, loud, noisy; goose, duck, quail; king, queen, lady.*

nickel, dime, quarter

Connect Sound to Letter

Find Words That Begin with Q or q

Have children look at "A Quilt." Ask them to identify pictures on the chart with names that begin with /kw/. Then help them find the /kw/ words in the rhyme. Ask a child to circle the Q's in red and another child to circle the q's in blue. Remind children that although the words begin with Q or q, the letters Qu or qu stand for the /kw/ sound in each word.

CD 2/Tape 14, Side 1
Phonics Songs and Rhymes Audio

A Quilt

Queen will make a quilt today.
She'll work quickly all the day.

In the squares she'll stitch a Q
And a little quail that's blue.

She'll work quietly on this day.
Then she'll quit and go to play.

Phonics Songs and Rhymes Chart 27

Phonological Awareness

Listen for Same Ending Sound

Say: *Jump up if the two words I say have the same ending sound.* For example, use these word pairs: *quack/duck, quit/dog, quarter/ deer, queen/moon, quail/cat.*

Ongoing Assessment

Phonological Awareness

If... children have difficulty hearing sounds at the ends of words,

then... have them segment the sounds in each word and repeat the final sounds in both words.

Phonics and High-Frequency Words

Read Kindergarten Reader 27

- Read the title *One, Two, Three* as you track the print.
- Do a picture walk. Ask children to identify the characters and the setting.
- Turn to page 2. Ask children where you should begin reading. Read the story aloud. Have children track the print with their fingers to match spoken to printed words.

Kindergarten Reader 27

Phonics Consonant *Qq*

High-Frequency Words
one, two, three

One, two, three.
The duck can see the queen.

One, two, three.
The queen can see the duck.

What can the duck do?
The duck is bad.

What can the queen do?
The queen is mad.

Bad, bad duck.
Can duck win?

Mad, mad queen.
Can queen win?

One, two, three.
Two can win.

Modeled Writing

Demonstrate Writing a Sentence

Model writing a sentence based on *One, Two, Three*. For example, write *Two can win*.

As you write the sentence, model these strategies:

- Begin the sentence with a capital letter.

- Put correct punctuation at the end of the sentence.

- Point out that the sentence tells a complete thought, so it is a complete sentence.

Guided Writing

Ask children to read the sentence with you. Have them write their own sentences based on *One, Two, Three*.

ABC Wall

Ask a volunteer to find a word that begins with *qu* on the ABC Wall. Invite children to say the word and tell about it, using a complete sentence.

Day 3

Optional Resources

Phonics Sourcebook pp. 84–85

High-Frequency Word Cards

Phonics Workbook p. 133

Full Day Options...

Independent Writing 🚶

Write About an Adventure Have children draw a picture of themselves going "over the hills and far away" on an adventure. Ask children to write or dictate a sentence about where they would go or what they would do.

Phonics 🚶🚶

Draw /kw/ Pictures Have children draw pictures of things with names that begin with /kw/. Help them label their pictures. Display the pictures around the room while children learn *qu*/kw.

Sequence 🚶🚶🚶

Put Steps in Order Demonstrate a simple activity, such as putting on a shoe, but mix up the steps. (For example, tie the shoe before you put it on.) Ask children to correct your mistakes by telling the correct order of the steps in the activity.

Day
3

Objectives

Children will

- ☞ read a rhyme chorally
- ☞ sequence story events
- • dictate questions to investigate

Sequence
Practice Book, p. 174
Teacher's Resource Book, p. 174

Oral Language

Discuss Choral Reading	Ask children what they remember about choral reading. Elicit that choral reading means reading together with a partner or in groups. Discuss what they enjoy about reading together and what they find difficult about it.
Practice Choral Reading	Assign small groups pages 6, 10, 14, 18, and 22 of *Five Little Ducks* to practice reading aloud. Then ask children to help you reread the book. Have each group read its section chorally with you, while the whole class joins in on the the repeated pattern.

Shared Reading

Big Book

Ongoing Assessment

Choral Reading

If... children have difficulty staying together while reading chorally,

then... play the selection audio and have children listen to it and practice reading along.

Comprehension

Apply Sequence by Ordering Events

Remind children that events in stories happen in a certain order. Ask questions such as:

- **Which happened first, mother duck said, "Quack, quack, quack, quack" or five little ducks went out?** (Five little ducks went out.)

- **Which happened last, five little ducks came back or sad mother duck went out?** (Five little ducks came back.)

Encourage children to verify their responses by returning to the big book.

Reader Response

Recall the Story

Have children recall *Five Little Ducks.* Ask:

- **Are the ducks in this story real or make-believe? How do you know?**

- **What do you know about real ducks? What would you like to know?**

Have children dictate questions about ducks that they could investigate. For example, write the question *What do ducks eat?*

Model Writing Questions

As you write the question, model these strategies:

- Begin each sentence with a capital letter.

- Make sure each sentence is a complete thought.

- Put a question mark at the end of the question.

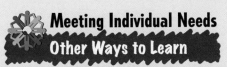

Meeting Individual Needs
Other Ways to Learn

Kinesthetic Have children make a mother duck stick puppet using paper, markers, and craft sticks. Children can use the puppet to act out what mother duck says and does in the story.

Self-Selected Reading D.E.A.R. *Drop Everything And Read*

From your self-selected reading collection, have children choose their own books to read. You might suggest *The Enormous Turnip* by Kathy Parkinson.

Day 3

Full Day Options...

Independent Writing 🚶

Mother Duck's Call Invite each child to write or dictate something mother duck might have said besides "quack, quack, quack, quack" to make her little ducks come home.

Oral Language 👫

Read Together Have each group select a familiar nursery rhyme and practice reading it together before presenting the choral reading to the class.

Vocabulary 🚶

Show the Number Ask children to use clay to create a number of animals doing something such as two fish swimming or four birds flying. Have children count their animals and write that number somewhere on a piece of paper. Let them place their animals on the paper next to the number. Invite children to tell the class about their creations.

Sequence 👫👫

Order Classroom Activities Tell about three activities the class usually does each day, but list them in the wrong sequence. Have children correct you by listing them in the correct order. Repeat with three more activities.

Objectives

Children will

↻ identify words with /kw/
- write number words
- distinguish verb forms
- complete sentences
- uses high-frequency words

Daily Phonics Routine

Review
Consonant v/v/

Phonemic Awareness

Ask children: *Which of these words begins with /v/: hill, mountain, volcano?* (volcano) Continue with the following word groups: *hat, vest, boots; van, taxi, car; eggs, meat, vegetables; dish, vase, bottle; violin, piano, horn.*

Ongoing Assessment

Phonemic Awareness

If... children have difficulty hearing initial /v/,	**then...** have them say *very* several times. Ask them to feel the lower lip vibration that the sound produces.

Identify Words with /kw/ and /v/

Ask children to identify words in the following sentences that begin /v/ or /kw/.

The quail is hidden in the grass.

Our vegetables are the highest quality.

My old vest became part of a quilt.

Connect Sound to Letter

Make a /kw/ Quilt

Give each child a sheet of paper with a six-box grid on it. Have children write *Qu* and *qu* in two boxes. Ask them to draw pictures of /kw/ words in two boxes and then color the last two boxes. Invite children to share their quilts so that classmates can name the /kw/ words.

Phonological Awareness

Build Silly Sentences

Brainstorm *qu* words with children. Have pairs make up a silly sentence using several of the *qu* words: *Queen Quack asked a quick question.* Ask pairs to share their sentences.

High-Frequency Words

Make Number Cards

Give each child three index cards. Have them use the ABC Wall to write a number word on each card. (You may want to provide handwriting models for *one, two,* and *three.* See pages AR45–AR46 of this Teacher's Edition.) On the back, have children write the number or draw that many objects.

Day 4

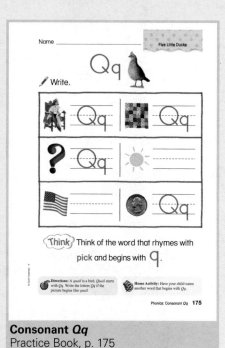

Consonant *Qq*
Practice Book, p. 175
Teacher's Resource Book, p. 175

Interactive Writing

Verbs Ending in -s Ask two volunteers to skip across the room. Say: *They skip.* Write *skip* on the board. Have only one child skip across the room. Say: *He (she) skips.* Exaggerate the -s ending. Write *skips* under *skip.* Point to the words and remind children that action words that tell what one person is doing end in -s.

Use Verbs Ending in -s Write *One duck quacks.* Point to each word as you read it. Have children find the action word and explain why it ends in -s. (Action words that tell what one person or thing does end in -s.) Ask children to suggest another action word that completes the sentence, such as *swims.* Write the word as children segment its sounds, /s/ /w/ /i/ /m/ /s/. Read the new sentence with children.

> One duck quacks.
> One duck swims.

Ongoing Assessment
Writing

If... children cannot suggest the correct form of the verb,	**then...** ask a child to perform the action and have children say a sentence that tells what the child is doing.

ABC Wall

Have three children children go to the ABC Wall. Ask one child to point to a word beginning with *qu.* The other two read the word with your help if needed. Continue until all have had a chance to go to the wall.

Meeting Individual Needs
Challenge

Display *A Good Day* and identify the title, author, and illustrator. Encourage children to look for familiar words as you read the story together.

Independent Reader 27

Optional Resources

Phonics Sourcebook pp. 84–85

Phonics Workbook p. 134

High-Frequency Word Cards

Full Day Options...

Phonics 👫

Revisit Kindergarten Reader 27, *One, Two, Three* For more practice in high-frequency word recognition, have children reread *One, Two, Three.* Let partners take turns reading the pages out loud or read together.

Kindergarten Reader 27

Phonics 👫👫

Shared Poetry Have children sing or recite "A Quilt." Review the sounds of *qu, w,* and *d.* Ask children to find *quail.* Point out that it begins with *qu,* which has the sound /kw/. Have children say the word with you. Repeat the activity for the words *will* and *day.*

Independent Writing 🚶

Write About Ducks Ask children to draw and write a descriptive sentence about one of the following:

- what one little duck misses while far from home
- how five little ducks come home

Day 4

READING ABC

Objectives

Children will

- ⟳ identify sequence
- ⟳ read a poem chorally
- • listen for enjoyment

Name _____

✎ Draw.

Five Little Ducks

Check children's drawings.

Directions: Draw a picture to show what happens last in the story.

Home Activity: Have your child tell you the story of the five little ducks using first, second, and last.

176 Comprehension: Sequence

Sequence
Practice Book, p. 176
Teacher's Resource Book, p. 176

Day 4

Comprehension

Activate Prior Knowledge

Display *Shoes Like Miss Alice's* from Unit 4. Ask:

- **What do you remember about Miss Alice?**

- **Why did the little girl feel sad sometimes?**

Read Aloud

Shoes Like Miss Alice's by Angela Johnson, paintings by Ken Page

Trade Book

Reread *Shoes Like Miss Alice's.* After reading, ask:

What did Miss Alice do first to help the girl forget her sadness? (dance)

Assess Sequence

To assess children's ability to sequence story events, have children act out what Miss Alice and the little girl do after they

- **eat a snack** (take a walk)

- **go for a walk** (take a nap)

- **take a nap** (draw pictures of what they did all day)

Ongoing Assessment

Sequence

If... children have difficulty sequencing events,	then... use the Sequence reteaching lesson on page AR15 of this Teacher's Edition.

Oral Language

Establish a Purpose for Speaking

Remind children that when they read a poem together, they must practice saying it together. Ask children to listen carefully as you read "Once I Saw a Little Bird."

Read Aloud

Once I Saw a Little Bird

Once I saw a little bird
Come hop, hop, hop,
And I cried, "Little bird,
Will you stop, stop, stop?"

I was going to the window
To say, "How do you do?"
But he shook his little tail
And away he flew.

Copy "Once I Saw a Little Bird" onto chart paper. Ask children to read the poem chorally with you. Read the first stanza together several times until children are comfortable with it. Then practice the second stanza.

Won't you stop, stop, stop?

Once children feel confident reciting the poem, you may wish to add actions to represent hopping, stopping, hat tipping, tail shaking, and flying away.

Ongoing Assessment

Choral Reading

If... children have difficulty participating in the choral reading,	**then...** assign small groups two lines each to practice reading together. Then have each group read its part.

Meeting Individual Needs
Other Ways to Learn

Kinesthetic Have children make up a tune for "Once I Saw a Little Bird" and sing the rhyme together. Encourage them to keep time to the rhythm (tap foot, clap hands) to help them stay together.

Optional Resources

Assessment Handbook

Full Day Options...

Sequence

Sequence the Poem Have partners draw three pictures showing what happened first, next, and last in the rhyme "Once I Saw a Little Bird." Pairs can exchange pictures and put them in the correct order.

Shared Writing

Finish a Sentence On the board, write *A bird ___.* As children list things a bird does, write their suggestions on the board. Have a volunteer fill in the blank with an action from the list. Then read the sentence with children, pointing to each word. Repeat, substituting another word from the list until all words are used.

flies
hops
pecks

A bird _____.

Vocabulary

Count Birds Give each child a sheet of paper. Have children draw a group of birds from one to five. Then ask them to count the birds and write the word *one, two, three, four,* or *five* on their page.

Oral Language

Choral Reading Have each group practice reading a favorite Kindergarten Reader or part of one together. Invite groups to present their choral reading to the class.

Day 4

 **PHONICS** A Z

Daily Phonics Routine

 Objectives

Children will

- recognize *qu*/kw/
- recognize complete sentences
- write number words to label pictures
- participate in a shared writing activity

Prepare to Assess

Phonemic Awareness

Stretch a word into onset and rime, such as /kw/–*it*. Ask children to repeat the sounds after you and then blend them together to say the word. Repeat with *quick, queen, quack, quail.*

Assess *qu*/kw/

Connect Sound to Letter

Give each child an index card. Ask children to write *qu* on one side and *v* on the other. One at a time, show the picture cards for *quarter, van, queen, vegetables, vest,* and *quilt.* *Ask: What letter or letters stand for the beginning sound of this picture?* Have children hold up the appropriate letters.

Ongoing Assessment

Phonics

| **If...** children have trouble identifying initial /kw/, | **then...** use the Consonant *Qq* reteaching activities on page AR14 of this Teacher's Edition. |

Count the Words

Phonological Awareness

Give children counters, such as buttons or snap cubes. Have Alphapotamus say: *The quail ran quickly.* As Alphapotamus repeats the sentence, model how to count the words using one counter for each word. Repeat with sentences of varying lengths.

 The quail ran quickly.

High-Frequency Words

Assess

Help children make counting books. Give each child three sheets of paper. Have them draw a group of objects on each page, one for each number 1 through 3. Have children label their pictures with the number and naming word. Since the vocabulary words are also numbers, you may wish to extend this activity to include the numbers *four* and *five.* Compile their pages to make individual books to take home.

Day 5

Independent Writing

Assess Writing Development

Recall with children that in *Five Little Ducks* the little ducks go out and don't come back. Tell children they are going to write a news story about the missing little ducks.

Think ALOUD

> **I'm a newspaper reporter. My paper wants a report on the little ducks. I will write "Five little ducks went over the hills. They have not come home."**

Remind children that a complete sentence begins with a capital letter, ends with a punctuation mark, and tells a complete thought.

Have children continue the news story, telling about the mother duck going to find her little ducks and the little ducks coming home. Encourage them to use pictures or transitional spelling for words they do not know. You may wish to assess each child's writing using the scoring guide.

Select Work for Portfolio

Encourage children to choose a piece of work to add to their portfolio.

Shared Writing

Add to the Class Diary

Encourage children to use complete sentences as they recall and dictate the week's news. Ask them which activity they did first, next, and last. Then write the sentences on chart paper in the order children note. Invite them to help by writing beginning letters or entire words. Add the pages to the class diary.

Scoring Guide

Not every child will be able to write sentences expressing complete thoughts.

3 Competent
The child uses spelling approximations and pictures to write a complete sentence about the ducks.

2 Developing
The child uses initial letters and pictures to represent word groups about the ducks.

1 Emerging
The child is beginning to understand that writing communicates ideas.

Meeting Individual Needs
Intervention

Help children strengthen their concept of words and print-meaning connections by reading the class diary with them. Point to each word as you say it. Help children segment and blend the sounds of words that give them difficulty.

Optional Resources

Phonics Sourcebook pp. 79–82, 84–85, 86–129

Phonics Workbook p. 135

High-Frequency Word Cards

Phonics Kit

Assessment Handbook

Full Day Options...

Phonics

Hunt for *Qq* Give each child a piece of lined paper, a pencil, and a clipboard. Tell children they are going to hunt for capital and lowercase *q*'s in the school hallways and library. When children find a *Q* or *q*, have them write the letter on their piece of paper.

Independent Writing

Write About Exploring Invite children to draw a picture of themselves exploring. Ask them to write a descriptive sentence telling where they would like to explore.

Reading

Read Aloud Invite children who have beginning reading skills to read *A Good Day* aloud to you. Listen for evidence of decoding strategies.

Independent Reader 27

Day **5**

Comprehension

Drawing Conclusions

Remind children that in stories, animals and things can be characters and talk and act like people. Introduce "Sunshine Stories" by asking children to describe sunshine, wind, and rain— what they look, feel, and sound like. As they listen to the story, ask children to think about the gifts the swan gives people.

Read Aloud

TE Volume 5, p. AR6

After reading, ask:

- **Who was the most powerful: the Sunshine, the Wind, or the Rain? Why do you think so?** (Possible answer: The Sunshine. It tells the story. It shines on people.)

- **How did the poor woman know the rings were for her sons?** (She had four sons and there were four rings.)

Ongoing Assessment

Drawing Conclusions

If... children cannot draw conclusions about story characters, events, and ideas,	**then...** reread appropriate parts of the story and ask children what they learned from those parts.

Draw Conclusions About the Swan

Have children suggest words that describe the swan. Discuss the gifts the swan gave and why the swan gives gifts to people. Invite volunteers to do a dance that shows what they think the swan is like.

beautiful   giving
golden   wise

Oral Language

Listen for Rhyming Words

Remind children that rhyming words have the same ending sounds. Say these pairs of words and ask children to stand up if they rhyme: *ring/sing; gold/gone; clay/day; book/took.*

Objectives

Children will

- draw conclusions about a story
- listen for rhyming words
- generate rhymes about a story

Meeting Individual Needs

Intervention

To help children follow the events in the story, break it down into smaller parts. Paraphrase some of the events and ask questions to help children fill in the rest. For example, say: *First the swan flew over the sea. It dropped a feather. Who got the feather? What did the feather become? How did the pen help the young man?*

Day 5

Practice Listening for Rhyming Words

Make a "golden ring" by taping the ends of a strip of yellow construction paper together. Say: *Whoever wears the golden ring gets to name the rhyming words.* Give the ring to a child. Say a rhyme and ask the child to name the two rhyming words and give a third rhyming word. Then have him or her pass the ring to another child. Use rhymes such as:

- **Sunshine *told* the story of a swan of *gold.*** (bold, fold, hold, mold, sold)

- **Please take a *look* at this most wonderful *book.*** (cook, hook, shook, took)

- **What did the little swan *bring*? A shiny golden *ring.*** (sing, wing, thing, king)

Self-Selected Reading

Help children look for books that they can read independently. One story you might suggest is *Rosie's Walk* by Pat Hutchins.

Full Day Options...

Reading

Reader Response: "Sunshine Stories"
Recall with children that the Rain and the Wind both wanted to tell a story. They said they didn't like the Sunshine's stories. Ask: *Why do you think the Rain and the Wind said that? Did you like the Sunshine's stories? Why or why not?*

TE Volume 5, p. AR6

Oral Language

Identify Rhyming Words Have children listen, then tell which words in each sentence rhyme:

- The leaf fell into a little boy's *hand* and turned into a book that was very *grand.*
- The woman gave each ring a *kiss* and Sunshine saw all of *this.*

Independent Writing

Write About the Characters Have children draw a picture of the Sunshine and the swan from the story. Invite them to write a sentence about these characters.

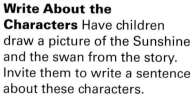

The sun shone on the swan

Drawing Conclusions

What's the Feeling? Give each group a picture from a book or magazine of people expressing an emotion. Have the group decide how each person feels and tell why they think the person feels this way.

Day
5

Theme Launch
Make a Wish

Value of the Theme

Make a Wish refers to the things kindergartners wish for and dream about doing, seeing, and learning. Through their wishes and dreams, kindergartners transform their environments—all things are possible. Wishes and dreams encourage children to explore and speculate on what could be as they investigate their world.

Discuss the Theme Question

How do dreams keep us going?

Read the theme question to children. Discuss with them what they think this question means. Encourage children to discuss

- dreams they have had
- why they think people dream
- why wishes are important

Setting Up the Classroom

The theme *Make a Wish* can be supported by setting an art center where children can create representations of their dreams and wishes. Provide a variety of materials, including cut paper, yarn, fabric, pipe cleaners, glitter, buttons, and so on. Display the finished artwork in the classroom.

Launch the Theme

Explain to children that they will be reading stories and doing projects about characters' wishes and dreams. Ask children:

- **If you were a toy, what might you wish for?**
- **What do you think every sports team dreams about?**
- **Have you ever wished for something and then gotten it? How did you feel?**

Ask children about things they have wished for. Ask if anyone has ever wished for a new bicycle. Then introduce the finger play "My Bicycle" and encourage children to join in the actions of the rhyme.

Finger Play: My Bicycle

One wheel, two wheels on the ground;
(Revolve hands in a forward circle to form each wheel.)

My feet make the pedals go 'round and 'round.
(Move feet in a pedaling motion.)

Handlebars help me steer straight,
(Pretend to steer a bicycle.)

Down the sidewalk, through the gate.

Crossing Cultures

 Use the following selections to help children learn about their own and other cultures.

Corduroy Explain that children all over the world love toys. Many children around the world have toys that they or their families have made.

I Need a Lunch Box In other parts of the world, rice and meat are very common lunch foods. Ask volunteers to tell about favorite foods from their cultures.

Poster Activities

Topic Activities

Use the poster to build background on the weekly topics.

Activity 1 Ask a volunteer to describe what is happening in the first panel. Ask children what the boy might be wishing for at that moment.

Activity 2 Explain that odd things may happen in dreams. Ask volunteers to point to unusual things that are happening in the boy's dreams on the second and third panels.

Activity 3 Have children look at the fourth panel. Ask them why they think the boy is dreaming about flying airplanes, flying ships, and flying eggs. What might he want to do?

Language Arts Connection

Types of Sentences Ask volunteers to point to an item on the poster and say a telling sentence and then an asking sentence about the item. For example, *The boat is on the road. Why is the boat on the road?*

Project

On the floor on butcher paper, draw a running-track-style game board. It should have spaces large enough for children to stand on. Label the game board "Things We Wish For" and label one place "Start" and "Finish." Children can draw pictures of things they wish for in the sections of the game board and around the border. Give small groups a 1–3 spinner. They take turns spinning, moving that many spaces, and pantomiming and/or describing what's in or around the space they land on.

Lesson Overview

Trade Book

Corduroy

Selection Audio

Genre
Classic Animal Fantasy

☞ **Phonemic Awareness/Phonics**
Vowel *e*

☞ **Comprehension**
Drawing Conclusions

High-Frequency Words
one   two   three

About the Author

Don Freeman
earned his living playing the trumpet in jazz bands while studying art. Torn between art and music, he decided on art when he lost his trumpet on the subway. This forced him to distribute his sketches of New York theater life, which appeared in many newspapers and magazines. Author William Saroyan saw his drawings and asked him to illustrate his books. He illustrated other authors' books and published his first children's book, *Chuggy and the Blue Caboose*, which he wrote for his son. He wrote books until his death in 1978.

Leveled Books

Easy

Wordless Story 28

On–Level

Kindergarten Reader 28

Challenge

Independent Reader 28

Trade Books for Self-Selected Reading and Read Aloud

A Pocket for Corduroy
by Don Freeman

Dogger
by Shirley Hughes

Mama Bear
by Chyng Feng Sun

The Runaway Bunny
by Margaret Wise Brown

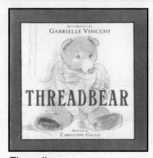

Threadbear
by Christophe Gallaz

The Complete Tales of Winnie-the-Pooh
by A.A. Milne

Theme Make a Wish   **Lesson Topic** A New Friend

5-Day Planner

Customize your week with the Teacher's Resource Planner CD-ROM!

Reading

Comprehension

Vocabulary

Phonics

Phonemic Awareness

Day 1

Activate Prior Knowledge p. 131

Poem "My Teddy Bear"

Reading pp. 132–139

Read Aloud *Corduroy*

Reader Response: Show What a Character Feels

 Comprehension: Drawing Conclusions

Solve Riddles to Draw Conclusions

Phonics pp. 140–141

✓ Short *e*

Phonemic Awareness: Listen for /e/ Words
• Phonics Songs and Rhymes Chart 28

Identify /e/ Picture Cards

Connect Sound to Letter: Match /e/ to *e*

Phonological Awareness: Blend Sounds with /e/

✔ High-Frequency Words

one	two	three

Day 2

Phonics pp. 142–143

✓ Short *e*

Phonemic Awareness: Sing a Song with /e/ Words
• Phonics Songs and Rhymes Chart 28

Identify /e/ Words
• Wordless Story 28 *Em, Ed, and Jet*

Connect Sound to Letter: Match /e/ to *e*

Phonological Awareness: Identify Words with /e/

✔ High-Frequency Words: Write *one, two* and *three*

Reading pp. 144–145

 Comprehension: Drawing Conclusions

Recall Book's Main Character

Use Vocabulary in Sentences

Drawing Conclusions About Corduroy

Oral Language

Speaking, Listening, and Viewing

Oral Language pp. 138–139

Introduce Vocabulary: Furniture Words

beds   tables   chairs   lamps   sofas

Use Furniture Words to Complete Sentences

Oral Language pp. 144–145

 Speaking: Speak with Proper Grammar
• Oral Language Chart 28

Writing

Grammar, Usage, and Mechanics

Writing pp. 140–141

 Shared Writing: Write Sentences Together

Writing pp. 142–143

 Modeled Writing: Write About a New Friend

Guided Writing

Handwriting: Practice Writing *Ee*

Self-Selected Reading
Read Aloud

Self-Selected Reading p. 139

Have children select books to read. They might like to read another book about Corduroy by Don Freeman, such as *A Pocket for Corduroy*.

Self-Selected Reading p. 145

Because they have been reading about a toy bear who finds a home, children might be interested in reading *Threadbear* by Christophe Gallaz.

 Target Skill   **Review** **Review Skill**

Target Skills of the Week

Reading Drawing Conclusions
Phonics Short *e*
Oral Language Speak with Proper Grammar
Writing Complete Sentences

Day 3

Phonics pp. 146–147

 Short *e*

Phonemic Awareness:
Identify Names with /e/

Connect Sound to Letter:
Find *e* Words That
Have /e/ Sound
• Phonics Songs and
Rhymes Chart 28

Phonological Awareness:
Count Words

Read Kindergarten Reader 28: *Sick in Bed?*

Reading pp. 148–149

 Comprehension:
Drawing Conclusions

Draw Conclusions to
Describe Characters

Reader Response:
Recall the Story

Model Writing Sentences

Oral Language pp. 148–149

 Speaking: Use Proper
Grammar to Retell Story

Practice Using
Proper Grammar

Writing pp. 146–147

 Modeled Writing: Demonstrate
Writing Sentences

Guided Writing

Self-Selected Reading p. 149

If children enjoy reading stories
about animals, you might
suggest *The Runaway Bunny* by
Margaret Wise Brown.

Day 4

Phonics pp. 150–151

 Consonant *qu* /kw/

 Short *e*

Phonemic Awareness:
Consonant *qu* /kw/

Segment and Blend Words
with /e/ and /kw/

Connect Sound to Letter: Find
Pictures with /e/

Phonological Awareness:
Distinguish /e/ from Other
Vowel Sounds

✔ **High-Frequency Words:**
Build Words

Challenge: Independent
Reader 28

Reading pp. 152–153

 Comprehension:
Drawing Conclusions

Activate Prior
Knowledge

 **Assess Drawing
Conclusions**

Oral Language pp. 152–153

 Speaking: Speak with
Proper Grammar
• Read Aloud

 **Assess Speak with Proper
Grammar**

Writing pp. 150–151

 Interactive Writing:
Verbs

Use Verbs

Self-Selected Reading p. 153

Have children choose books to
read. They might like to read
other books about lovable bears,
such as *The Complete Tales of
Winnie-the-Pooh* by A.A. Milne.

Day 5

Phonics pp. 154–155

 Short *e*

Phonemic Awareness:
Prepare to Assess

 Connect Sound to Letter:
Assess *e* /e/

Phonological Awareness:
Count Syllables

 High-Frequency Words: Assess

Reading pp. 156–157

Comprehension: Sequence
• Read Aloud "How Matti Almost
Taught the Bear to Play the
Fiddle"

Sequence Story Illustrations

Oral Language pp. 156–157

Speaking: Choral Reading

Practice Choral Reading

Writing pp. 154–155

 Independent Writing: Assess
Writing Development

Shared Writing: Add to the
Class Diary

Self-Selected Reading p. 157

Have children choose books to
read. They might like to read
another book about stuffed
animals, such as *Dogger* by Shirley
Hughes.

 Assessment   ✔ **Benchmark Assessment of Target Skills and Skills Assessment**

Cross-Curricular Work Stations

Community Link

Ideas for bringing the school and community together

Field Experiences
department store
toy store

Guest Speakers
toy maker
department store personnel
magician

Letters and Sounds

Short *e* Families 10 minutes

Materials: paper, pencils, consonant cards and phonogram cards for *-et* and *-en*

Learning Styles Kinesthetic, Logical

Place the two phonogram cards one above the other. Mix the consonant cards and give one to each child. Have children take turns placing their consonant card in front of each phonogram card to see if the combination makes a word. If it does, children write the word on paper. Continue until all consonants have been tried.

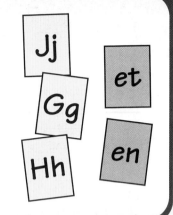

Science

Compare Animals 10 minutes

Materials: stuffed animals, books and other reference materials about real animals

Learning Styles Logical, Verbal, Visual

Children choose a stuffed animal and compare it with its real counterpart. How are they alike? How are they different? Individually, or during group time, record children's observations.

ESL Ask questions about children's observations and encourage them to answer in complete sentences, for example, *Which animals have long tails? Which lion can roar loudly?*

Math

Solve the Problem 10 minutes

Materials: shelves, toys, problem cards

Learning Styles Kinesthetic, Logical, Visual

Arrange various numbers of toys on several shelves. Have children solve simple problems such as *How many toys are on the top shelf? Which toy is first on the bottom shelf? How many cars and trucks are there in all?* Children can take turns answering the questions.

Challenge Children can arrange toys on shelves and write problems for classmates to solve.

INTERNET SAFETY

Establish guidelines for your students' safe and responsible use of the Internet. See the Scott Foresman Internet Guide for tips.

Technology

Multimedia Presentation three days for 10 minutes

Learning Styles Auditory, Verbal

Have each child share a favorite toy or stuffed animal. Record children on video or audio tape and include the recordings in a hypermedia presentation about new friends.

Web Site two days for 10 minutes

Learning Styles Individual, Visual

sfreading.com

Visit the Scott Foresman Web site (sfreading.com) for current hyperlinks to sites that can be used by children for an Internet Workshop investigation of new friends. Also see the Scott Foresman Internet Guide for additional information on the Internet Workshop method.

Art

Make Stuffed Animals 10 minutes

Materials: bear outline (front and back), construction paper, crayons, glue, scissors, buttons, stapler, newspaper

Learning Styles Kinesthetic, Individual

Provide a large bear outline for children to trace and cut or precut bear shapes for children. Have children decorate their bear. When they are finished, they can crush newspaper to stuff the bear before stapling it closed.

Social Studies

Toys from Around the World 10 minutes

Materials: toys or books showing toys from around the world, drawing materials

Learning Styles Visual, Kinesthetic

Provide books that show toys from different countries or, if possible, display the actual toys. Encourage children to note similarities and differences between these toys and the toys they have at home. Have children choose a toy that they would like to play with and draw a picture of themselves with the toy.

Introduce the Reading Road Show Activity Stations to reinforce this week's skills.

Phonemic Awareness & Phonics
Literacy Activities

Use these activities during the week to reinforce skills.

Phonemic Awareness

Red Light   15 minutes

Learning Styles Kinesthetic, Auditory, Spatial

Have a small group of children stand shoulder to shoulder in a line. Designate a goal line some distance away from the children. Say *red*. As you say the word, children are to say another word that has the same middle sound. Whoever gives a correct answer first takes one step forward. Say another word with a short *e* sound and the game proceeds. If any child gives an incorrect answer, he or she hits a "red light" and must go back to the starting line. The first child to reach the goal line is the winner.

The game can be made less competitive by calling on children one at a time rather than having them try to be the first to say a word. It can also be played to practice beginning or ending consonant sounds.

Working with Letters

Letter Puzzles 10 minutes

Materials: cardboard pieces, large envelopes

Learning Styles Visual, Logical, Kinesthetic

Write a capital *B* and a lowercase *b* on one side of a piece of cardboard. On the other side, paste a picture whose name begins with *b*. Cut the cardboard into medium-sized puzzle pieces. Have several children work together to assemble the puzzle. Have them name the letter and the picture.

Children may enjoy creating their own puzzles for other children to put together.

Working with Words

Rhyming Ball Game 10 minutes

Materials: heavy shelf paper or bulletin board paper

Learning Styles Visual, Kinesthetic, Spatial, Auditory

Tape heavy shelf paper to the floor or sidewalk and divided it into six sections. Write one of these words in each section: *cat, bag, hen, top, pig, pet*. Have children form a line. Give a ball to the first child. Have the child bounce the ball on each word, read the word, and say a rhyming word. Continue until many children have turns.

ABC Wall

Point to the Word 10 minutes

Materials: ruler

Learning Styles Visual, Social

Have children stand in a semicircle facing the ABC Wall. Give the child at one end a ruler. Tell children to pass the ruler along the line until you say "Stop" and say a sentence that contains one of the words from the ABC Wall. The child points to the word with the ruler and reads the word. Continue the game by having children pass the ruler again.

(ESL) Encourage children to use each ABC Wall word in a sentence. Help them make simple sentences more complex by changing a simple sentence, such as *I have a cat*, into a more descriptive one, such as *I have a black cat named Smoky.*

Daily Warm-Up

Message Board

Day One

Today we will read about Corduroy. He is a toy bear.

Ask children to tell about their favorite stuffed animal or toy.

Ask children: "What words do you know that begin like *elephant?*"

Day Two

We will look and listen for words with Ee.

Day Three

We will read the words one, two, and three.

Ask children to show you *one, two,* and *three* fingers.

Discuss with children why it is important to use words correctly.

Day Four

Today we will work on using correct words when we speak.

Day Five

Today we will write a note to a friend.

Ask children: "What do you want to tell a friend?"

Getting Ready
for the Week

Day One
stuffed animal
pictures of people showing
   emotions (Full Day)
version of the story *Henny Penny* (Full Day)

Day Two
"sticky" notes
magazines, coathangers, yarn
   (Full Day)
pictures of children doing
   different activities
   (Full Day)

Day Three
paper egg shapes

Day Four
chart paper, magazines
pennies, lunch bags

Day Five
large index cards

Family Times

Send home the newsletter with fun instructional activities to reinforce this week's target skills.

Practice Book, pp. 177–178
Teacher's Resource Book, pp. 177–178

Activate Prior Knowledge

Objectives

Children will

- listen and respond to a poem
- get meaning from illustrations
- connect literature to a real-life experience

Talk About Toy Animals

Tell children that this week's story is about a teddy bear. Talk about the stuffed animals and toys they have at home. Ask:

- **What are your favorite things to play with? Why?**

- **How do you feel when you get a new stuffed animal or toy? When a stuffed animal or toy gets old or lost?**

Introduce a stuffed animal to the class. Let children hold it and invite them to tell what they would call it and how they would play with it if it were theirs.

Build Background

Choose one or more of these activities to build background for concepts presented in this week's selection, *Corduroy*.

Read Aloud a Poem

Share this poem. Invite children to think about what the teddy bear means to the speaker.

My Teddy Bear
by Margaret Hillert

A teddy bear is nice to hold.
The one I have is getting old.
His paws are almost wearing out
And so's his funny furry snout
From rubbing on my nose of skin,
And all his fur is pretty thin.
A ribbon and a piece of string
Make a sort of necktie thing.
His eyes came out and now instead
He has some new ones made of
   thread.
I take him everywhere I go
And tell him all the things I know.
I like the way he feels at night,
All snuggled up against me tight.

Use Illustrations to Develop Oral Language

Hold up *Corduroy* and show children the cover. Then show them pages 6–7. Ask them to describe what they see in the pictures. Elicit that the toy bear is in a store and that the little girl seems interested in him. Have children make up a conversation between the little girl and her mother in which they talk about the bear.

Use Audio to Develop Story Concepts

Ask:

- **What kind of stuffed animal is on the cover of this week's story?** (teddy bear)

- **How do children play with teddy bears?**

Share the Background-Building CD/tape, which presents the history of the teddy bear.

CD 5/Tape 14, Side 2
Background-Building Audio

Day 1

Children will

- identify author and illustrator
- use illustrations to make predictions about the story
- listen to a story

Read Aloud Routine

Day 1

- Read the story through for enjoyment.
- To practice the reading strategy predicting, use the stopping point on TE page 133.

Day 2

- Reread the entire story, using the activities found in the margins on pages 133–137.

Days 3–5

- Reread selected pages for specific purposes as suggested in the lessons.

Concepts of Print

Author and Illustrator

As children examine the cover of *Corduroy*, read the title and the author and illustrator's name. Help children understand that Don Freeman is both the author and illustrator of the book.

Model Reading Behaviors

Picture Walk and Predict

Turn through the pages and ask questions to help children set a purpose for reading:

- **Where does most of the story take place?** (in a store)

- **Who seems to be the main character in the story?** (a stuffed bear)

- **What do you think will happen to the bear? Let's read to find out.**

Read Aloud

Trade Book

Corduroy is a bear who once lived in the toy department of a big store. Day after day he waited with all the other animals and dolls for somebody to come along and take him home.

page 5

The store was always filled with shoppers buying all sorts of things, but no one ever seemed to want a small bear in green overalls.

Then one morning a little girl stopped and looked straight into Corduroy's bright eyes.
"Oh, Mommy!" she said. "Look! There's the very bear I've always wanted."
"Not today, dear." Her mother sighed. "I've spent too much already. Besides, he doesn't look new. He's lost the button to one of his shoulder straps."

pages 6–7

Corduroy watched them sadly as they walked away.

"I didn't know I'd lost a button," he said to himself. "Tonight I'll go and see if I can find it."

pages 8–9

Day 1

Language Development

Explain to children that *corduroy* is a material used to make clothing. The ribbed fabric is often used to make shirts, pants, or jackets. If possible, bring in a piece of *corduroy* material or clothing and allow children to feel it.

corduroy

Language Development

a small green bear in overalls

What does the word *overalls* mean? How do you know? How can you use other words and the pictures to figure out what *overalls* means?

overalls

average

Guiding the Reading

Critical Thinking

Why hasn't Corduroy been bought yet? What in the story lets you know this?
Possible answers: He is small. He has a missing button.

Stopping Point

Predict On the first reading, you may want to stop at the bottom of page 9 and ask children to predict what will happen next.

Guiding the Reading

Critical Thinking

Why do you think Corduroy wants to find his button?
Possible answer: Maybe he thinks that if he had his button back, someone would buy him and take him home.

Guiding the Reading

Critical Thinking

Why did Corduroy decide to wait until nighttime to go look for his button?
Possible answer: He didn't want shoppers and people working in the store to see him leave the toy department.

Content Connection: Social Studies

- An escalator is a set of moving stairs. They are moved by electricity.
- Some escalators carry you up. Others carry you down. The same escalator cannot do both.

pages 10–11

pages 12–13

pages 14–15

He wandered around admiring the furniture.
"This must be a bed," he said. "I've always wanted to sleep in a bed." And up he crawled onto a large, thick mattress.

All at once he saw something small and round.
"Why, here's my button!" he cried. And he tried to pick it up. But, like all the other buttons on the mattress, it was tied down tight.

pages 16–17

Language Development

Share with children the meaning of the word *admiring*.

Corduroy was admiring the furniture, looking at everything with wonder.

admiring

challenge

Day
1

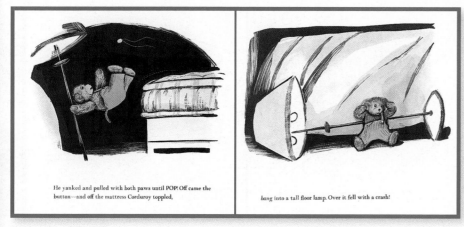

He yanked and pulled with both paws until POP! Off came the button—and off the mattress Corduroy toppled,

bang into a tall floor lamp. Over it fell with a crash!

pages 18–19

Content Connection: Social Studies

- A night watchman is a type of guard for a business.
- A night watchman stands guard while the store is closed and makes sure it stays safe.
- A night watchman walks all around the building. This is called "making the rounds."

Corduroy didn't know it, but there was someone else awake in the store. The night watchman was going his rounds on the floor above. When he heard the crash he came dashing down the escalator.

"Now who in the world did that!" he exclaimed. "Somebody must be hiding around here!"

pages 20–21

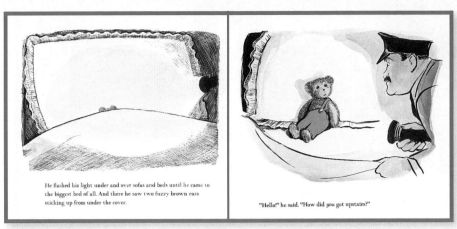

pages 22–23

pages 24–25

Guiding the Reading

Critical Thinking

Why does the little girl come back? Why does she spend her own money to buy Corduroy?
Possible answers: She wants the bear very much. She is willing to give up other things to have the bear.

pages 26–27

pages 28–29

pages 30–31

Share with children the meaning of the word *blinked*.

Corduroy blinked; he opened and closed his eyes quickly.

blinked

average

Guiding the Reading

Critical Thinking

What parts of this story could be true? What parts are make-believe?
Possible answers: The teddy bear could really be in the store and be sold to a little girl who loved it. The teddy bear could not wander around the store or think to itself or talk.

page 32

Objectives

Children will

 draw conclusions

- develop vocabulary by completing sentences
- relate events in a story to own life

Day **1**

 Meeting Individual Needs
Other Ways to Learn

Visual Provide sheets of paper with a picture of each vocabulary word shown at the top. Have children cut out pictures of furniture, sort them, and paste examples of each kind on the appropriate paper.

Skills Trace

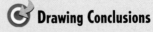 **Drawing Conclusions**

Introduce	TE: K.5 64–65
Teach	PB: 168, 170, 180, 182, 218, 220
Reteach/ Review	TE: K.5 71, 74, 78, 118, **138–139**, 145, 148, 152, 192, AR13, AR17 K.6 138–139, 145, 148, 152, 194, AR17
Skills Assessment	Skills Assessment Unit 5 TE: K.5 AR1–AR3 K.6 AR1 AR3

Reader Response

Show What a Character Feels

Ask: *What was your favorite part of this story? Tell me your favorite part.*

How did Lisa feel about Corduroy? How do you know? Have you ever felt this way? Show me how you would show Corduroy this feeling. Make a teddy bear or other stuffed animal available.

Continue by having children show how Lisa felt when

- She first saw Corduroy (excited)
- She had to leave him at the store (sad)
- She carried him home (happy)

Oral Language/Vocabulary

Use Furniture Words to Complete Sentences

The vocabulary words name kinds of furniture. Have children use these words to complete sentences.

beds   tables   chairs   lamps   sofas

- **We sit in ___.** (chairs)
- **We sleep in ___.** (beds)
- **When we want light, we turn on ____.** (lamps)
- **Another name for couches is ____.** (sofas)
- **When we want to eat or do work we sit at ____.** (tables)

Ongoing Assessment

Vocabulary

If... children cannot complete the sentences,

then... have them use the pictures on pages 14 and 15 to identify the furniture.

Comprehension

Solve Riddles to Draw Conclusions Say riddles, such as the following:

> **I am soft and furry. I have a long tail and whiskers. I say, "Meow." What am I?**

Have children draw a picture to show their answer or write the word. Ask children to show each other their papers. Ask:

> **How did everyone know that the answer to the riddle was a cat?**

Elicit that children know what a cat looks like and how it sounds. Therefore, they were able to figure out that you were talking about a cat.

Tell children: *Stories are like riddles. The author doesn't tell you everything, so you have to figure out some things yourself. You can look at pictures in the story, use information in the story, and use what you know from real life. For example, you know what an escalator and a mountain are. You can also see a picture of an escalator in the story. All of this helped you figure out why Corduroy thought the escalator was a mountain—they both go up.*

Self-Selected Reading **D.E.A.R.** Drop Everything And Read

Have children select books to read. They might like to read another book about Corduroy by Don Freeman, such as *A Pocket for Corduroy*.

Day **1**

Full Day Options...

Oral Language

Tell a Story Have children choose a prompt.

- Tell a story about one of the other toys in the toy department.
- Corduroy went to the furniture floor. Tell what would have happened if he had gone to the children's clothing floor instead.
- Lisa wanted to buy Corduroy. Which toy would you want to buy? Why?

Vocabulary

Make Furniture Riddles Have children choose a vocabulary word and make up a riddle about it. For example, *I have a flat top and four legs. What am I?* (table) Call on volunteers to say their riddles for classmates to answer.

Drawing Conclusions

Look at Faces Give each group a picture of a person that clearly shows an emotion. Have children work together to figure out what the person is feeling and perhaps why the person is feeling that way. Have children share their conclusions with the class.

Drawing Conclusions

Act Out Situations Have volunteers act out situations that you whisper to them, such as eating a banana or getting caught in the rain. Have classmates identify what is happening and how they were able to figure it out.

DRAMA CONNECTION

PHONICS A–Z

Children will

- recognize /e/
- recognize the letters *Ee*
- blend sounds into words
- participate in a shared writing activity

Meeting Individual Needs
Intervention

Display picture cards for *bed, fan, hat, jet, leg, map, nest,* and *cap.* Have children name each picture with you. Help them choose the cards in which the picture name has the /e/ sound in the middle.

Skills Trace

Vowel *Ee*

Introduce	TE: K.5 **140**
Practice	PB: 179, 181
Reteach/ Review	TE: K.5 142, 146–147, 150, 154, 190, AR16
Skills Assessment	Skills Assessment Unit 5 TE: K.5 AR1–AR3

140 **Phonics** and Writing

Daily Phonics Routine

Listen for /e/ Words

Display "Big Enough for Ten!" and read the title. Say *ten*, emphasizing /e/. Sing "Big Enough for Ten!" or play the CD/tape. Have children listen for and name other words that have /e/ in the middle like *ten*. (let's, pen, hen, nest, them, rest, tent, best)

Big Enough for Ten!

Let's build a little pen
For the chicks and mother hen.
Let's build a little nest for them
That's big enough for ten!

Let's put the little nest
Where everyone can rest.
Let's build a tent where we can play.
We really did our best!

CD 2/Tape 14, Side 2
Phonics Songs and Rhymes Audio

Phonics Songs and Rhymes Chart 28

Identify /e/ Picture Cards

Show picture cards for *egg, elephant,* and *escalator.* Have children identify each picture by name. Ask: *What sound do you hear at the beginning of each name?* (/e/)

Ongoing Assessment
Phonemic Awareness

If... children have trouble hearing /e/,

then... have them echo you as you say the word *egg*, emphasizing /e/.

Connect Sound to Letter

Match /e/ to *e*

Have Alphapotamus show the alphabet card for *Ee*. Have Alphapotamus say *elephant* slowly, segmenting the sounds and emphasizing the initial /e/ sound. Write *elephant* and *Elephant* on the board. Point out that /e/ is spelled *e* and *E*. Have children say /e/ several times as you point to the initial *e*. Tell children that *e* is special because it has two sounds: /e/ as in *elephant* and the sound of its name as in *eagle.*

Ee

Alphabet Cards

Phonological Awareness

Blend Sounds with /e/

Say: *I am going to say three sounds. I want you to blend them together and say the word:* /s/ /e/ /t/. Continue with /b/ /e/ /d/, /p/ /e/ /n/, and /j/ /e/ /t/.

High-Frequency Words

Recognize *one, two,* and *three*

Write the high-frequency words *one, two,* and *three* on the board. Hold up large index cards with 1, 2, and 3 on them. Have volunteers place the numeral on the ledge under the correct word. Then ask children to locate the words on the ABC Wall.

Day 1

Invite children to look in magazines for pictures with names that have /e/ at the beginning or in the middle. Add the words to this week's panel of the ABC Wall.

Optional Resources

Phonics Sourcebook pp. 16–17, 84–85

High-Frequency Word Cards

Phonics Workbook p. 136

Shared Writing

Write Sentences Together

Say: *We are going to write three sentences about what the mother hen and her chicks do in the pen.* Ask children to try to use the numbers *one, two,* and *three* in their sentences.

Mother Hen and Her Chicks

One hen builds a nest.

Two chicks rest.

Three chicks play.

As children respond, they can

• Use words that have /e/

• Use high-frequency words

• Attempt to sound out words as you write them

When you finish writing, do a choral reading of the sentences. Track the print as you read.

Full Day Options...

Phonics

Listen for /e/ Words Ask children to listen for words with /e/ as you read a familiar story such as *Henny Penny.* Have them clap when they hear a word with /e/.

Drawing Conclusions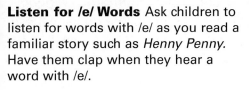

Why Build a Pen? Have children look at Phonics Songs and Rhymes Chart 28. Ask them why the children needed to build a pen for the hen and chicks.

Independent Writing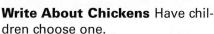

Write About Chickens Have children choose one.

• Write or dictate a sentence about a hen.

• Write or dictate a sentence about baby chicks.

• Write or dictate a sentence about building a pen.

Objectives

Children will

- 🗘 recognize initial and medial *e*/e/
- 🗘 write complete sentences
- • recognize the letters *Ee*
- • write number words

Day 2

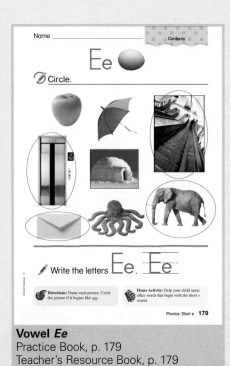

Vowel *Ee*
Practice Book, p. 179
Teacher's Resource Book, p. 179

Skills Trace

🗘 Complete Sentences

Introduce	TE: K.3 33
Teach	TE: K.3 39, 43 K.5 105, 113, 117, **143**, 151, 155, 227 K.6 189, 221, 229, 233
Reteach/ Review	TE: K.3 119 K.5 155 K.6 225 PB: 220, 228
Skills Assessment	Skills Assessment Unit 3, Unit 5, Unit 6 TE: K.3 AR1–AR3 K.5 AR1–AR3 K.6 AR1–AR3

142 **Phonics** and Writing

Daily Phonics Routine

Phonemic Awareness

Sing a Song with /e/ Words

Have children pretend their pencils are hammers. As they sing along with the CD/tape of "Big Enough for Ten!" children can tap their "hammers" on their desks for every /e/ word they hear. Then have them identify things in the picture with names that have /e/ in the middle. (tent, hen, pen, nest)

Phonics Songs and Rhymes Chart 28

CD 2/Tape 14, Side 2
Phonics Songs and Rhymes Audio

Identify /e/ Words

Share *Em, Ed, and Jet* with children. Ask: *Who is Jet?* (a dog) *Who are Em and Ed?* (a boy and a girl) *What sound do you hear at the beginning of* Em *and* Ed? (/e/) *What sound do you hear in the middle of* Jet? (/e/) As they look at the pictures, ask children to tell the story in their own words. You may wish to have them dictate or write the story in the take-home version.

Wordless Story 28

Connect Sound to Letter

Match /e/ to *e*

Show children the *Ee* alphabet card and say *elephant*, emphasizing the beginning sound in the middle. Display picture cards for *jet, hat, egg, leg, pan, bed, pig, ten, nest,* and *box*. Have children write *Ee* on a "sticky" note. Say the name of each picture, emphasizing the vowel sound. Have children place a "sticky" note on any picture that has an /e/ sound at the beginning or in the middle of its name.

Alphabet Cards

Phonological Awareness

Identify Words with /e/

Say: *I'm going to say three words. One of the words begins with* /e/ *or has the* /e/ *sound in the middle. When you hear me say that word, write an e in the air. Say these words: bell, ball, bill; pot, pat, pet; sat, sit, set; egg, at, ox.*

High-Frequency Words

Write *one*, *two*, and *three*

Have children find *one*, *two*, and *three* on the ABC Wall. Model writing each word on the board. (See pages AR45–AR46 of this Teacher's Edition.) Distribute writing paper and have children write the words.

Modeled Writing

Write About a New Friend

Recall that Corduroy met a new friend in the department store. Invite children to tell where they met a new friend. Write a sentence: *Meg and Raul met at school.* Say:

- **A sentence should tell a complete thought about someone or something and what they do.**

- **My sentence is about two friends: *Meg and Raul.* It tells what they did: *met at school.***

Guided Writing

Help children write a complete sentence about where they met a new friend. Some may need to dictate or draw.

Handwriting

Practice Writing *Ee*

Distribute writing paper and have children practice writing *e* and *E*. Children who are already proficient writing *e* and *E* can write *bed* and *egg*.

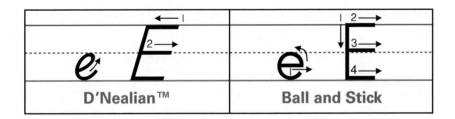

D'Nealian™	Ball and Stick

Help children find two or three words with /e/ from Phonics Songs and Rhymes Chart 28 to add to this week's panel of the ABC Wall. Ask children who have names with /e/ to add them to the wall.

❄ Meeting Individual Needs

ESL

Write simple sentences, such as *Tom runs, Maria sings, Jesse plays.* Read each sentence and ask children who the sentence is about and what that person is doing.

Day 2

Optional Resources

Phonics Sourcebook pp. 16–17, 84–85

Phonics Workbook p. 137

High-Frequency Word Cards

Full Day Options...

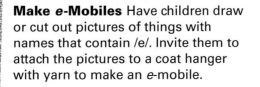

Independent Writing 🧍

Write About What You Want
Remind children that Corduroy often says "I have always wanted . . ." Have them write about something they have always wanted to have or do.

Phonics 👪

Make *e*-Mobiles Have children draw or cut out pictures of things with names that contain /e/. Invite them to attach the pictures to a coat hanger with yarn to make an *e*-mobile.

Handwriting 🧍

Practice Have children choose one.

- Write these rhyming words: *vet, jet, wet.*
- Write this sentence: *Ed gets one egg.*

Oral Language

Speak with Proper Grammar

Explain that some action words (verbs) tell what one person or thing does and other action words tell what more than one person or thing does. Ask children which sentence uses the correct action word: *The girl like Corduroy. The girl likes Corduroy.*

Ask children to listen to the chant "Teddy Bear, Teddy Bear" for the actions the teddy bear is supposed to do. After reading, have children complete sentences such as: *One teddy bear ___ the ground.* (touches) *Two teddy bears ___ the ground.* (touch) Point out that it is important to use correct words when we speak and write so that others can understand us.

Teddy Bear, Teddy Bear
a Mother Goose rhyme

Teddy bear, teddy bear
Touch the ground.
Teddy bear, teddy bear
Turn around.
Teddy bear, teddy bear
Show your shoe.
Teddy bear, teddy bear
That will do.

Oral Language Chart 28

Comprehension

Recall Book's Main Character

Hold up *Corduroy* and ask children how Corduroy felt when Lisa and her mother left the store. Have children make a face to show how Corduroy felt.

Use Vocabulary in Sentences

Have children imagine they are Corduroy getting off the escalator on the furniture floor. Ask: *What do you say when you see the sofas?* Encourage children to answer with a complete sentence, using the word *sofas.* Continue the activity with *beds, chairs, tables,* and *lamps.*

Listen to Trade Book for Information

Ask children to listen as you reread the story. Ask them to listen to decide why Corduroy and Lisa are so happy at the end of the story.

While reading, you may wish to use the ideas in the *Guiding the Reading* and *Language Development* boxes on pages 133–137 of this Teacher's Edition.

Read Aloud

Trade Book

Objectives

Children will

 draw conclusions

 use proper grammar when speaking

- listen to a rhyme

Day 2

Draw Conclusions About Corduroy

Remind children that the author of a story does not tell them everything. Children can use story pictures, information in the story, and what they know from real life to figure out things about characters and what happens to them. Help children draw conclusions about Corduroy:

- **Why is Corduroy sad when the girl and her mother leave?** (He hoped they were going to take him home with them.)

- **Why does Corduroy search for his button?** (He thinks that if he has his button back, he will look better and someone might take him home.)

- **How does Corduroy feel when Lisa buys him?** (He is very happy.)

- **How does Lisa feel when she buys Corduroy?** (She is happy to be able to take Corduroy home.)

Self-Selected Reading

Have children choose their own books to read from your self-selected reading collection. Because they have been reading about a toy bear who finds a home, children might be interested in reading *Threadbear* by Christophe Gallaz.

Day 2

Ongoing Assessment
Drawing Conclusions

If... children have difficulty drawing conclusions about story events and characters,	**then...** prompt them with specific questions: *What had Corduroy been waiting for? Did the little girl seem interested in him?*

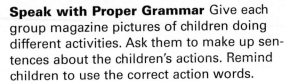

Full Day Options...

Drawing Conclusions 👫

Look at Pictures Invite partners to page through an unfamiliar picture book. They can take turns describing the characters and what they do. Then ask each pair to tell what they think one character is like and explain how they know this.

Oral Language 👫

Speak with Proper Grammar Give each group magazine pictures of children doing different activities. Ask them to make up sentences about the children's actions. Remind children to use the correct action words.

Phonics 👬👬

Repeat /e/ Words Say a pair of words and have children repeat the word with /e/: *bell, cot; ant, egg; hit, ten; red, rob; mad, leg; get, big.*

Modeled Writing 👬👬

Change a Chant Copy Oral Language Chart 28 on the board, leaving the even-numbered lines blank. Ask children to make up new directions for the teddy bear. Model writing the directions as children say them. Invite volunteers to demonstrate the new directions.

Daily Phonics Routine

Day 3

❄ Meeting Individual Needs
ESL

Have children work with fluent English-speaking partners to name the animals shown in *Sick in Bed?* Children can draw a picture of their favorite animal to show and identify for the rest of the class.

Phonemic Awareness

Identify Names with /e/

Give each child a paper egg shape. Say: *Listen to these names. When you hear a name that has /e/, wave your egg in the air:* Meg, Bob, Ann, Ed, Ashley, Ben, Emily, Jamahl, Ned.

Connect Sound to Letter

Find *e* Words That Have /e/ Sound

Have children read or sing the first stanza of "Big Enough for Ten" as you track the print. Ask children to clap each time they hear a word that has the /e/ sound they hear in *egg*. Invite volunteers to circle the /e/ words.

Big Enough for Ten!

Let's build a little pen
For the chicks and mother hen.
Let's build a little nest for them
That's big enough for ten!

Let's put the little nest
Where everyone can rest.
Let's build a tent where we can play.
We really did our best!

Phonics Songs and Rhymes Chart 28

CD 2/Tape 14, Side 2
Phonics Songs and Rhymes Audio

Phonological Awareness

Count Words

Have children say a word with /e/ and make up a sentence using the word. Write the sentences. Say: *Read this sentence with me. How many words does it have? Which word has /e/?*

Ongoing Assessment
Phonological Awareness

If... children have difficulty distinguishing and counting words in a sentence,

then... point out the spaces between the words. Read the sentence slowly, pointing to each word and holding up fingers showing how many words have been counted.

Phonics and High-Frequency Words

Read Kindergarten Reader 28

- Read the title, pointing to each word as you say it. Make sure children understand that the title asks a question. Point out that *bed* has an e that stands for the sound /e/.

- Do a picture walk and have children predict what the book will be about.

- Read the story aloud. Have children track the print with their fingers as you read.

Kindergarten Reader 28

Phonics Vowel *Ee*

High-Frequency Words
one, two, three

Peg Pig got Hen.
Hen, Hen! Ben is in bed!
2

Ben is red.
One in bed.
3

Peg Pig got Cat.
Cat, Cat! Jen is in bed!
4

Jen is red.
Two in bed.
5

Peg Pig got bear.
Bear! Bear! Len is in bed.
6

Len is red.
Three in bed.
7

One, two three! Not sick!
Not in bed! Not red!
8

Modeled Writing

Demonstrate Writing Sentences

Model writing using sentences based on Kindergarten Reader 28 *Sick in Bed?* For example, write *Ben is red.*

As you write the sentences, model these strategies:

- Begin each sentence with a capital letter.
- Leave spaces between words.
- Put punctuation at the end of each sentence.
- Make sure each sentence tells a complete thought.

Guided Writing

Ask children to read the sentences with you. Help children write their own sentences based on *Sick in Bed?*

ABC Wall

Ask a volunteer to find a word that begins with *e* on the ABC Wall. Help the child give clues about the word. Have other children name the word.

Day 3

Optional Resources

Phonics Workbook p. 138

Full Day Options...

Independent Writing

Use a Writing Journal Have children choose one.

- Draw or write about a time you were sick.
- Draw or write about a trick someone played on you or you played on someone.

Phonics

Build Words Give children letter cards for *B, L, J, e,* and *n* and word cards *for Ben, Len,* and *Jen.* Have them make the names by matching the letters to the word cards. Have children read each name as it is made.

Drawing Conclusions

What Is Happening? Have children page through *Sick in Bed?* Ask them to describe what is happening and explain how they figured out that Ben, Jen, and Len are not really sick.

Trade Book

Objectives

Children will

- use proper grammar when speaking
- draw conclusions
- relate the story to life experiences

Meeting Individual Needs
Intervention

Day 3

To help children draw conclusions from pictures, prompt with questions: *What look do you see on the night watchman's face? How does he carry Corduroy? What does Lisa do for Corduroy? Why does she do this?*

Drawing Conclusions
Practice Book, p. 180
Teacher's Resource Book, p. 180

Oral Language

Use Proper Grammar to Retell Story

Display pages 12–19 and have children recall what Corduroy does first when he leaves the toy department: *Corduroy rides the escalator.* Ask children to pretend they are with Corduroy and tell what the two of them do: *We ride the escalator.* Help children recognize that they used a different action word in each sentence: *rides* and *ride.* Continue with: *Corduroy sees lots of furniture. We see lots of furniture. Corduroy yanks on a button. We yank on a button.*

Practice Using Proper Grammar

Have groups of one, two, and three children carry out simple directions, such as clap twice. Have children who are watching use a complete sentence to tell what each individual or group is doing, for example, *Maria claps. Bret and Carmen clap.* When children use action words correctly, group members give a thumbs up sign.

Ongoing Assessment
Speak with Proper Grammar

If... children have difficulty using proper grammar,

then... repeat the child's sentence correctly and have the child echo it.

Comprehension

Draw Conclusions to Describe Characters

Reread pages 20–32 of *Corduroy.* Encourage children to act out how the night watchman and Lisa treated Corduroy. Talk about what kind of person each character is. Ask:

- **What kind of person is the night watchman? What did he do that makes you think this?** (He is a nice person. He spoke kindly to Corduroy. He carefully carried Corduroy back to where he belonged.)

- **What kind of person is Lisa? What did she do that makes you think this?** (She is kind and loving. She sewed a button on Corduroy's overalls, got a little bed for him, and gave him a hug.)

Reader Response

Recall the Story

Recall *Corduroy* with children. Ask:

- **How would you feel if you saw Corduroy in a store?**
- **Would you like to have Corduroy as your teddy bear?**

Write a sentence on the board such as *Corduroy is nice to hug.*

Model Writing Sentences

As you write the sentence, model these strategies:

- Begin the sentence with a capital letter.
- Write words from left to right.
- Be sure the sentence tells a complete thought.
- Use correct end punctuation.

Day
3

Self-Selected Reading

D.E.A.R. Drop Everything And Read

From your self-selected reading collection, have children choose their own books to read. If children enjoy reading stories about animals, you might suggest *The Runaway Bunny* by Margaret Wise Brown.

Full Day Options...

Independent Writing 🧍

Write a Sentence Invite each child to write or dictate a descriptive sentence about

- what you would buy with money you saved in a piggy bank
- what you would do to be kind to Corduroy
- what you would do if you were the night watchman and found Corduroy

Drawing Conclusions 👪

Tell About Character's Feelings
Ask children how they think Corduroy felt when he knocked over the lamp. Have children draw a picture showing how Corduroy looked after he and the lamp fell down. Encourage children to use spelling approximations to write a word that tells how Corduroy felt.

Oral Language 👥

Use Proper Grammar Have Alphapotamus ask: *Were Lisa and her mother shopping?* Have children answer the question, using proper grammar: *Lisa and her mother were shopping.* Continue with other questions about *Corduroy.*

> Were Lisa and her mother shopping?

PHONICS A2

Objectives

Children will

 recognize /e/ spelled *e*

 recognize complete sentences

• spell number words

❄ **Meeting Individual Needs**
Challenge

Have children write a sentence for each number word: *one, two,* and *three.* Encourage children to write sentences for any of the other number words that they also know.

Day 4

↙ Draw a picture of the word that rhymes with **wet** and begins with P.

Vowel *Ee*
Practice Book, p. 181
Teacher's Resource Book, p. 181

Daily Phonics Routine

Phonemic Awareness

Review
qu/kw/

Say: *quick, game, queen.* Ask children to identify the words that begin with /kw/. (quick, queen) Continue having children identify the words that begin with /kw/ in these groups: *question, quill, pie; cat, quarter, quilt.*

Segment and Blend Words with /e/ and /kw/

Have children stand in a row and listen as you segment a word into its sounds. Ask them to blend the sounds to make a word. When they hear /e/ in a word, have them take a step forward. When they hear /kw/ in a word, have them take a step backward. Use these words:

/kw/ /i/ /t/   /p/ /e/ /n/   /kw/ /a/ /k/   /l/ /e/ /t/

Connect Sound to Letter

Find Pictures with /e/

Draw a large egg shape on chart paper and write *Ee* above it. Have children draw or cut out pictures with names that have short *e* and tape or paste them inside the egg shape. As each child adds a picture, ask him or her to name the picture, emphasizing the /e/, and to say a sentence: *I put a ___ in the egg.* You may want to help children label their pictures.

Phonological Awareness

Distinguish /e/ from Other Vowel Sounds

Give each child five pennies and a lunch bag. Say: *I'm going to say some words. If I say a word with /e/, throw a penny into the bag.* Say these words: *bell, top, fish, leg, pig, red, van, jet, hot, hen, cap.*

High-Frequency Words

Build Words

Give children letter cards that can be used to spell *one, two,* and *three.* Write the words and the numerals they represent on the board. Ask children to write *1* or draw one object on a sheet of paper. Have children arrange letters to spell *one* next to the numeral or object. Have them continue this process for *two* and *three.*

Interactive Writing

Review
Verbs

Have volunteers pantomime actions, such as skipping, hopping, and jumping. Have other children tell what the volunteers are doing, for example, *Isabel skips* and *Lee and Kim sit*. List the action words (verbs) on the board as children say them.

Use Verbs

Write these incomplete sentences: *One bear ____. Two bears ____.* Have children choose an action word from the list to complete each sentence: *One bear skips. Two bears skip.* Invite volunteers to help write the verbs in the blanks. Read the completed sentences together.

skip	skips
hop	hops
jump	jumps

One bear _____.
Two bears _____.

Ongoing Assessment

Writing

If... children have trouble completing sentences with action words,

then... model using both forms of the verb: *One bear skips. Two bears skip.*

Meeting Individual Needs
Challenge

Display *Party at the Pond* and identify the title, author, and illustrator of the story. Have children look for familiar words as you share the story. Challenge children to find words that have /e/.

Independent Reader 28

Optional Resources

Phonics Sourcebook pp. 79–82, 84–85, 86–129

Phonics Workbook p. 139

High-Frequency Word Cards

Phonics Kit

Day 4

Full Day Options...

Independent Writing 🚶

Write About Good Health Ask children to write informational text about one of the following:

- What can you do to keep from getting sick?
- What do you do to get well when you are sick?

Phonics 🚶🚶

Revisit Kindergarten Reader 28, *Sick in Bed?* For more practice in high-frequency word recognition, have children reread *Sick in Bed?* Let partners read together or take turns reading the pages aloud.

Kindergarten Reader 28

Phonics 🚶🚶🚶

Shared Poetry Have children sing or recite "Big Enough for Ten!" Review the sounds that *e, n, t, h,* and *p* stand for. Ask children to find *hen*. Point out that its middle letter is *e*, which stands for the sound /e/. Have children say the word with you. Repeat the activity for the words *pen* and *ten*.

Phonics Songs and Rhymes Chart 28

READING

Objectives

Children will

- ☑ draw conclusions
- ☑ use proper grammar when speaking
- listen to a rhyme

❄ Meeting Individual Needs
Challenge

Have children choose a favorite storybook character. Invite them to tell the class about the character. Encourage children to explain what helped them figure out what the character is like.

Day 4

Drawing Conclusions
Practice Book, p. 182
Teacher's Resource Book, p. 182

Comprehension

Shared Reading

Activate Prior Knowledge

Display last week's story, *Five Little Ducks*. Ask:

What happens each day the little ducks go out?

Reread the book. Then ask:

Are the little ducks used to exploring on their own? How do you know? (Yes; Mother duck does not go with them.)

Big Book

Assess Drawing Conclusions

To assess children's ability to draw conclusions, have children recall how mother duck felt when no little ducks come back. (sad, lonely; She missed them.) Ask children to tell how they figured out how she felt. (She looked sad in the picture on page 26; their mothers would be sad if they didn't come home.) Have children draw a picture to show how mother duck felt

- when no little ducks came back.

- when all her little ducks came back.

Children's pictures should show mother duck looking sad and mother duck looking happy.

Ongoing Assessment
Drawing Conclusions

If... children have difficulty drawing conclusions,

then... use the Drawing Conclusions reteach lesson on page AR17 of this Teacher's Edition.

Oral Language

Establish a Purpose for Listening

Read the title of the rhyme, "The Very Nicest Place." Ask children what they think of when they think of the very nicest place. Have them listen as you read to find out what the very nicest place in the rhyme is.

The Very Nicest Place
The fish lives in the brook,
The bird lives in the tree,
But home's the very nicest place
For a little child like me.

Have children choose books to read. They might like to read other books about lovable bears, such as *The Complete Tales of Winnie-the-Pooh* by A.A. Milne.

Optional Resources

Assessment Handbook

Assess Speaking with Proper Grammar

Check children's understanding of using correct grammar by having them answer these questions with complete sentences:

- **Who lives in the brook?** (The fish lives in the brook.)

- **Who lives in the tree?** (The bird lives in the tree.)

- **What is the very nicest place?** (Home is the very nicest place.)

Ongoing Assessment

Speak with Proper Grammar

If... children have difficulty answering the questions,	**then...** reread the parts that answer the questions, repeat the questions, and model the answers.

Full Day Options...

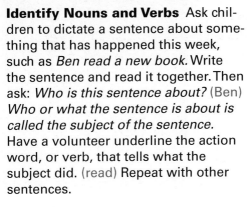

Oral Language

Identify Nouns and Verbs Ask children to dictate a sentence about something that has happened this week, such as *Ben read a new book.* Write the sentence and read it together. Then ask: *Who is this sentence about?* (Ben) *Who or what the sentence is about is called the subject of the sentence.* Have a volunteer underline the action word, or verb, that tells what the subject did. (read) Repeat with other sentences.

Drawing Conclusions

What Do Actions Tell? Whisper to a volunteer a reaction you want him or her to show without words. For example, you might say, *You just saw something really funny.* Children then conclude how the person is feeling and what might have just happened. Encourage children to explain how they could decide this.

Interactive Writing/Phonics

Write Words with /e/ Write *A teddy bear would like a ____.* Have children read the words with you. Invite them to offer words with /e/ to complete the sentence. As children dictate words, invite volunteers to help by writing a letter or the entire word. Read the sentences with children, tracking the words.

Objectives

Children will

 recognize e/e/ in beginning and medial positions

 write complete sentences

- count syllables in words
- write number words

Daily Phonics Routine

Prepare to Assess

Phonemic Awareness

Say the word *ten* and ask children to repeat it. Have them identify the onset and rime by asking: *What sound do you hear in the beginning of ten?* (/t/) *What sound do you hear in the end?* (-en) Continue with: *jet, bed, net, red, den.*

 **Assess e/e/**

Connect Sound to Letter

Have children write an *e* on a large index card. Say the following words and ask children to hold up their *e* cards when they hear a word with /e/: *wet, fan, web, lid, set, net, sip, men, jam, fed, dot, den, beg, box.* Write the /e/ words on the board, leaving out the *e*'s. Have volunteers write the *e*'s to complete the words.

Ongoing Assessment

Phonics

| **If...** children cannot correctly identify the *e* in words, | **then...** use the Vowel *Ee* reteaching activities on page AR16 of this Teacher's Edition. |

Count Syllables

Phonological Awareness

Write *one, two,* and *three* on the board. Have Alphapotamus say *elephant* slowly, emphasizing the syllables. Have children tell how many syllables they hear. Write the word under the appropriate number word. Repeat with *egg, penguin, bed, letter.*

elephant

High-Frequency Words

 Assess

Have children think about what they need when they come to school. Invite them to make a list. Direct them to use the number words *one, two,* and *three* as they write their lists. They can draw, dictate, or write the items.

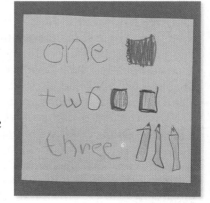

Independent Writing

Assess Writing Development

Think ALOUD

Recall with children that in *Corduroy* a toy bear gets a friend. Tell children they are going to write a note to a friend.

I want to tell my friend about something I did. I am going to write, "I got a new pen."

Remind children that a complete sentence tells about someone or something and tells what that someone or something does.

Have children write a note to a friend. Ask them to write complete sentences. Encourage them to use pictures or spelling approximations for words they do not know. You may wish to assess each child's writing using the scoring guide.

Shared Writing

Add to the Class Diary

Ask children to recall some activities they did this week.

Encourage children to use complete sentences. Write the sentences on chart paper. Children can dictate beginning letters or entire words. Add the pages to the class diary.

Optional Resources

Phonics Sourcebook   Assessment
pp. 1–78   Handbook

Phonics Workbook
p. 140

Full Day Options...

Phonics

Shared Poetry
Make copies of the first stanza of "Big Enough for Ten!" on blank paper and give one to each child. Invite children to draw pictures of things with names that have /e/ to illustrate the page.

Phonics Songs and Rhymes Chart 28

Independent Writing

Write About Friends Invite children to draw a picture of themselves with a friend. Ask them to write a sentence telling what they like to do with their friend. Invite children to share their work with someone at home.

Reading

Read Aloud Ask children who have beginning reading skills to read *Party at the Pond* aloud to you. Listen for evidence of decoding strategies.

Independent Reader 28

Day 5

READING

Objectives

Children will

- recognize sequence of events
- illustrate story events
- participate in choral reading

Comprehension

Review Sequence

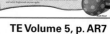

Read Aloud

To introduce "How Matti Almost Taught the Bear to Play the Fiddle," tell children that you are going to tell them a story about two brothers and a bear. Ask them to think about what happens first, next, and last as you read the story.

TE Volume 5, p. AR7

After reading, ask:

- **Who went into the forest first?** (Toivo) **What happened?** (Toivo made a lot of noise chopping wood. A bear woke up growling and Toivo ran out of the forest.)

- **Who went into the forest next?** (Matti) **What happened?** (Matti played his fiddle and the bear woke up again and danced. The bear asked Matti to teach him to play the fiddle.)

- **What happened after the bear asked Matti to teach him to play the fiddle?** (The bear couldn't play the fiddle and Matti told him it was because his fingers were too fat. He told the bear to put his paws in a tree and they got pinched. Matti said that he would let the bear go if he didn't scare people anymore. The bear agreed and went back to his home.)

Ongoing Assessment

Sequence

If... children have trouble answering the questions about sequence,	**then...** read the story in sections, pausing to insert the questions in the spot where the answers occur.

Sequence Story Illustrations

Assign each pair of children a part of the story to illustrate. Put mural paper on a wall. Display children's pictures in random order. As you reread the story in parts, have children find the picture for each part and attach it to the mural paper in the correct sequence. Invite children to tell the story in their own words, using the pictures as a guide.

Day 5

Oral Language

Review

Choral Reading

Remind children that choral reading is reading together as a group. Point out that all members of a group need to speak loudly, clearly, and at the same speed.

Practice Choral Reading

Write the following couplet on chart paper. Read it several times to familiarize children with it. Divide the class into two groups. Have one group read the first line and the other group read the second line as you track the print.

"Young man, teach me to play the fiddle, too."
"Why not, you can try till your face turns blue."

Self-Selected Reading   D.E.A.R.

Have children choose books to read. They might like to read another book about stuffed animals, such as *Dogger* by Shirley Hughes.

Full Day Options...

Independent Writing 🚶

Write About Matti's Fiddle Have children draw a picture of Matti and his fiddle. Invite them to write a descriptive sentence about how the fiddle sounded.

Oral Language 🚶

Tell a Story Have children choose a prompt.

- Tell about Toivo and Matti trying to win the hand of a princess.
- Tell about Matti and a fire-breathing dragon.

Sequence 👥👥

Put Events in Order Describe two story actions, such as Toivo running home and Matti going into the forest. Have children tell which happened first. Continue pairing events in random order. Then give three events and have children put them in order.

Reading 👥👥

Reader Response: "How Matti Almost Taught the Bear to Play the Fiddle" Ask: *Do you think Matti ever intended to teach the bear to play the fiddle? Why or why not?* Invite children to show the expression on Matti's face when he watched the bear run away.

Volume 5, p. AR7

Day **5**

Lesson Overview

Big Book

I Need a Lunch Box!

Genre
Realistic Fiction

Phonemic Awareness/Phonics
Consonant *x* /ks/

Comprehension
Author's Purpose

High-Frequency Words
red   yellow   blue

About the Illustrator

Pat Cummings
spent her childhood moving every few years because of her father's army career. She lived in Germany and Japan as well as Illinois, New York, and other states. She met many people of different backgrounds, and as a result, she tries to include people of all races in her books. She has illustrated dozens of books and has written her own as well.

Leveled Books

Easy

Wordless Story 29

On-Level

Kindergarten Reader 29

Challenge

Independent Reader 29

Trade Books for Self-Selected Reading and Read Aloud

Cherries and Cherry Pits
by Vera B. Williams

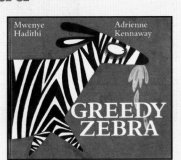

Greedy Zebra
by Mwenye Hadithi

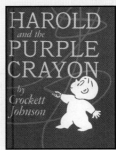

Harold and the Purple Crayon
by Crockett Johnson

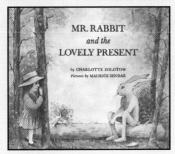

Mr. Rabbit and the Lovely Present
by Charlotte Zolotow

On Monday When It Rained
by Cherryl Kachenmeister

My Yellow Ball
by Dee Lillegard

Theme Make a Wish   **Lesson Topic** Something New

5-Day Planner

 Customize your week with the Teacher's Resource Planner CD-ROM!

Reading

Comprehension

Vocabulary

Phonics

Phonemic Awareness

Oral Language

Speaking, Listening, and Viewing

Writing

Grammar, Usage, and Mechanics

Self-Selected Reading
Read Aloud

Day 1

Activate Prior Knowledge p. 167
Poem "Yesterday's Paper"

Reading pp. 168–175
Shared Reading
I Need a Lunch Box

Reader Response:
Relate to Story Character

 Comprehension:
Author's Purpose

Recall Books to Understand
Author's Purpose

Phonics pp. 176–177

 Consonant *x* /ks/

Phonemic Awareness:
Listen to a Song
• Phonics Songs and
Rhymes Chart 29

**Connect Sound to
Letter:** Match /ks/ to *x*

Phonological Awareness:
Repeat the Sentence

✔ **High-Frequency Words**

 red   yellow   blue

Oral Language pp. 174–175
Introduce Vocabulary:
sandwich   peanut butter   jelly
oranges   apples
Use Food Words to Answer
Questions

Writing pp. 176–177
 Shared Writing: Write a
Poem Together

Self-Selected Reading p. 175
Have children select books to
read. They might like to read
other books about imagining
things. See page 159 for suggestions.

Day 2

Phonics pp. 178–179

 Consonant *x* /ks/

Phonemic Awareness:
Play Musical Chairs with
/ks/ Words
• Phonics Songs and
Rhymes Chart 29

Use /ks/ Words in
a Story
• Wordless Story 29
Six Monkeys

Connect Sound to Letter:
Match /ks/ to *x*

Phonological Awareness:
Match Ending Sounds

✔ **High-Frequency Words:** Find
red, yellow, and *blue* on ABC Wall

Reading pp. 180–181
 Comprehension:
Author's Purpose

Recall Big Book's
Main Idea

Use Vocabulary in
Sentences

Answer Questions
About Author's Purpose

Oral Language pp. 180–181
 Speaking: Speak Well

Use a Rhyme to Speak
Well
• Oral Language
Chart 29

Writing pp. 178–179
 Modeled Writing: Write About
Present and Past
Guided Writing
Handwriting: Practice Writing *Xx*

Self-Selected Reading p. 181
Children might like to read
another book about feelings:
On Monday When It Rained by
Cherryl Kachenmeister.

 **Target Skill**   **Review Skill**

Target Skills of the Week

Reading	Author's Purpose
Phonics	Consonant *x* /ks/
Oral Language	Speak Well
Writing	Past Tense

Day 3

Phonics pp. 182–183

 Consonant *x* /ks/

Phonemic Awareness:
Listen for /ks/

Connect Sound to Letter:
Find Words with *x*
• Phonics Songs and
  Rhymes Chart 29

Phonological Awareness:
Listen for /ks/

Read Kindergarten Reader 29: *A Big Blue Box*

Reading pp. 184–185

 Comprehension:
Author's Purpose

Think About Author's Purpose to Answer Questions

Reader Response:
Connect Story to Own Experiences

Model Writing Past-Tense Sentences

Oral Language pp. 184–185

 Speaking: Speak Well

Discuss Speaking Well

Retell Story by Speaking Well

Writing pp. 182–183

 Modeled Writing:
Demonstrate Writing Sentences

Guided Writing

Self-Selected Reading p. 185

If you think children might like another book about colors, suggest *Mr. Rabbit and the Lovely Present* by Charlotte Zolotow.

Day 4

Phonics pp. 186–187

 Short *e* /e/

 Consonant *x* /ks/

Phonemic Awareness:
Vowel *e* /e/

Listen for /e/ and /ks/

Connect Sound to Letter:
Sort Word Cards

Phonological Awareness:
Listen for Ending Sounds

✔ **High-Frequency Words:**
Make Color Labels

Challenge: Independent Reader 29

Reading pp. 188–189

 Comprehension:
Author's Purpose

Activate Prior Knowledge

 Assess Author's Purpose

Oral Language pp. 188–189

 Speaking: Speak Well
• Read Aloud "Rain"

 Assess Speaking Well

Writing pp. 186–187

 Interactive Writing:
More Than One

Use Plural Nouns

Self-Selected Reading p. 189

Have children choose books to read. They might enjoy reading *Cherries and Cherry Pits* by Vera B. Williams in which a girl tells her story and shares her art.

Day 5

Phonics pp. 190–191

 Consonant *x* /ks/

Phonemic Awareness:
Prepare to Assess

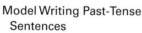 **Connect Sound to Letter:**
Assess *x* /ks/

Phonological Awareness:
Identify Syllables

High-Frequency Words:
Assess

Reading pp. 192–193

Comprehension:
Drawing Conclusions
• Read Aloud "The Fox and the Crow"

Match Feelings and Faces

Oral Language pp. 192–193

Speaking: Speak with Proper Grammar

Practice Speaking Using Proper Grammar

Writing pp. 190–191

 Independent Writing: Assess Writing Development

Shared Writing: Add to the Class Diary

Self-Selected Reading p. 193

Have children find books that they can read independently. One possibility is *Harold and the Purple Crayon* by Crockett Johnson.

 **Assessment** ✔ **Benchmark Assessment of Target Skills and Skills Assessment**

Cross-Curricular Work Stations

Community Link

Ideas for bringing the school and community together

Field Experiences
art gallery
craft store
museum
flower shop

Guest Speakers
artist
painter
inventor

Letters and Sounds

What Is It? 10 minutes

Materials: drawing paper, crayons

Learning Styles Visual, Kinesthetic

Children use their imagination to create something new that has a name with the letter *x* in it. Point out that this new something can be a person, a place, or a thing. Encourage children to label it. Have them introduce their creation at group time.

Flix

Writing

If I Could Talk 10 minutes

Materials: writing materials

Learning Styles Individual, Kinesthetic

Children choose an object and write or dictate what they think the object would say if it could talk. *What if your paper and pencil could talk? the clock? the water fountain?*

Challenge Children can write sentences about a talking object.

I can go fast.

Social Studies

Make a Pot two days for 10 minutes

Materials: clay, small bowl of water, plastic knives and spoons

Learning Styles Kinesthetic, Visual, Spatial

Tell children that people all over the world make pottery for use or for pleasure. Share examples of pots, either in pictures or the actual objects from different cultures. Children can work with clay to create their own pots. Model how to use your fingers to press, punch, roll, and twist the clay. Allow pots to air-dry for several days, and then have children paint their pots.

INTERNET SAFETY Establish guidelines for your students' safe and responsible use of the Internet. See the Scott Foresman Internet Guide for tips.

Technology

AstroWord   15 minutes

Learning Styles Visual, Auditory

AstroWord reinforces children's understanding of phonemic awareness. Children can work individually or collaboratively.

Web Site two days for 10 minutes

Learning Styles Individual, Visual

sfreading.com

Visit the Scott Foresman web site (sfreading.com) for current hyperlinks to sites that can be used by children for an Internet Workshop investigation of making new things. Also see the Scott Foresman Internet Guide for additional information on the Internet Workshop method.

Science

Mix Colors   10 minutes

Materials: red, yellow, blue paint; paintbrushes; water; smocks

Learning Styles Logical, Verbal, Visual

Children experiment with mixing paints to make other colors. Encourage them to mix just two paints at one time. Have children record their findings.

ESL Children can orally describe how they mix the paints to make other colors.

Math

Large Number Match   10 minutes

Materials: number cards for 11–30; 30 crayons

Learning Styles Logical, Social, Spatial

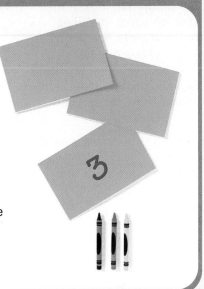

Have children mix the number cards and place them face down. One child picks a card, reads the number, and displays that number of crayons. The partner counts to verify the number shown. Partners switch roles and continue the activity. To extend the activity, children can arrange the number cards in order.

Challenge Children mix the number cards and arrange them in descending order.

Introduce the Reading Road Show Activity Stations to reinforce this week's skills.

Phonemic Awareness & Phonics
Literacy Activities

> Use these activities during the week to reinforce skills.

Phonemic Awareness

Consonant Categories 15 minutes

Materials: letter cards or shapes

Learning Styles Social, Auditory, Kinesthetic

Have children name items in various categories, such as the following, to reinforce initial sounds represented by different consonants:

- foods whose names begin like *banana:* beans, butter, beets, biscuits, beef, bagels

- animals whose names begin like *cat:* cow, caterpillar, calf, canary, coyote, camel

- toys whose names begin like *jacks:* jack-in-the-box, jump rope, jungle gym, juggling balls, jeep, jigsaw puzzle

- people whose names begin like *Tony:* Tim, Ted, Tara, Tanya, Tom, Teresa

As a variation, assign categories to small groups to work on independently and have them share their lists with the class.

Working with Letters

Describing Letters 10 minutes

Materials: letter cards

Learning Styles Visual, Verbal, Auditory

Give each child a letter card. Tell children to look at their letter and think of a clue they can give that identifies their letter. Give several examples: *It looks like a zigzag.* (z) *It looks like a v with a long tail.* (y) *It is two lines across each other.* (x) Call on a volunteer to begin and give the first clue. When the letter is identified, the child places the letter on the chalk ledge. Continue until all the clues are given.

(ESL) If children have difficulty giving clues, prompt with questions such as these: *Does it have any slanted lines?* If the child answers correctly, have him or her use that question to make a statement that can be a clue such as *It has two slanted lines.*

Working with Words

Hidden Words 🕐 10 minutes

Learning Styles Visual, Kinesthetic, Spatial

Have children make a word search puzzle by writing a high-frequency word on a sheet of paper with the letters spaced a short distance apart. At both ends of the word, have children write letters that do not make words. When the puzzles are complete, have children exchange puzzles and find the word in the puzzle. Then have them take turns showing the puzzle and reading the word.

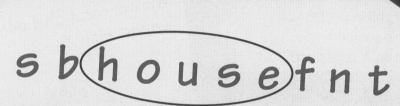

ABC Wall

ABC Wall 👥👥 🕐 10 minutes

Learning Styles Visual, Kinesthetic

Divide the class into teams of four to play a Spelling Bees Relay. On the board, draw a simple outline of a bee for each team. Say a word from the ABC Wall and have the first child from each team go to the board and write the first letter of the word on his or her team's bee. Those children go back to their teams. Then the second child from each team goes to the board and writes the second letter of the word and so on. Each team that spells the word correctly scores a point.

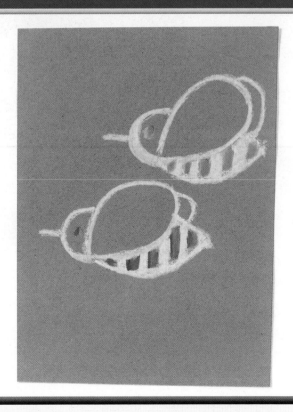

Daily Warm-Up

Message Board

Day One

Today we will read about a boy who wants a lunch box.

Discuss with children times when they have really, really wanted something.

Ask children: "Do you know someone who has had an X ray taken?"

Day Two

We will read and say words with Xx.

Day Three

We will read and write red, yellow, and blue.

Ask children: "Who is wearing something *red* today? *Yellow? Blue?*"

Discuss with children why they need to speak well in school and elsewhere.

Day Four

Today we are working on speaking well.

Day Five

Today we will write a story about a person who wanted and got something.

Ask: "How do you feel when you get something you want?"

Getting Ready
for the Week

Day One

peanut butter, jelly, bread, apples, oranges (ESL)
"sticky" notes (Challenge)
chart paper

Day Two

tape recorder, blank tape (Auditory)
beanbag (Full Day)

Day Three

"sticky" notes

Day Four

shoebox
red, blue, and yellow construction paper
sand table or chart paper (Kinesthetic)
magazines (Full Day)

Day Five

red, blue, and yellow construction paper (ESL)

Family Times

Send home the newsletter with fun instructional activities to reinforce this week's target skills.

Practice Book, pp. 183–184
Teacher's Resource Book, pp. 183–184

Activate Prior Knowledge

Talk About Wanting Something

Tell children that this week they will read about a boy who wants a lunch box so badly that he dreams about it at night! Say: *Tell about something that you really wanted. How did you feel when you got it?* Then ask children to

- **think of something they wish they had**

- **imagine what they would do with that thing**

- **draw a picture of themselves with that thing**

Build Background

Choose one or more of these activities to build background for this week's selection *I Need a Lunch Box.*

Read Aloud a Poem

Share this poem with children. Then invite them to think of other things they could do with "Yesterday's Paper."

Yesterday's Paper
by Mabel Watts

Yesterday's paper makes a hat,
    Or a boat,
    Or a plane,
    Or a playhouse mat.

Yesterday's paper makes things
    Like that—
    And a very fine tent
    For a sleeping cat.

Use Illustrations to Develop Oral Language

Hold up *I Need a Lunch Box.* Have children look at the illustration on the cover. Ask: *What is the boy doing? What kind of boxes are those?* Ask children to tell a story about the boy and the lunch boxes.

Use Audio to Develop Story Concepts

Show children a brown paper lunch bag and a lunch box. Ask:

- **How are these things alike?**

- **How would people use them?**

Share the Background-Building CD/tape, in which children in a school cafeteria tell what is in their lunch boxes and talk about their favorite foods.

CD 5/Tape 15, Side 1
Background-Building Audio

Concepts of Print

Read Left to Right and Top to Bottom

Display *I Need a Lunch Box*. Turn to page 5. Point to the first word, *My,* and read it aloud. Ask:

Who can point to the next word I should read?
(Let a child demonstrate by pointing to *sister.*)

Continue reading the sentence and the rest of the page. Then reread the page, tracking the print and pointing out that we read from left to right and from top to bottom.

Model Reading Behaviors

Picture Walk and Predict

Read the title again. Have children look at the illustrations in the book. Ask:

• **Who seems to be the main character in the story?**
(a boy)

• **What does he spend a lot of time thinking about?**
(lunch boxes)

• **Do you think the boy will get a lunch box? Why or why not? Let's read to find out.**

Big Book

objectives

Children will

• recognize that text is read from left to right and from top to bottom

• listen to a story

• use illustrations to predict

Shared Reading Routine

Day 1

• Read the story through for enjoyment.

• To practice the reading strategy predicting, use the stopping point on TE page 173.

Day 2

• Reread the entire story, using the activities in the margins on pages 169–173.

Day 3–5

• Reread the entire book or portions of it each day, using the activities as suggested in the lessons.

pages 4–5

My sister Doris got a brand new lunch box.
I need a lunch box too.
But Mommy said no lunch box until I start school.

pages 6–7

Last week Daddy bought us new shoes.
Brown school shoes for Doris.
Black sneakers with yellow laces for me.

pages 8–9

We walked past the lunch box counter, twice.
I need a lunch box!

Day 1

Guiding the Reading

Critical Thinking

Who is telling the story? How do you know? What in the story lets you know this?
Possible answers: The boy shown on the cover is telling the story. The pictures and story make me think the boy is a storyteller.

Why does the little boy think he needs a lunch box?
Possible answer: His sister is getting one, so he thinks he needs one too.

Guiding the Reading

Critical Thinking

Why do you think Doris got new pencils, erasers, and a pencil case as well as a new lunch box?
Possible answer: She is getting ready to start a new school year. She needs school supplies.

Doris got a pencil case with a ruler, two new pencils, and two pink erasers.

pages 10–11

Guiding the Reading

Critical Thinking

Why isn't the little boy satisfied with his new coloring book and crayons?
Possible answer: He really wanted a lunch box instead.

All I got was a coloring book about space men and a box of crayons— but no lunch box.

pages 12–13

Yesterday Doris got book covers, a raincoat, and an umbrella—all because she's going to first grade.

pages 14–15

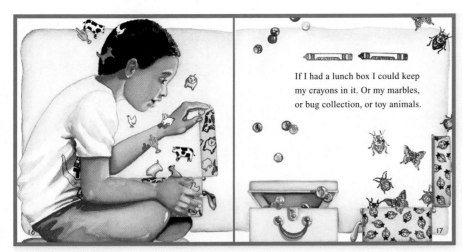

pages 16–17

pages 18–19

pages 20–21

Guiding the Reading

Critical Thinking

Why does the boy dream about having five lunch boxes?
Possible answer: With five lunch boxes, he would have one for every school day of the week.

Guiding the Reading

Critical Thinking

Why is the boy's lunch box for Wednesday shaped like a fire engine?
Possible answer: He dreams that his lunch box for Wednesday is red, and fire engines are often red.

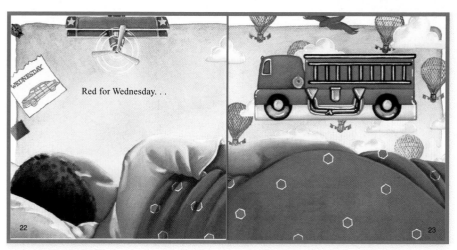

pages 22–23

pages 24–25

Guiding the Reading

Critical Thinking

What is unusual about the boy's lunch box for Friday?
Possible answer: The lunch box is shaped like a banana.

Do you think a banana is a good shape for a lunch box?
Possible answers: Yes, because it is different; it is funny. No, because it would be hard to put anything inside; it is small.

pages 26–27

pages 28–29

I filled them with peanut butter and jelly sandwiches, apples, oranges, chocolate cake, cookies and pies and donuts.
And then we had a lunch box parade.

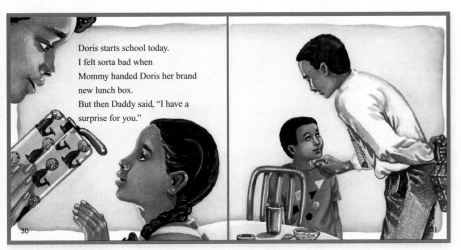

pages 30–31

Doris starts school today.
I felt sorta bad when Mommy handed Doris her brand new lunch box.
But then Daddy said, "I have a surprise for you."

page 32

Wow!
I got a lunch box too!

Stopping Point

Predict On the first reading, you may want to stop at the bottom of page 29 and ask children to predict whether the boy will get a lunch box or not.

Day 1

Language Development

Explain that sometimes when we say *sort of,* we combine the two words together and do not pronounce them clearly. *Sort of* ends up sounding like *sorta. Sort of* means "a little bit."

sorta

average

Objectives

Children will

Day 1

- recognize the author's purpose for writing a story
- respond to a story
- develop vocabulary by answering questions

Meeting Individual Needs
ESL

Bring in apples, oranges, bread, peanut butter, and jelly. Peel the oranges and make sandwiches for a snack. Talk about the foods and let children help with the preparation so they can experience the food words *sandwich, peanut butter, jelly, apples,* and *oranges.*

Skills Trace

Author's Purpose

Introduce	TE: K.5 174–175
Practice	PB: 186, 188
Reteach/ Review	TE: K.5 181, 184, 188, 228, AR19
Skills Assessment	TE: K.5 AR1–AR3

Reader Response

Check Predictions

Say: *Did you think the boy would or would not get a lunch box before we read the story? Were you right?*

Relate to Story Character

Ask: *What is the theme of this story? What is it all about?*

Suppose you have five lunch boxes. What would you put in each one? A peanut butter and jelly sandwich? Some oranges? What else?

Provide children with outlines of five lunch boxes. Suggest they draw pictures of what they would put in the lunch boxes.

Oral Language/Vocabulary

Use Food Words to Answer Questions

The vocabulary words are some of the foods in the story. Have children use these words to answer questions.

sandwich   peanut butter   jelly   oranges   apples

- **What is made of two slices of bread with something in between?** (a sandwich)

- **What two things go between the bread in a peanut butter and jelly sandwich?** (peanut butter and jelly)

- **What are two fruits you could put in a lunch box?** (oranges and apples)

Ask children whether they have ever had peanut butter and jelly sandwiches or apples and oranges for lunch. Let them talk about other foods they eat for lunch.

Ongoing Assessment
Vocabulary

If... children cannot answer questions with the words *sandwich, peanut butter, jelly, oranges,* and *apples,*

then... show them examples of those foods or pictures of the foods and identify each one.

174 **Reading** and Oral Language

Comprehension

Recall Books to Understand Author's Purpose

Ask children to choose a book from your reading table that they especially like. Point out that you have read many different kinds of books together. Ask:

- **Which books made you laugh? Hold up your book if it made you laugh.**

- **Which books told you about some interesting real things or animals? Hold up those books for us to see.**

Tell children: *People write books for different reasons. Sometimes they want to explain things or give information. Sometimes they want to entertain us by sharing a good story and making us happy or sad. Sometimes they want to give information and entertain at the same time.*

Ask children who have books that they think entertain to stand in one group and children who have books that give information to stand in another group. Then discuss which group is larger and why that might be.

Self-Selected Reading

Have children select books to read. They might like to read other books about imagining things. See page 159 for suggestions.

Day 1

Full Day Options...

Oral Language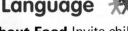

Talk About Food Invite children to choose one of the following prompts.

- Tell what you like best to eat for lunch.
- Tell what you like best to eat for dinner.
- Tell what you like to eat as a snack after school.

Oral Language

Tell a Story Have children choose a prompt.

- Tell about the kind of lunch box you would really like to have.
- Tell about your own lunch box and why you like it.

Author's Purpose

TV Shows Inform and Entertain Discuss television shows with children. Include some that inform as well as some that entertain. You may want to list the names on the board. Lead children to see that TV shows have different purposes. Some entertain us, some give us information, and some do both.

Vocabulary

Play House Let children pretend they are a family and take turns "making lunch" for each other. Encourage them to use the vocabulary words *sandwich, peanut butter, jelly, oranges,* and *apples,* as well as other food words.

Daily Phonics Routine

Objectives

Children will

 recognize x/ks/
- recognize words with the same ending sounds
- identify high-frequency words
- participate in a shared writing activity

Meeting Individual Needs
Challenge

Remind children that some words end with x/ks/. Give them the picture cards for *box, bus, duck, fox, goose, lock,* and *ox.* Ask them to say each picture name and use "sticky" notes to label those pictures with names that end with x/ks/.

Skills Trace

 **Consonant Xx**

Introduce	TE: K.5 176
Practice	PB: 185, 187
Reteach/ Review	TE: K.5 178, 182–183, 186, 190, 222 AR18
Skills Assessment	Skills Assessment Unit 5 TE: K.5 AR1–AR3

Phonemic Awareness

Listen to a Song

Sing "Maximilian X. Mox Has Chicken Pox" to the tune of "There's a Hole in the Bucket" or play the CD/tape. Have children listen for and name words with /ks/. (Maximilian, X, Mox, pox, X ray, fix)

CD 2/Tape 15, Side 1
Phonics Songs and Rhymes Audio

Identify /ks/ Picture Cards

Show the picture card for *box* and have children identify it and tell the ending sound. (/ks/)

Maximilian X. Mox Has Chicken Pox

There are six bumps on your nose
Maximilian X. Mox.
Do they itch a whole lot?
Oh, you have chicken pox.

Do you need an X-ray
Maximilian X. Mox?
Oh, what can we do to
Fix your chicken pox?

Phonics Songs and Rhymes Chart 29

Ongoing Assessment

Phonics

If... children have difficulty hearing the sound /ks/,

then... say word pairs such as *fox box* and *six fix,* emphasizing the ending sound, and have children repeat the words.

Connect Sound to Letter

Match /ks/ to x

Have Alphapotamus show children the alphabet card for *Xx* and say the word *X ray.* Explain that the X in *X ray* stands for the sound /eks/, just as the name of the letter *x* is pronounced. Say *X ray* slowly as you write it on the board. Circle the X. Write the word *fox* on the board, saying it slowly. Explain that the x in *fox* stands for the sound /ks/. Circle the x and say the word again.

Xx

Alphabet Cards

Phonological Awareness

Repeat the Sentence

To accustom children to listening for the ending sounds of words, say the following silly sentence. First ask children to listen for the ending sounds of the words. Next, have children count how many words end with /ks/. Last, have the class repeat the sentence, emphasizing /ks/.

The fox can fix the wax box and relax.

High-Frequency Words

Add *red, yellow,* and *blue* to ABC Wall

Say each of the high-frequency words *red, yellow,* and *blue* as you show a crayon that is that color. Write each word on an index card and show the card as you use the word in a sentence. Have volunteers add the cards to the ABC Wall.

Day
1

ABC Wall

Ask children to think of words that have /ks/ in them, such as *next, relax, fix,* and *taxi.* On a large index card, write each word in which *x* stands for /ks/. Add those words to this week's panel of the ABC Wall.

Optional Resources

Phonics Sourcebook
pp. 75, 84–85

High-Frequency
Word Cards

Phonics Workbook
p. 141

Shared Writing

Write a Poem Together

Say: *We are going to write a poem about Maximilian X. Mox and his chicken pox. We will call him Max Mox for short. Let's imagine that when Max was sick, he dreamed about things that are red, yellow, and blue.* Ask children to think of red, yellow, and blue things.

Max Mox and His Chicken Pox

Max Mox had the chicken pox.
He dreamed about a yellow dish.
He dreamed about a red lunch box.
He dreamed about a big blue fish.

As children say sentences that tell things Max dreamed about, they can

* Help you think of words that rhyme
* Use the high-frequency words *red, yellow,* and *blue*
* Draw the red, yellow, and blue things Max dreamed about

Full Day Options...

Independent Writing 🧍

Write Sentences Have children write or dictate descriptive sentences about one of these:

* an exciting dream you remember
* something red, yellow, or blue that you like to eat

Phonics 🧍

Draw a /ks/ Picture Write the sentence *The fox fixed six boxes* on the board and read it aloud. Have children copy the sentence on a sheet of paper and illustrate it. Display the finished papers.

Oral Language/ Author's Purpose 🧍🧍

Learn from Books Have each pair choose a nonfiction book and look at it carefully, thinking about the information the author wanted them to find out. Ask the pairs to report to the class something they learned from the book.

Objectives

Children will

- recognize the letters *Xx*
- use the past-tense forms of action words
- use high-frequency words

Day 2

Consonant *Xx*
Practice Book, p. 185
Teacher's Resource Book, p. 185

Skills Trace

Past Tense

Introduce	TE: K.5 179
Reteach/ Review	TE: K.5 187, 191
Skills Assessment	Skills Assessment Unit 5 TE: K.5 AR1–AR3

Daily Phonics Routine

Phonemic Awareness

Play Musical Chairs with /ks/ Words

Have children march around a circle of chairs as they sing or listen to the CD/tape "Maximilian X. Mox Has Chicken Pox." Play the CD/tape again, this time without children joining in. Stop the tape at each word with /ks/, have children sit down on the chairs, and have a volunteer name the word.

CD 2/Tape 15, Side 1
Phonics Songs and Rhymes Audio

Phonics Songs and Rhymes Chart 29

Use /ks/ Words in a Story

Ask children to look through *Six Monkeys*. Encourage them to use words with /ks/, such as *six, mix, extra,* and *excited,* to tell what the six monkeys are doing. Some children may know that the word *xylophone* begins with *x* although the sound is /z/. You may wish to have children dictate or write a story in the take-home version.

Wordless Story 29

Connect Sound to Letter

Match /ks/ to *x*

Display the *Xx* alphabet card, pointing out to children that the letter *x* usually does not come at the beginning of a word as it does in the word *X ray.* Show children the picture cards for *fox, box,* and *ox* and say the words to model *x*/ks/ at the end of words. Write *fox, box,* and *ox* on the board and have volunteers circle each *x* as you say the word together.

Phonological Awareness

Match Ending Sounds

Using Alphapotamus, say: *Listen to three words and think about the ending sound of each word: ax, box, house. Which one does not have the same sound at the end as the other two?* (house) Have Alphapotamus continue with these sets of words: *cake, mix, sick* (mix); *six, dish, fax* (dish); and *top, map, fox* (fox).

ax, box, house

High-Frequency Words

Use *red*, *yellow*, and *blue*

Have children find *red*, *yellow*, and *blue* on the ABC Wall. Ask them to use the words in sentences that tell about what others in the class are wearing today.

Modeled Writing

Write About Present and Past

Discuss with children things they could do now and things they did yesterday or a long time ago. On the board, write: *I can jump rope. Yesterday I jumped rope all afternoon.* Say:

Think ALOUD

- **First, I told about something I can do now.**

- **In my second sentence, I told about something I did yesterday. I added the letters *-ed* to the action word (verb) *jump* to show that this happened in the past.**

Guided Writing

Say: *Write about something you did yesterday or last week and something you can do now.* Some children may need to dictate or draw instead of write.

Handwriting

Practice Writing *Xx*

Distribute writing paper and have children practice writing *x* and *X*. Have children who are already proficient writing *x* and *X* write *Max fixes boxes.*

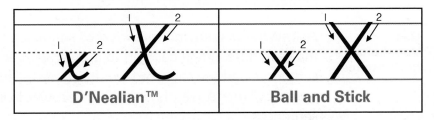

| D'Nealian™ | Ball and Stick |

Ask children to find the color words *red, yellow,* and *blue* on the ABC Wall. Help them write other color words on large index cards and add them to the wall.

Optional Resources

Phonics Sourcebook pp. 75, 84–85

Phonics Workbook p. 142

High-Frequency Word Cards

Day **2**

Full Day Options...

Independent Writing

Write About a New Thing Have children dictate or write one or more narrative sentences about something new they have or would like to have. Let them illustrate their sentences.

Handwriting

Practice Have children choose one.

- Write *six foxes* and draw a picture of them.
- Write the words *next, mix, fix,* and *taxi.*

Phonics

Make an *Xx* Collage Have children draw or cut out pictures whose names include the letter *x*, such as *X ray, fox, box,* or *taxi.* Have them use glue to draw a large *X* on paper and paste the pictures to the letter.

Objectives

Children will

- practice speaking well
- discuss the author's purpose for writing
- listen to a nursery rhyme

Day 2

❄ Meeting Individual Needs
Other Ways to Learn

Auditory Tape record individual children as they tell you about the story *I Need a Lunch Box*. Then let them listen to themselves to help them recognize any poor speaking habits they may have, such as pausing unnecessarily, adding sounds that aren't words, and so on.

Oral Language

Use a Rhyme to Speak Well

Direct children to listen carefully as you say: *Now we are* [pause] *going to* [pause] *read the, the, ummmm, rhyme poster.* Then say: *Now we are going to read the rhyme poster.* Ask: *Which sentence sounded better? Why?* Help children recognize that a good speaker does not pause too often, repeat words, or use unnecessary sounds.

The Flying Pig
a Mother Goose rhyme

Dickory, dickory, dare,
The pig flew up in the air;
The man in brown
Soon brought him down,
Dickory,
Dickory,
Dare.

Oral Language Chart 29

Display "The Flying Pig" and read it aloud. Ask children: *What did you like about the rhyme?* Remind them to practice being good speakers as they answer.

Comprehension

Recall Big Book's Main Idea

Hold up *I Need a Lunch Box* and ask why the boy dreamed about lunch boxes. (He wanted a lunch box so badly that he even dreamed about it.) Have children hold up a crayon or color card for each color lunch box that the boy dreamed about. (blue, green, red, purple, yellow)

Use Vocabulary in Sentences

Ask: *What is your favorite kind of sandwich? How do you make it?* Encourage children to answer with complete sentences and use the word *sandwich.* Ask: *What is your favorite fruit?* Again, have children answer in complete sentences.

Listen to Big Book for Information

Invite children to listen while you reread *I Need a Lunch Box.* Ask them to think about what the boy receives throughout the story instead of a lunch box.

Shared Reading

While reading, you may wish to use the ideas in the *Guiding the Reading* and *Language Development* boxes on pages 169–173 of this Teacher's Edition.

Big Book

Answer Questions About Author's Purpose

Recall with children that the person who is telling the story is a little boy. Say:

Jeannette Caines, the author of the book, is a woman. Why do you think she wrote the story as if a little boy were telling it?

Discuss possible reasons for authors to write stories, such as to entertain readers, to give information, or to express an idea. Ask:

- **How did the little boy feel at the beginning of the story? In the middle? At the end? Could telling you about those feelings be one reason the author wrote the story?**

- **Could telling you about colors and days of the week be another reason she wrote the story?**

- **Did you enjoy the story? Did you learn something?**

Guide the discussion so that children understand Ms. Caines wrote the book mostly to entertain readers, but also to tell them about colors and days of the week.

Day
2

Ongoing Assessment
Author's Purpose

If... children have difficulty identifying the author's purpose,

then... ask: *Who is telling the story? What is the character feeling? Have you ever felt this way? Why might the author write about such feelings?*

Full Day Options...

Author's Purpose

Which Face? Give small groups sets of books that children have already read, such as *Corduroy, Miss Bindergarten Gets Ready for Kindergarten, On the Go,* and *Follow the Leader.* Ask children: *Did the author of this book want to entertain you or give you information?* Have each group sort their books according to author's purpose.

Oral Language

Beanbag Sentences Have children sit in a circle on the floor. Say: *Here is something I can do. I can count. Now I pass it on to you.* Toss the beanbag to a child who repeats the rhyme but changes the middle line to tell a different action. Continue until all children have had a turn. Remind children to speak in complete sentences as they tell what they can do.

Reader Response

Tell About Feelings Ask children how they think the boy in the story felt. Then ask: *What would you do if you had the same problem as the boy in the story?* Have children develop and verbalize their own solutions to the problem.

Daily Phonics Routine

Objectives

Children will

↻ recognize *x*/ks/

↻ recognize the letters *Xx*

• identify high-frequency words

• count phonemes

Day 3

Meeting Individual Needs
Intervention

If children say /a/ /ks/ instead of /a/ /sk/ for the word *ask,* they may have difficulty distinguishing between /ks/ and /sk/. Write the words *ask* and *ax* on the board and pronounce them carefully, emphasizing the final sounds represented by *sk* and *x.* Have children repeat the words with you.

Phonemic Awareness

Listen for /ks/

Have Alphapotamus say word pairs to children. Ask them to make an *x* with their hands when they hear /ks/ in a word. Use these word pairs: *Mexico, puzzle; mask, fax; cookie, extra; taxi, extra.*

Ongoing Assessment
Phonemic Awareness

| **If...** children have difficulty hearing the words with /ks/, | **then...** say each word again, emphasizing /ks/ and asking after each word whether children hear /ks/. |

Connect Sound to Letter

Find Words with *x*

Have children write an *X* on a "sticky" note. Reread "Maximilian X. Mox Has Chicken Pox" with children, beginning with the title. As you read, have volunteers place their *X* notes on the chart over the words that have *x*/ks/, or *X*/ks/.

Phonics Songs and Rhymes Chart 29

CD 2/Tape 15, Side 1

Phonics Songs and Rhymes Audio

Phonological Awareness

Count Phonemes

Draw four sound boxes on the board. Say *six* and have children echo you. Then say /s/ /i/ /ks/ and place one magnet or "sticky" note in a box to stand for each sound. Count the sounds together and ask children if they hear the /ks/ at the beginning, middle, or end of *six*. Repeat with *taxi, mix, fox,* and *ax.*

Phonics and High-Frequency Words

Read Kindergarten Reader 29

• Track the print as you read the title aloud. Ask children how many words are in the title.

• Do a picture walk and have children predict what might be in that big blue box.

• Read the book aloud to children, having them track the print with their fingers as you read.

Kindergarten Reader 29

Phonics Consonant *Xx*

High-Frequency Words
red, yellow, blue

In a big blue box,

sat a big, big fox,

and a big, yellow hat,

and a big, yellow cat,

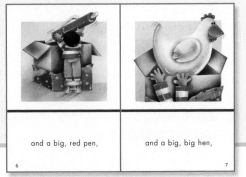

and a big, red pen,

and a big, big hen,

and six little, little chicks.

Modeled Writing

Demonstrate Writing Sentences

Model writing using sentences based on Kindergarten Reader 29 *A Big, Blue Box*. For example, write *A big, blue box dropped on the floor.*

As you write the sentence, model these strategies:

- Notice the color word *blue* is on the ABC Wall.

- Use an action word (verb) such as *dropped* to tell what happened in the past.

Guided Writing

Have children read the sentence with you. Help children write their own sentences based on *A Big, Blue Box*.

ABC Wall

Help children choose several words with *x*/ks/ to add to the ABC Wall. You might suggest *six* or *next*.

Day
3

Optional Resources

Phonics Sourcebook pp. 84–85

High-Frequency Word Cards

Phonics Workbook p. 143

Full Day Options...

Independent Writing 🚶

Write About Boxes Have children write or dictate descriptive sentences about one one of these:

- something you found in a box
- what you found inside a make-believe box that could hold anything

Phonics 👪

Segment and Blend Sounds Say a word segmented into its sounds, such as /m/ /i/ /ks/. Have children repeat the sounds and then blend them together to say the word *mix.* Repeat with the sounds for the words *fox, tax, box,* and *six.*

Author's Purpose 👬

Review a Book Have partners each choose a favorite book and take turns telling about their book and explaining why they think the author wrote it.

Objectives

Children will

⟳ practice speaking well

⟳ discuss the author's purpose for writing

• write using past-tense verbs

• use prewriting strategies

✳ Meeting Individual Needs

Intervention

Reread a familiar story to children. Ask them how the story made them feel or what they learned from it. Help them conclude that the author's purpose was probably to make them feel that way or to learn those things.

Author's Purpose
Practice Book, p. 186
Teacher's Resource Book, p. 186

Day 3

Oral Language

Shared Reading

Big Book

Discuss Speaking Well
Recall that in *I Need a Lunch Box* the boy tells the story. Reread the sentences on pages 8–9. Invite volunteers to imagine they are the boy telling the story and repeat the lines. Remind them to speak clearly and to avoid mumbling or adding extra sounds, such as "ummm" or "uh."

Retell Story by Speaking Well
Let children take turns retelling the main parts or events of *I Need a Lunch Box* until the whole story has been retold. Comment when a child speaks clearly. Point out how easy it is to hear and follow the story line when the speaker speaks well.

Ongoing Assessment

Speak Well

If... children are repeating words, pausing, or saying sounds that are not words,	then... tell them to speak slowly and to think about what they are going to say before they say it.

Comprehension

Think About Author's Purpose to Answer Questions
Reread pages 30–32 of *I Need a Lunch Box*, encouraging children to think again about the author's purpose for writing the story. Ask:

• **How do you think the author wanted you to feel about the ending?** (Children will probably say the author wanted readers to be happy for the boy.)

• **Can you think of another way the author could have ended the story?** (The boy could have gotten something else, such as a set of marbles; he could have gotten two lunch boxes, or even five.)

• **Would you change any part of this story? Why or why not?**

Reader Response

Connect Story to Own Experiences

Recall with children that in *I Need a Lunch Box* the boy was sad when he did not have a lunch box and happy when he got a lunch box. Ask:

- **How did you feel when you got something you really wanted?**

- **What did you do to show how you felt?**

Ask children to tell a classmate how they felt when they got something they really wanted.

Write on the board a sentence demonstrated by children such as [child's name] *smiled and cheered.*

Model Writing Past Tense Sentences

As you write the sentence, model these strategies:

- Begin each sentence with a capital letter.

- Add *-ed* to *smile* and *cheer* because those action words (verbs) tell about things that happened in the past.

- End the sentence with a period.

Self-Selected Reading **D.E.A.R.** *Drop Everything And Read*

From your self-selected reading collection, have children choose their own books to read. If you think they might like another book about colors, suggest *Mr. Rabbit and the Lovely Present* by Charlotte Zolotow.

Day 3

Full Day Options...

Independent Writing

What I Wanted Ask children to dictate or write their own sentence that begins *I wanted a ____.* Have them complete the sentence by writing a naming word, or noun.

Oral Language

Rhymes and Stories Ask volunteers in small groups to recite nursery rhymes or poems they know. Others may prefer to retell stories. Encourage children to speak without unnecessary pauses or extra words.

Author's Purpose

What's the Purpose? Ask children why they think the author wrote each of these books:

- a book about an imaginary space creature (entertain)
- a book about the planets in our solar system (inform)
- a book about three kittens that lose their mittens (entertain)
- a book about how to take care of kittens and cats (inform)

Handwriting

Practice Ask children to write one of these sentences.

- Many foxes live in Texas.
- Max sat next to Dex.
- I made six extra boxes.

Objectives

Children will

 recognize *x*/ks/
- review *e*/e/
- use high-frequency words
- review plural nouns

Meeting Individual Needs
Other Ways to Learn

Kinesthetic Show children how to play tic-tac-toe on a large grid on a sand table or chart paper. Let them take turns writing the *x*'s and *o*'s. Every time a child writes *x*, ask him or her to think of a word with *x*/ks/ and say it aloud.

Day 4

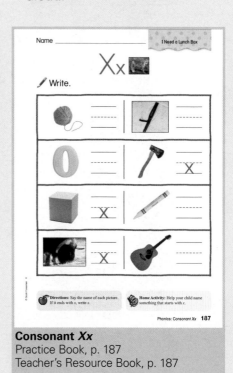

Consonant *Xx*
Practice Book, p. 187
Teacher's Resource Book, p. 187

Daily Phonics Routine

What sound do you hear?

Phonemic Awareness

Review **Vowel *e* /e/**

Using Alphapotamus, say: *Listen to this word:* men. Have children repeat the word. Then have them identify the onset and rime by asking: *What sound do you hear in the beginning of* men? (/m/) *What sound do you hear in the end?* (–en) Continue with *peg, get, set, net,* and *pen.*

Listen for /e/ and /ks/

Show the picture cards for *bed* and *box.* Say each of the following words and have children say /e/ if the word has /e/ and /ks/ if the word has /ks/. Use these words: *fix, fed, tax, pen, fox, pet, wax, web, six, ten, ox.*

Connect Sound to Letter

Sort Word Cards

Have children write *x*'s in different sizes and colors on the outside of a box with a lid, such as a shoebox. Make word cards for *ax, bus, fax, dish, fix, horse, mix, lock, tax, fox, mask, six, nest,* and *box.* Read each word and ask: *Does this word have the /ks/ sound in it?* If children answer *yes,* let a volunteer trace the *x* in the word with a red marker and put the card into the box.

Phonological Awareness

Listen for Ending Sounds

Tell children that you will say three words. Ask them to say the two words that have the same ending sound. Use these groups: *fox, bus, six; rod, mad, man; hot, bat, did;* and *box, fix, did.*

High-Frequency Words

Make Color Labels

Give each child squares of red, blue, and yellow construction paper. Have children write the word *red, blue,* or *yellow* on the appropriate square. Ask them to find things in the classroom that are those colors and put their color squares near those things.

Interactive Writing

Review

More Than One

Remind children that some words name people, places, animals, and things. Those words called naming words, or nouns, can mean one or more than one. Say the following words and ask children whether each word means one or more than one: *boys, girl, box, chairs, tables.*

Use Plural Nouns

Write on the board *We have six boxes,* saying each word as you write it. Point to the word *boxes* and ask children whether it means one or more than one box. Then have them review the words *red, yellow,* and *blue* on the ABC Wall.

> We have six boxes.
> Two boxes are red.
> Two boxes are yellow.
> Two boxes are blue.

Under the first sentence, write *Two boxes are _____.* Ask children to complete the sentence by writing one of the color words or parts of the word. Have children complete sentences for the other color words.

Ongoing Assessment
Writing

If... children have difficulty deciding whether a word names one or more than one,

then... point out that naming words that mean more than one usually end in the letter *s*.

ABC Wall

Have children check the ABC Wall for words that have the letter *x*. Invite them to add *x* words from Phonics Songs and Rhymes Chart 29 to the wall.

Meeting Individual Needs
Challenge

Show children *My Big Yellow Hat* and read the title, author's name, and illustrator's name aloud. As you read the story together, ask children to tell words they recognize.

Independent Reader 29

Optional Resources

Phonics Sourcebook pp. 1–78, 86–129

High-Frequency Word Cards

Phonics Workbook p. 144

Full Day Options...

Independent Writing 🚶

Use a Writing Journal Ask children to choose one of the following words and write a descriptive sentence in their writing journal that includes it: *foxes, crayons, pencils, books, shirts.*

Phonics 👥

Revisit Kindergarten Reader 29, *A Big, Blue Box* For more practice in high-frequency word recognition and phonics skills, have children reread *A Big, Blue Box.* Encourage partners to read the book together or take turns reading one page at a time.

Kindergarten Reader 29

Phonics 👥

Shared Song Sing "Maximilian X. Mox Has Chicken Pox" with children. Review *x*/ks/ and *o*/o/. Ask children to circle the two words on the chart that have both *x*/ks/ and *o*/o/. (Mox, pox) Then have them draw a line under the other words that have either /ks/ or /o/. (Maximilian, X, fix; on, lot)

Phonics Songs and Rhymes Chart 29

Day 4

Objectives

Children will

- recognize the author's purpose for writing
- practice speaking well
- listen to a poem
- recite a poem in pairs

Meeting Individual Needs

Intervention

Point out to children that what they like about a book usually gives them a clue to the author's purpose. If it was funny, the author meant to entertain them. If they learned many things, the author meant to give them information. Have children choose a book and figure out the author's purpose using this method.

Day 4

Name _____   I Need a Lunch Box

Draw.

Check children's drawings.

Directions: If you had a brand-new lunch box, what would you put in it? Draw a picture to show what would be in a new lunch box.   **Home Activity:** Ask your child to tell why the boy in the story wanted a lunch box.

188 Comprehension: Author's Purpose

Author's Purpose
Practice Book, p. 188
Teacher's Resource Book, p. 188

Comprehension

Activate Prior Knowledge

Display *On the Go* from Unit 4. Ask:

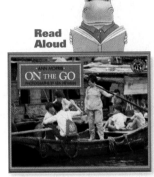

Read Aloud

ON THE GO

Trade Book

- **What do you remember about this book?**

- **What did the book tell you about how people move from place to place?** (People get from place to place in many different ways.)

Reread *On the Go.* After reading, ask:

What are some of the ways that people use to move themselves and other things around? (They carry things; they have animals carry things; they use bicycles, carts, baby strollers, buses, cars, trains, airplanes, and so on.)

Assess Author's Purpose

To assess children's understanding of author's purpose, ask:

Why do you think the author wrote *On the Go?* Was it to give you information or to entertain you? (Children will probably respond that it was to give information. If children choose entertain, ask them to tell what parts of the book entertained them.)

Have each child draw a picture of something he or she learned from the story.

Ongoing Assessment

Author's Purpose

If... children have difficulty recognizing the author's purpose,

then... use the Author's Purpose reteaching lesson on page AR19 of this Teacher's Edition.

Oral Language

Establish a Purpose for Speaking

Remind children that it is important to speak well so that others understand you. Review what they need to do to speak well: think about what you will say, do not say sounds that are not words, and do not repeat words. Ask them to listen to the poem "Rain" and then speak well as they tell what they like or do not like about the poem.

Read Aloud

> **Rain**
> by *Robert Louis Stevenson*
> The rain is raining all around,
> It falls on field and tree,
> It rains on the umbrellas here,
> And on the ships at sea.

Assess Speaking Well

Ask children to speak clearly and tell what they like or don't like about the poem or about rain. Reread the poem several times, emphasizing the rhythm. Invite children to say the poem in pairs or by themselves. Monitor how well they are speaking.

Ongoing Assessment

Speak Well

If... children do not speak in complete sentences or if they use unnecessary words or pauses,	**then...** say several complete sentences and have children echo you.

Self-Selected Reading

Have children choose books to read. They might enjoy reading *Cherries and Cherry Pits* by Vera B. Williams in which a girl tells her story and shares her art.

Optional Resources

Assessment Handbook

Full Day Options...

Author's Purpose

I'm an Author! Ask children to make a book cover for a book they might like to write. They can dictate or write the title, write their name as the author, and decorate the cover to support the title. Let them display their covers and tell what their purpose for writing the book would be.

Vocabulary

Use Story Words Write the color words *red, yellow,* and *blue* on the board. Ask children to choose one of the words and write it in that color. Children will need help spelling the words.

Writing

What's in Our Lunch Box? Ask partners to choose real or silly things they would put in a lunch box. Have them draw a big lunch box, cut out magazine pictures of items for their lunches, and glue them in the lunch box. Have them dictate or write a descriptive sentence that tells what is in their lunch box.

Oral Language/ Vocabulary

Talk About Colors Have children cut out pictures of things in their favorite colors and use the pictures to make a collage. Let them show their collages and talk about the colors and pictures they used. Remind them to speak clearly.

Day **4**

 PHONICS

Daily Phonics Routine

Children will

- use past-tense verbs
- identify ending sounds in words
- use high-frequency words
- participate in a shared writing activity

Phonemic Awareness

Prepare to Assess

Have Alphapotamus say the following words to children. Ask children to repeat each word after Alphapotamus and clap when they hear a word with /ks/. Use: *mix, buzz, yes, rush, next, rock, neck, gas, six, extra, basket,* and *jacket.*

Mix

Connect Sound to Letter

Assess x/ks/

On the board, write *mix, cat, tax, top, box, pig,* and *fix,* omitting the last letter in each word. Point to *mi-* and say *mix.* Ask children to identify the ending sound and the letter that stands for the sound in *mix.* Have a volunteer write the letter to complete the word. Continue with the other words.

Ongoing Assessment

Phonics

If... children cannot correctly identify the ending sounds,

then... use the Consonant *Xx* reteaching activities on page AR18 of this Teacher's Edition.

Meeting Individual Needs

ESL

Show children sheets of red, yellow, and blue construction paper. Write the appropriate color word on each sheet as you say the word aloud. Invite children to say the color word in their native language as they point to the sheet that is that color.

Phonological Awareness

Identify Syllables

Tell children that you will say several words. Each time they hear a syllable they should tap on their desk or table—one tap for each syllable. Model by tapping with them for the first one or two words, and then let them do it on their own. Use the following words: *taxi, children, stay, baseball, chalk, tablecloth, exercise.*

High-Frequency Words

Assess

Invite children to make their own color books. Have them write *This is a* on three sheets of paper. Ask them to write *red, blue,* or *yellow* and draw or cut out and paste a picture to complete each sentence. Have them write *Colors* and their name on another sheet of paper to use as the cover. Fasten the sheets together to make a book for them to take home.

This is a yellow

Independent Writing

Assess Writing Development

Recall with children that in *I Need a Lunch Box* the boy wanted a lunch box. Tell children they will write a story about another character that wanted something.

I think I'll write a story about a girl named Alex who wanted a pet. I am going to write "Alex really wanted a puppy. She liked puppies very much."

Point out that adding *-ed* to *want* and *like* shows the actions happened in the past.

Have children write about what a character wanted and how that character got it. Help them write past-tense verbs. Encourage children to use transitional spelling. You may wish to assess each child's writing using the scoring guide.

Scoring Guide

Not every child will be able to write a story.

3 Competent
The child uses spelling approximations and directionality of print and may include a past-tense verb. The sentence begins with a capital letter and ends with a period.

2 Developing
The child uses spelling approximations and directionality of print and may include a verb. Beginning capitalization and end punctuation are sometimes correct.

1 Emerging
The child writes a sentence with one to two sounds represented in the words spelled phonetically, and is beginning to use spaces between words.

Optional Resources

Phonics Sourcebook pp. 84–85

High-Frequency Word Cards

Phonics Workbook p. 145

Assessment Handbook

Shared Writing

Add to the Class Diary

Ask children to recall what they have done in class this week. Remind them to use the rules for speaking clearly as they tell about their activities. Have children sequence the events to tell you the order in which to write them. Write their sentences on chart paper. Add the pages to the class diary.

Full Day Options...

Phonics

Sort Picture Cards Show small groups the picture cards for *box, fox, monkey, ox, pickle, sock,* and *sandwich.* Have them say the name of the picture and put the card in a box if the word ends in *x*/ks/.

Independent Writing

Write in Color Have children choose either a red, yellow, or blue crayon to write with. Ask them to use the crayon to write a persuasive sentence telling why that color is the best. Encourage transitional spelling.

Reading

Read Aloud Ask children who have good beginning reading skills to read *My Big Yellow Hat* aloud to you. Notice their decoding skills as they read.

Independent Reader 29

Day **5**

Meeting Individual Needs
Intervention

Write sentence pairs on the board, such as: *The boy needs help. Two boys need help.* Read the sentences aloud and track the print as children watch and listen. Then have children repeat the sentences. Continue with other examples as necessary.

Day 5

Comprehension

Review Drawing Conclusions

Remind children that some stories, called fables, teach a lesson. Help them recall the fable "Belling the Cat" in Unit 4. Explain that you are going to read them another fable called "The Fox and the Crow." Ask children to think about what the fox does and what the crow learns as they listen to the story.

Read Aloud

TE Volume 5, p. AR8

After reading, ask:

- **How did the crow lose the piece of cheese?** (She let the fox trick her into opening her mouth and dropping it.)

- **What do you think is the lesson of the story?** (Don't believe everything you hear.)

- **How do you think the crow felt at the end of the story? How do you think the fox felt?** (The crow probably was sorry, disappointed, or mad. The fox may have felt happy and even proud.)

Ongoing Assessment
Drawing Conclusions

If... children have difficulty drawing conclusions about the story,

then... reread the appropriate part of the story and ask the question again.

Match Feelings and Faces

Have children talk about the fox and the crow in the story. Ask: *If they were people, how would their faces look at the beginning of the story? At the end of the story?* Invite volunteers to pretend they are the fox and the crow. Have them use facial expressions to show how the characters felt at the beginning and the end of the story.

Oral Language

Speak Using Proper Grammar

Review with children what it means to speak with proper grammar. Write *sit* and *sits* on the board. Say the following sentences and have children tell which word belongs in each: *In the tree, one crow _____. In the tree, two crows _____.*

Remind children that action words, or verbs, change to show whether they are telling about one or more than one person, place, animal, or thing. Say: *When you tell about one, you usually add –s to the action word (verb).*

Practice Speaking Using Proper Grammar

Recall with children "The Fox and the Crow." Say:

- **The crow believes the fox. Does *the crow believes* sound correct, or should it be *the crow believe the fox?* **("The crow believes the fox" is correct.)

- **Which of these sentences is correct? *The crow flies to the top of the tree. The crow fly to the top of the tree.* **(the first sentence)

- **Which sentence is right? Why? *The crow and the fox meets in the woods. The crow and the fox meet in the woods.* **(the second sentence; The sentence describes more than one and so there is no –s added to the action word, or verb.)

Self-Selected Reading

Help children find books that they can read independently. One possibility is *Harold and the Purple Crayon* by Crockett Johnson.

Full Day Options...

Reading

Reader Response: "The Fox and the Crow" Recall with children that the crow lost the cheese because she believed what the fox told her. Ask them to tell what they think the crow should have done when the fox talked to her.

TE Volume 3, p. AR8

Oral Language

Foxes and Crows Ask children to draw a picture that shows one fox talking and two foxes talking. Have them use action words, or verbs, to tell about the pictures; for example, *A fox talks. Two foxes talk.* Let them continue with *One crow sings* and *Two crows sing.*

Author's Purpose

Favorite Books Ask children to choose a book they like that gives information and another book they like that made them laugh. Have them show the book, state the author's purpose for writing it, and tell how they recognized that purpose.

Independent Writing

Write About the Fox Ask children to dictate or write two expository sentences—one that tells what the fox in the story wanted and one that tells why he wanted it. Encourage children to share their work with someone at home.

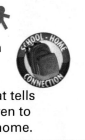

Day 5

Lesson Overview

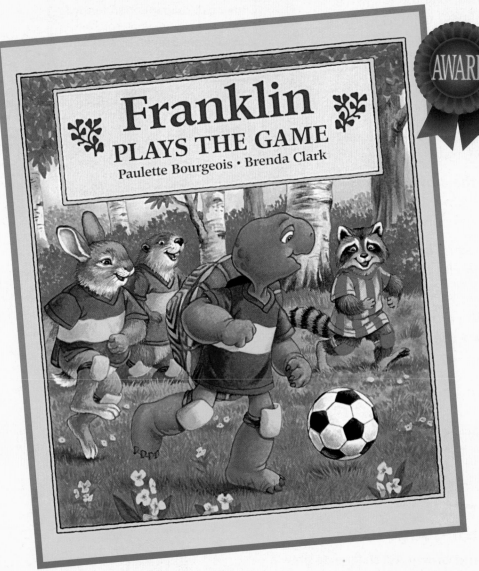

Trade Book

Franklin Plays the Game

Selection Audio

Genre
Animal Fantasy

↻ **Phonemic Awareness/Phonics**
Consonant *y* /y/

↻ **Comprehension**
Character

High-Frequency Words
red   yellow   blue

About the Author and Illustrator

Paulette Bourgeois
grew up in Winnipeg, Canada, with a family who loved storytelling. There are more than 15 million Franklin books in print, a television series, and other activities and merchandise bearing the Franklin name. She writes about four Franklin books each year.

Brenda Clark
has said that making a living as a full-time artist had always been her ambition in life. She achieved her goal, quickly establishing herself as a successful children's book illustrator. She has illustrated twenty-eight books and is best known for her illustrations of Franklin the Turtle.

Leveled Books

Easy

Wordless Story 30

On–Level

Kindergarten Reader 30

Challenge

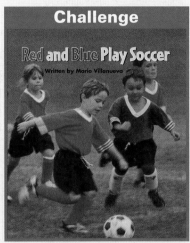

Independent Reader 30

Trade Books for Self-Selected Reading and Read Aloud

Albert's Ballgame
by Leslie Tryon

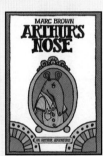

Arthur's Nose
by Marc Brown

Bedtime for Frances
by Russell Hoban

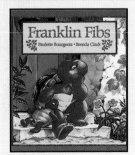

Franklin Fibs
by Paulette Bourgeois

Franklin in the Dark
by Paulette Bourgeois

Franklin Rides a Bike
by Paulette Bourgeois

Theme Make a Wish   **Lesson Topic** A New Way to Win

5-Day Planner

Customize your week with the Teacher's Resource Planner CD-ROM!

Reading
Comprehension
Vocabulary

Phonics
Phonemic Awareness

Oral Language
Speaking, Listening, and Viewing

Writing
Grammar, Usage, and Mechanics

Self-Selected Reading
Read Aloud

Day 1

Activate Prior Knowledge p. 203
Poem "Rope Rhyme"

Reading pp. 204–211
Shared Reading
Franklin Plays the Game

Reader Response:
Show Feelings of the Soccer Players

 Comprehension:
Character

Create Puppets to
Understand Character

Phonics pp. 212–213
 Consonant *y* /y/

Phonemic Awareness:
Listen to a Song
• Phonics Songs and
Rhymes Chart 30

**Connect Sound to
Letter:** Match /y/ to *y*

**Phonological
Awareness:** Blend Sounds

✔ **High-Frequency Words**

red   yellow   blue

Oral Language pp. 210–211
Introduce Vocabulary
Soccer Words
soccer dribbled bounced team goal
Use Soccer Words to
Answer Questions

Writing pp. 212–213
 Shared Writing: Write
Sentences Together

Self-Selected Reading p. 211
Have children select books to
read. They might enjoy reading
other books that feature sports.
See page 195 for suggestions.

Day 2

Phonics pp. 214–215
 Consonant *y* /y/

Phonemic Awareness:
Listen for /y/ Words
• Phonics Songs and
Rhymes Chart 30

Find Picture
Names with /y/
• Wordless Story 30
Yoki and Yum Yum

**Connect Sound to
Letter:** Match /y/ to *y*

Phonological Awareness:
Name Words with Matching
Sounds

✔ **High-Frequency Words:**
Spell *red, yellow,* and *blue*

Reading pp. 216–217
 Comprehension: Character

Recall Book's Theme

Use Soccer Words
in Sentences

Describe Main
Character

Oral Language pp. 216–217
 Listening: Listen for
Main Idea

Listen for Main Idea
• Oral Language
Chart 30

Writing pp. 214–215
 Modeled Writing: Write About
Ways to Win

Guided Writing

Handwriting: Practice Writing *Yy*

Self-Selected Reading p. 217
Have children choose their own
books to read from your self-
selected reading collection.
Children might be interested in reading
Arthur's Nose by Marc Brown.

 **Target Skill**    **Review Skill**

Day 3

Phonics pp. 218–219

 Consonant y /y/

Phonemic Awareness:
Choose Initial /y/ Words

Connect Sound to Letter:
Underline /y/ Words
• Phonics Songs and Rhymes Chart 30

Phonological Awareness:
Change Initial Sounds

Read Kindergarten Reader 30:
Yes! We Get Wet!

Reading pp. 220–221

 Comprehension:
Character

Identify Characters from Clues

Reader Response:
Learn Information from Pictures

Model Writing Sentences

Oral Language pp. 220–221

 Listening: Listen for Main Idea

Discuss Listening for Main Idea

Listen to Find Main Idea

Writing pp. 218–219

 Modeled Writing:
Model Writing Telling Sentences

Guided Writing

Self-Selected Reading p. 221

Children may enjoy reading other books about Franklin, such as *Franklin Rides a Bike* by Paulette Bourgeois.

Day 4

Phonics pp. 222–223

Review Consonant x /ks/

 Consonant y /y/

Phonemic Awareness:

Consonant x /ks/

Identify Initial /y/ or Final /ks/

Connect Sound to Letter: Identify Initial /y/ Words

Phonological Awareness:
Delete Phomemes

✔ **High-Frequency Words:**
Match Words to Colors

Challenge: Independent Reader 30

Reading pp. 224–225

 Comprehension:
Character

Activate Prior Knowledge

 Assess Character

Oral Language pp. 224–225

 Listening: Listen for Main Idea

Establish a Purpose for Listening
• Read Aloud "The Playful Crickets"
 Assess Listen for Main Idea

Writing pp. 222–223

✔ *Review* **Interactive Writing:**
Complete Sentences

Write Complete Sentences

Self-Selected Reading p. 225

Have children choose books to read. Children might enjoy other stories about coaches and team sports, such as *Albert's Ballgame* by Leslie Tryon.

Day 5

Phonics pp. 226–227

 Consonant y /y/

Phonemic Awareness:
Prepare to Assess

 Connect Sound to Letter:
Assess y /y/

Phonological Awareness:
Count the Syllables

 High-Frequency Words:
Assess

Reading pp. 228–229

Review **Comprehension:** Author's Purpose
• Read Aloud "Why the Monkey and the Turtle Are Cold at Night"

Draw a New Ending

Oral Language pp. 228–229

Review **Speaking:** Speak Well

Practice Speaking Well

Writing pp. 226–227

 Independent Writing: Assess Writing Development

Shared Writing: Add to the Class Diary

Self-Selected Reading p. 229

Help children look for books that they can read independently. One book you might suggest is *Bedtime for Frances* by Russell Hoban.

 Assessment ✔ Benchmark Assessment of Target Skills and Skills Assessment

Cross-Curricular Work Stations

Community Link

Ideas for bringing the school and community together

Field Experiences
football, baseball, soccer fields
gymnasium
tennis courts

Guest Speakers
athletes
coaches
parents
adults who have participated in team training

Letters and Sounds

Create Silly Sentences 10 minutes

Materials: word cards

Learning Styles Visual, Auditory, Individual

Provide children with groups of word cards that have a rhyming word written on each of them, such as *cat, hat, mat, vet, set, jet, big, pig, jig, hot, pot, cot, bug, rug, tug.* Have children choose two cards from a rhyming group and use them to write or dictate a silly sentence, for example, *I did a jig with a pig. The cat wears a hat.*

cat
bug
hat
The cat wears a hat.
The bug is on the rug.

Social Studies

Rules of the Game 10 minutes

Materials: beanbags, balls, other sports equipment

Learning Styles Social, Kinesthetic, Spatial, Logical

Talk with children about the importance of rules in games. What would happen if there were no rules? Give small groups a ball and have them play a game with no rules or directions. After several minutes, gather children together and make a list of reasons why it is important to have rules.

Challenge Children can create a simple board game or a game using sports equipment and write or draw the rules to play the game.

Science

Roll Away 10 minutes

Materials: balls of various sizes, an incline plane

Learning Styles Logical, Kinesthetic, Spatial, Social

Children explore using different balls and inclines. First set up an incline and let children explore how far and fast different balls roll. Next compare balls using two inclines at the same height. Then raise one of the inclines to be steeper than the other. Children can make and write predictions on a chart.

 Children can play a variation of a game played in Italy called *bocce* in which balls are rolled toward a stone to see which player comes closest. Place a stone on a flat surface, and have children take turns rolling a ball toward the stone.

Technology

AstroWord 👥 ⏱ **10 minutes**

Learning Styles Visual, Auditory

AstroWord reinforces children's understanding of phonemic awareness. Children can work individually or collaboratively.

Web Site 🚶 ⏱ **two days for 10 minutes**

Learning Styles Individual, Visual

sfreading.com

WWW Visit the Scott Foresman web site (sfreading.com) for current hyperlinks to sites that can be used by children for an Internet Workshop investigation of sports and winning. Also see the Scott Foresman Internet Guide for additional understanding of the Internet Workshop method.

Social Studies

Who Is Winning? 👥 ⏱ **10 minutes**

Materials: heavy paper, sports stickers or markers, two lengths of yarn

Learning Styles Logical, Kinesthetic, Social

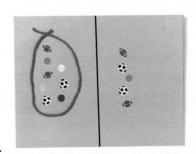

Create scoreboards similar to the one shown. Draw simple pictures or use stickers to represent each team's score. Children can take turns ringing the score that is higher with a piece of yarn. Partners can check by counting to see that the ringed group has more objects.

Writing

Work as a Team 👥 ⏱ **two days for 10 minutes**

Materials: writing materials, crayons, markers

Learning Styles Social, Verbal, Kinesthetic

As a group, children pick a topic for a storybook. They decide how the pages will get written and illustrated. Will each person do one page? Will one person write the words and another illustrate? Suggest that the entire team create the cover and sign their names as authors.

(ESL) Children talk about making the storybook. Encourage them to use the words *first,* *next,* and *last.*

CTW

Reading Road Show

Introduce the Reading Road Show Activity Stations to reinforce this week's skills.

Phonemic Awareness & Phonics
Literacy Activities

Use these activities during the week to reinforce skills.

Phonemic Awareness

Card Pick-Up 10 minutes

Materials: picture cards

Learning Styles Visual, Kinesthetic, Auditory, Spatial

Gather picture cards; one card for each child. Ask children to stand in a circle. Arrange the picture cards face down in a small inner circle. Have children skip around the circle. When you clap your hands, each child stops and picks up a card. The child identifies the picture, says a word that begins with the same sound, and replaces the card in the inner circle. After each child responds, have children skip around the circle again.

Challenge children to also name a word that rhymes with or has the same ending sound as their picture name.

Working with Letters

Racetrack 10 minutes

Materials: letter cards or shapes, spinner

Learning Styles Social, Visual, Kinesthetic, Spatial

Draw a racetrack on a large sheet of heavy paper. Divide the track into equal spaces and write a letter in each space. Place the racetrack on a table or the floor. Cut cars from different colored construction paper, one car for each child. Make a spinner by dividing a small cardboard circle into four sections, writing the numbers 1 through 4 in the sections, and fastening a pointer to the center of the circle. Each child has a turn to spin the pointer and read the number in the section where the pointer stops. The player then moves that number of spaces on the racetrack. If he or she can name the letter in that space, the player moves his or her car to that space. If he or she cannot name the letter, the car remains where it is. Another child then has a turn. The first child to reach the finish line wins the game.

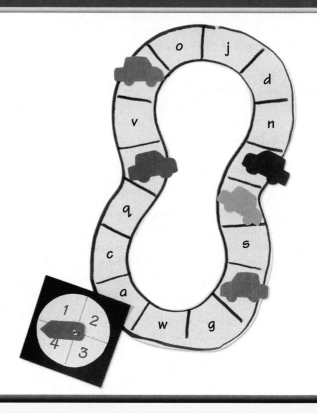

Working with Words

Travel the Rhyme Trail 15 minutes

Learning Styles Visual, Verbal, Kinesthetic

Draw a trail on the board. Along the trail make signs with rhyming word patterns such as these: ___ed, ___at, ___en, ___ot, ___ig, ___ap, ___op, ___ed, ___an. Have a child begin "traveling the rhyme trail" by writing a word that has the pattern on the first sign and reading the word. He or she then chooses someone to have the next turn at the next sign. Continue along the trail until many rhyming words have been made.

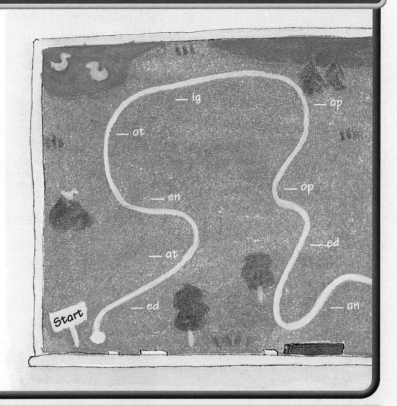

ABC Wall

ABC Wall 15 minutes

Learning Styles Verbal, Visual, Logical

Have a child come to the front of the room and read a word from the ABC Wall, for example, the word *red*. Call on another child to read a word from the ABC Wall that begins with the final letter in the word the first child read (the *d* in *red*), for example, *dog*. If correct, that child comes to the front of the room and holds hands with the first child to form a "word chain." The next child must read an ABC Wall word that begins with the final letter in the word *dog*, that is, a word that begins with *g*. Continue in the same way until a long chain of words has been made.

ESL The game can be modified for a small group. Give children a picture dictionary to use to find words. Encourage them to find words that are new to them.

Daily Warm-Up

Message Board

Day One

Today we will read about Franklin. He likes to play soccer.

Discuss with children sports that they enjoy playing or watching.

Ask children: "What words do you know that begin like *yellow?*"

Day Two

We will read and write words with Yy.

Day Three

We will read and spell the words red, yellow, and blue.

Ask children: "Which color do you like best—*red, yellow,* or *blue?*"

Discuss with children a favorite poem.

Day Four

Today we will listen to a poem.

Day Five

Today we will write a note to a friend.

Ask children: "Have you ever gotten a note from a friend?"

Getting Ready for the Week

Day One

paper lunch bags
construction paper, felt, glitter, pipe cleaners, buttons

Day Two

large index cards
small paper plates, bowls, sponges, tracers for soccer ball, turtle head and feet

Day Three

magazines (Full Day)

Day Four

craft sticks (Full Day)

Day Five

magazines
yarn (Full Day)

Family Times

Send home the newsletter with fun instructional activities to reinforce this week's target skills.

Practice Book, pp. 189–190
Teacher's Resource Book, pp.189–190

Activate Prior Knowledge

Go on a Scavenger Hunt

Say: *This week's story is about friends who learn to work together as a team.* Tell children they will work in teams to go on a scavenger hunt. Have children who have done a scavenger hunt explain it to classmates. Divide the class into small groups and give each group an illustrated list of simple objects that can be found in the classroom. After the hunt, ask questions such as:

- **Did everyone on your team work together to look for the objects?**

- **How is working in a team different from working by yourself?**

Objectives

Children will

- learn about teamwork by working in teams
- tell a story based on an illustration
- listen and respond to a poem

Build Background

Choose one or more of these activities to build background for concepts presented in this week's book, *Franklin Plays the Game.*

Read Aloud a Poem

Share this poem with children. Then invite them to talk about how the poet describes "jumping."

Rope Rhyme
by Eloise Greenfield

Get set, ready now, jump right in
Bounce and kick and giggle and
   spin
Listen to the rope when it hits the
   ground
Listen to that clappedy-slappedy
   sound
Jump right up when it tells you to
Come back down, whatever you do
Count to a hundred, count by ten
Start to count all over again
That's what jumping is all about
Get set, ready now,
   jump
      right
         out!

Use Illustrations to Develop Oral Language

Hold up *Franklin Plays the Game.* Ask children to describe what they see. Elicit that the animals are playing soccer and that three of them are on the same team because they are wearing matching shirts. Have children make up a story about the teammates.

Use Audio to Develop Story Concepts

Ask:

- **What games or sports do you like to play?**

- **Why is working as a team important in some games and sports?**

Share the Background-Building CD/tape, in which two children talk about playing soccer and basketball and the importance of teamwork. After listening, ask: *What do the children think makes a winning team?*

CD 5/Tape15, Side 2
Background-Building Audio

Day 1

Read Aloud Routine

Day 1

- Read the story through for enjoyment. Modulate your voice and use facial expressions to help convey the different feelings of the characters.

- To practice the reading strategy predicting, use the stopping point on page 208.

Day 2

- Reread the entire story, using the activities found in the margins on pages 205–209.

Days 3–5

- Reread selected pages for specific purposes, as suggested in the lessons.

Concepts of Print

Parts of a Book

Display *Franklin Plays the Game.* Read the title and the names of the author and the illustrator. Display and identify the title page. Read the information on the page. Discuss similarities and differences between the cover and title pages.

Model Reading Behaviors

Picture Walk and Predict

Preview the story and have children look at the illustrations. If any children are familiar with soccer, invite them to briefly explain the game to the class. Then ask:

- **Who do you think some of the characters are in this story?** (Different animals)

- **Where does most of this story take place?** (outside; on a soccer field)

- **Do you think this book is going to be about a winning soccer team? Why or why not? Let's read to find out.**

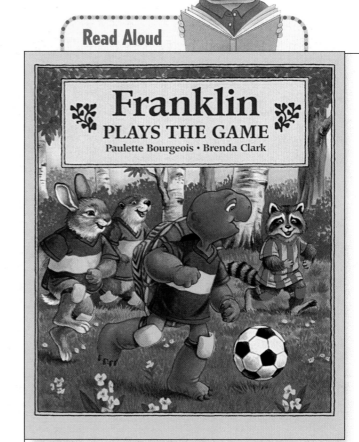

Read Aloud

Trade Book

FRANKLIN could slide down a riverbank. He could tie his shoes and count by twos. He could walk to Bear's house all by himself. But Franklin couldn't kick a soccer ball straight. That was a problem because Franklin wanted to be the best player on his team.

pages 4–5

Franklin loved soccer. He liked the running and the dribbling. He especially liked the uniforms. He wore his purple-and-yellow jersey and matching shin pads, even when he wasn't playing soccer. Sometimes he slept with his soccer ball and dreamed of scoring goals.

pages 6–7

Before every game, Franklin practiced in the park. He kicked the ball with the inside of his foot again and again. He did warm-up stretches and cool-down walks.

Still, Franklin had trouble. He couldn't run very fast...even without a soccer ball between his feet. And when Franklin kicked the ball, it never went where he intended.

pages 8–9

Day 1

Guiding the Reading

Critical Thinking

Why do you think Franklin couldn't run very fast?
Possible answer: He is a turtle. Turtles are very slow-moving animals.

Language Development

Share with children the meaning of the word *practiced.*

Franklin practiced kicking the ball before every game.

practiced

average

Content Connection: Science

- Tortoises are land turtles.
- Most turtles can pull their head, feet, and tail into their shells.
- Turtles do not have teeth.
- Some kinds of turtles can live to be more than 100 years old.

Guiding the Reading

Critical Thinking

Why are Franklin and Goose sad? How can you tell? What in the story lets you know that?

Possible answer: They think that they will never score a goal. The story says they have problems playing the game.

pages 10–11

Language Development

"No wonder we never win any games," grumbled Franklin.

What does *grumbled* mean in this sentence? How do you know? How can you use other words to figure out what *grumbled* means?

grumbled

challenge

pages 12–13

Guiding the Reading

Critical Thinking

Why doesn't losing bother the coach?

Possible answer: The coach felt that having fun was more important.

pages 14–15

"What's wrong?" asked Franklin's father.
"I never score a goal," answered Franklin.
"But you try and you have fun," said Franklin's
father. "That's the important thing."
    Franklin nodded. That's what all the grown-ups
said. But he really wanted everybody to cheer
for him. He wanted to score a goal.

pages 16–17

Critical Thinking

Why did the parents and the players feel differently about winning the game?
Possible answers: The children wanted to be known as winners. The parents wanted their children to learn the game and have fun playing it.

Day
1

It wasn't only Franklin who felt that way. Each of
Franklin's friends wanted to score a goal. But the
harder they tried, the worse they played. Franklin
forgot where to stand. Goose forgot what to do.
    Whenever the ball came to Franklin's teammates,
they rushed toward it. Players tripped over feet
and tails and long ears. They crashed into a heap.
    Coach helped untangle the players. "You have
to work together as a team. You have to share
the ball."

pages 18–19

But it wasn't easy to do. Their team lost again.
It made the players feel sad. Franklin huddled
inside his shell. Beaver tucked in her tail and
Goose folded her wings. The other team crossed
the field to shake hands.

"Nice try," said Bear.
Franklin didn't come out of his shell.
Bear bounced the soccer ball up and down.
"Come on out, Franklin," said Bear.

pages 20–21

Language Development

Share with children the meaning of the word *huddled.* Then help children demonstrate the word by huddling together.

Franklin huddled inside his shell. He would hide in the close space when he felt unhappy.

huddled

challenge

Franklin Plays the Game **207**

Language Development

Point out that the word *teamwork* is made up of the words *team* and *work*. Help children use what they know about the two words to develop the meaning of *teamwork*.

The team had to work together. If they used teamwork, they might score a goal.

teamwork

challenge

Guiding the Reading

Critical Thinking

Why was Franklin so excited about the next game?
Possible answers: He couldn't wait for his team to try out their special play. He thought that his team might finally score a goal.

 Stopping Point

Predict On the first reading, you may want to stop at the bottom of page 27 and ask children to predict whether Franklin and his team will score a goal.

pages 22–23

pages 24–25

pages 26–27

pages 28–29

pages 30–31

page 32

Critical Thinking

Why did Franklin's team finally score a goal?
Possible answers: The team members began using their strengths to play together as a team. They did not all rush after the ball at one time. They played their positions. They practiced and began thinking as much about having fun as about scoring.

Day
1

Objectives

Children will

- understand character
- use story events and life experiences to build vocabulary

Day 1

Meeting Individual Needs
ESL

Demonstrate the vocabulary words or show children pictures that illustrate the vocabulary words *soccer*, *dribbled*, *bounced*, *team*, and *goal*. Say each word aloud and have children echo you as you are demonstrating the word or pointing to a picture.

Skills Trace

Character

Introduce	TE: K.2 64–65
Practice	PB: 54, 56, 66, 68, 192, 194
Reteach/ Review	TE: K.2 71, 74, 78, 120, 142–143, 149, 152, 156, 196, AR13, AR17 K.5 210–211, 217, 220, 224, AR21 K.6 46
Skills Assessment	Skill Assessment Unit 2 TE: K.2 AR1–AR3, K.5 AR1–AR3

Reader Response

Show Feelings of the Soccer Players

Ask: *Do you think the mood at the end of the story is happy or sad? Why do you think so?*

Have children show how Franklin felt when

- They lost the first game (sad)
- His team worked out their special play (happy, excited)
- His team lost the second game (tired, proud, happy)

Oral Language/Vocabulary

Use Soccer Words to Answer Questions

The vocabulary words are related to soccer. Using the illustrations, discuss the meanings of the words. Then have children use them to answer questions.

 soccer dribbled bounced team goal

- **What game does Franklin play in the story?** (soccer)
- **He and his friends play on a soccer _____.** (team)
- **What did Franklin and his friends do with the soccer ball?** (dribbled and bounced it)
- **What does Franklin's team do that they had never done before?** (score a goal)

Encourage children to share their own experiences by using the vocabulary words to talk about playing sports.

Ongoing Assessment
Vocabulary

If... children have difficulty answering the questions with the vocabulary words,

then... show them the illustrations and reread passages in the trade book that provide clues.

Comprehension

Create Puppets to Understand Character

Tell children that characters are the people or animals in stories. Invite children to create their own character and make a puppet by decorating a paper lunch bag with construction paper, felt, glitter, pipe cleaners, or buttons. Have small groups of children use their puppets in a puppet show that demonstrates what each puppet is like. Ask children in the audience to describe the characters by answering questions such as:

- **What words would you use to describe this character?**

- **What did the character do or say to make you think that?**

Remind children that the people or animals in stories are called characters. Say: *Franklin and his friends were characters in the story we just read.*

Self-Selected Reading **D.E.A.R.** *Drop Everything And Read*

Have children select books to read. They might enjoy reading other books that feature sports. See page 195 for suggestions.

Day **1**

Full Day Options...

Character

Tell About Characters Show pictures of characters from a previously read trade book or big book. Help children recall the story and then ask them to tell about the characters.

Vocabulary

Pantomime Words Assign small groups one of the vocabulary words to pantomime for the rest of the class. Classmates should name the word the group is acting out.

Oral Language

Tell a Story Have children choose a prompt.

- Tell about a game you would like to play that involves running.
- Tell a story about how you learned to play a sport.
- Tell about something you practice so you will get better.

Independent Writing

Continue the Story Have children draw a picture to extend the story to another game. Encourage them to dictate or write narrative sentences that tell what the characters did to improve and whether or not they played well enough to win the game.

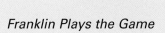

Daily Phonics Routine

Day 1

Objectives

Children will

- recognize initial /y/
- recognize the letters *Yy*
- blend sounds to make words
- participate in a shared writing activity

Meeting Individual Needs

Intervention

Place alphabet cards for *Yy*, *Jj*, and *Gg* on the chalk ledge. Show picture cards for *yak*, *jam*, *yarn*, *goose*, *yellow*, *gum*, *yo-yo*, and *jet*. Have children place each picture card near the alphabet card whose letters stand for the beginning sound in the picture name.

Skills Trace

Consonant *Yy*

Introduce	TE: K.5 212
Practice	PB: 191, 193
Reteach/Review	TE: K.5 214, 218–219, 222, 226, AR20 K.6 44
Skills Assessment	Skill Assessment Unit 5 TE: K.5 AR1–AR3

Phonemic Awareness

Listen to a Song

Sing "The Yak" or play the CD/tape. Have children listen for and name words that begin like *yak*. (yells, you, Yankee, yodels, yahoo, yogurt, yolks, yams, yellow)

CD 5/Tape 15, Side 2
Phonics Songs and Rhymes Audio

Identify /y/ Picture Cards

Display picture cards for *yak*, *yarn*, and *yellow*. Have children identify each picture by name. Ask: *What sound do you hear at the beginning of* yak, yam, *and* yellow? (/y/)

The Yak

Yak wears a hat of blue,
He yells to me and you.
He sings a Yankee Doodle doo
And yodels a yahoo.

Yak wants to eat some clams,
Yogurt, yolks, and yams.
He butters rolls with yellow jams
And eats lunch with the lambs.

Phonics Songs and Rhymes Chart 30

Ongoing Assessment

Phonemic Awareness

If... children have difficulty hearing initial /y/,

then... say phrases such as *your yellow yo-yo* and have children repeat them, listening to the beginning sound.

Connect Sound to Letter

Match /y/ to *y*

Show children the alphabet card and say *yo-yo* as you point to *Y* and *y*. Point out that the beginning sound in *yo-yo* is /y/ and that *Y* and *y* stand for the sound. Write *yo-yo* on the board. Point to each *y* and say the word slowly, emphasizing each /y/.

Alphabet Cards

Phonological Awareness

Blend Sounds

Using Alphapotamus say: *If I say /y/ellow, what word do you hear?* (yellow) Repeat with: /y/ams, /y/ogurt, /y/ou, /y/ard.

/y/ ellow

High-Frequency Words

Find *red, yellow,* and *blue* on the ABC Wall

Have children point to the words *red, yellow,* and *blue* on the ABC Wall. Point to something in the room that is each color and have children use the color word in a sentence identifying the item.

Optional Resources

Phonics Sourcebook pp. 76–77, 84–85

High-Frequency Word Cards

Phonics Workbook p. 146

Shared Writing

Write Sentences Together

Say: *Let's write silly sentences about a yak using words that begin with y/y/.* Ask children to think about some things a yak might do.

As children respond, they can

- Help you sound out the words as you write them
- Use high-frequency words
- Identify any words with initial /y/

When you are finished, read the sentences together as a volunteer tracks the print.

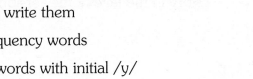

A Yak

The yak eats yams.

A yak has a blue yo-yo.

The yak eats yellow pears.

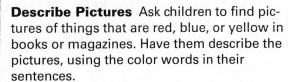

Full Day Options...

Independent Writing

Write About Feelings Have children write or dictate narrative text about one.

- How Franklin felt after the big game
- How you feel when you play a fun game

Oral Language

Describe Pictures Ask children to find pictures of things that are red, blue, or yellow in books or magazines. Have them describe the pictures, using the color words in their sentences.

Character

Who Am I? Have children take turns describing a character from a previously read big book or trade book without mentioning the character's name. The rest of the group can identify the character.

Phonics

Rhyming Pairs Ask children to use the words *red, yellow,* and *blue* to describe something that rhymes with the word. For example, *red bed, blue zoo, yellow fellow.*

Daily Phonics Routine

Objectives

Children will

↻ recognize initial /y/
- write the letters *Yy*
- match beginning sounds in words
- learn about two kinds of sentences

Day 2

Phonemic Awareness

Listen for /y/ Words

Have children stand in a circle and sing along with the CD/tape "The Yak." Ask them to put their arms up and stand like a *Y* each time they hear a word that begins with /y/.

CD 5/Tape 15, Side 2
Phonics Songs and Rhymes Audio

The Yak

Yak wears a hat of blue,
He yells to me and you.
He sings a Yankee Doodle doo
And yodels a yahoo.

Yak wants to eat some clams,
Yogurt, yolks, and yams.
He butters rolls with yellow jams
And eats lunch with the lambs.

Phonics Songs and Rhymes Chart 30

Find Picture Names with /y/

Have children look through *Yoki and Yum Yum.* Encourage them to find pictures of things whose names begin with /y/. You may wish to have children dictate or write a story in the take-home version.

Wordless Story 30

Connect Sound to Letter

Match /y/ to *y*

Give each child a large index card. Have children draw a picture that illustrates an initial /y/ word. Suggest words and pictures if necessary. Invite them to hold their picture cards next to the *Yy* alphabet card. Have the class identify the picture and verify that the beginning sound in the word is /y/.

Alphabet Cards

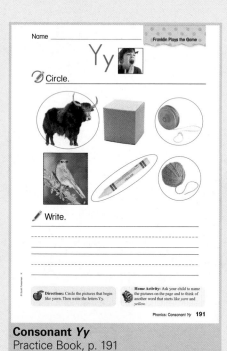

Name _____ Franklin Plays the Game

Yy

⊘ Circle.

✎ Write.

Directions: Circle the pictures that begin like *yawn.* Then write the letters *Yy.*

Home Activity: Ask your child to name the pictures on the page and to think of another word that starts like *yarn* and *yellow.*

Phonics: Consonant Yy **191**

Consonant *Yy*
Practice Book, p. 191
Teacher's Resource Book, p. 191

Phonological Awareness

Name Words with Matching Sounds

Have Alphapotamus say: *What sound do you hear at the beginning of the word* year? (/y/) *Say another word that has the same beginning sound.* Have Alphapotamus point to several volunteers who should say words that begin with /y/, such as *yes, yam,* and *yellow.* Have Alphapotamus continue in the same way with *violin* /v/ and *jump* /j/.

What's another /y/ word?

Skills Trace

↻ **Types of Sentences**

Introduce	TE: K.5 **215**
Reteach/ Review	TE: K.5 **223, 227** K.6 **113,151**
Skills Assessment	Skill Assessment Unit 5 TE: K.5 **AR1-AR3**

High-Frequency Words

Spell *red, yellow,* and *blue*

Have a volunteer spell *red* for classmates and ask them to say the word. Repeat with *yellow* and *blue*.

Modeled Writing

Write About Ways to Win

Discuss ways to win. Write a sentence and a question on the board: *Our team scored a goal. Did our team win?* Say:

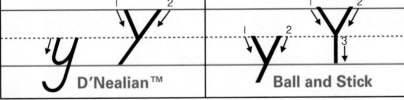

Think ALOUD

- **I wrote a sentence that tells about our team. A sentence that tells about a person, place, animal, or thing is called a telling sentence.**

- **I also wrote a sentence that asks about our team. A sentence that asks about a person, place, animal, or thing is called an asking sentence.**

- **I used a capital letter at the beginning of each sentence. I used a period at the end of the telling sentence and a question mark at the end of the asking sentence.**

Guided Writing

Help children write telling or asking sentences about winning. Remind them to use the correct end punctuation.

Handwriting

Practice Writing *Yy*

Distribute writing paper and have children practice writing *Y* and *y*. Have children who are already proficient writing *y* and *Y* write *Yaks ate yams*.

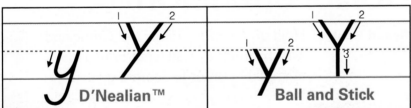

| D'Nealian™ | Ball and Stick |

Make up riddles with answers that are words that begin with /y/. Invite children to help you write the answer to the riddle on this week's panel of the ABC Wall after they guess it. Use riddles such as: *This word is the opposite of no.* (yes) *This word is the day before today.* (yesterday)

※ Meeting Individual Needs

Intervention

To help children who have difficulty writing letters, provide models of initial /y/ words, such as *yes, yam, yard,* and *yak*, that they can trace.

Optional Resources

Phonics Sourcebook pp. 76–77, 84–85

High-Frequency Word Cards

Phonics Workbook p. 147

Day 2

Full Day Options...

Independent Writing 🧍

Write About Winning
Encourage children to write a word to complete this sentence: *I felt like a winner when I ___.* Invite children to share their work with someone at home.

SCHOOL-HOME CONNECTION

Phonics 🧍🧍

Silly /y/ Sentences Together brain-storm a list of words with initial /y/. Ask partners to make up silly sentences in which many of the words begin with /y/.

Handwriting 🧍

Practice Have children choose one.

- Write *yellow yo-yo*. Draw a picture of a yellow yo-yo.
- Write this question: *Do yellow yaks yawn at you?*

Objectives

Children will

 describe characters and their feelings

 listen for the main idea of a rhyme

• listen for specific information

Oral Language

Listen for Main Idea

Say: *Every story, rhyme, and song tells about something.* Have children listen for what the rhyme "Come Out to Play" is about as you read it. After reading, ask:

• **What is the rhyme about?** (boys and girls coming out to play)

• **How do you know?** (The first sentence in the rhyme tells what the rhyme is about.)

Come Out to Play
a Mother Goose rhyme

Girls and boys, come out to play,
The moon doth shine as bright as day;

Leave your supper, and leave your sleep,
And come with your playfellows into the street.

Come with a whoop, come with a call,
Come with a good will or not at all.

Oral Language Chart 30

Ongoing Assessment

Listen for Main Idea

If... children have difficulty listening for the main idea of the rhyme,

then... reread two details of the rhyme and have children use the details to tell about the rhyme.

Comprehension

Recall Book's Theme

Hold up *Franklin Plays the Game* and ask children to recall what Franklin's team did in order to score a goal. (They learned to work as a team.) Divide children into groups of four and have each group act out the play that Franklin's team used to score their first goal.

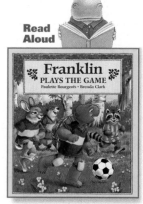

Read Aloud

Franklin PLAYS THE GAME
Paulette Bourgeois • Brenda Clark

Use Soccer Words in Sentences

Ask children what other sports have players on teams. Encourage them to answer with a complete sentence, using the word *team*. Repeat for *bounced, dribbled,* and *goal*.

Listen to Book for Information

Invite children to listen as you reread the trade book. Ask them to listen for clues about Franklin's feelings. While reading, you may wish to use the ideas in the *Guiding the Reading* and *Language Development* boxes on pages 205–209 of this Teacher's Edition.

Describe Main Character

Remind children that characters are the people or animals in stories and that characters can be real or make-believe. Ask:

- **Are the characters in this story real or make-believe?** (make-believe)

- **Who is the main character?** (Franklin, a turtle)

- **How did Franklin feel at the end of the first game? At the beginning of the second game?** (He was sad at the end of the game; He was excited before the next game.)

- **Was Franklin happy or sad at the end of the story?** (happy)

Tell children they are going to make a turtle. Have children trace and cut out a head and four feet from construction paper. Ask children to paste them onto a paper plate and then paste a bowl upside down on the plate. Invite children to decorate their turtle's shell by sponge painting. While turtles are drying, have children trace and cut out a soccer ball to glue on their turtle's head or foot.

Meeting Individual Needs
Other Ways to Learn

Auditory Children having difficulty with the characters in *Franklin Plays the Game* can listen to the selection audio several times as they look at the pictures in the book.

Self-Selected Reading

D.E.A.R. Drop Everything And Read

Have children choose their own books to read from your self-selected reading collection. Children might be interested in *Arthur's Nose* by Marc Brown.

Day 2

Full Day Options...

Character 👥

Describe Characters Gather familiar books whose covers show story characters. Showing one book at a time, ask children to tell what the cover illustration shows and help them recall the story characters. Ask: *Which story characters are make-believe? Which characters do things that could really happen?*

Oral Language 👥

Tell About Pictures Reread "Come Out to Play." Have children draw a picture to illustrate the rhyme. Encourage them to add details about the games the children will play or the sports equipment they will use. Ask children to describe their pictures.

Modeled Writing 👥

Write About Feelings Have each group find a picture of a person or animal that shows how the character feels. Ask each group to make up an asking sentence and a telling sentence about the character. For example, *Is the boy happy? Yes, the boy is happy.* Model writing the sentences on the board.

PHONICS

Meeting Individual Needs
Challenge

Invite children to make two-word phrases using one of the color words *red, yellow,* or *blue* and another word that begins with the same sound, for example, *red river, yellow yarn,* or *blue blankets.* You may wish to challenge children to expand their alliterative phrases into sentences.

Day 3

Phonemic Awareness

Choose Initial /y/ Words

Have Alphapotamus say: *I am collecting only words that begin with /y/. Help me choose the right words.* As Alphapotamus says the following words, have children say *yes* each time they hear a word that begins with /y/ and have them shake their heads *no* if it doesn't: *yak, watch, yarn, vest, yellow, nickel, yo-yo, yard, kitten, yawn, year.*

Ongoing Assessment

Phonemic Awareness

If... children have difficulty identifying words that begin with y/y/,

then... have Alphapotamus emphasize the initial sound of each word it names: /y/*ak,* /w/*atch.*

Connect Sound to Letter

Underline /y/ Words

Reread "The Yak" with children, tracking the print as you read. Invite volunteers to underline each word on the chart that begins with /y/ as they say the word.

CD 5/Tape 15, Side 2

Phonics Songs and Rhymes Audio

The Yak

Yak wears a hat of blue,
He yells to me and you.
He sings a Yankee Doodle doo
And yodels a yahoo.

Yak wants to eat some clams,
Yogurt, yolks, and yams.
He butters rolls with yellow jams
And eats lunch with the lambs.

Phonics Songs and Rhymes Chart 30

Phonological Awareness

Change Initial Sounds

Say: *Change the beginning sound in the word* tell *to /y/. What is the new word?* (yell) Write both words on the board and have a volunteer circle the beginning letter in each. Continue with: *ham, sank, card, barn, fellow.*

Phonics and High-Frequency Words

Read Kindergarten Reader 30

- Display Kindergarten Reader 30 and track the print as you read the title *Yes! We Get Wet!* Ask children to identify the word that begins with /y/.

- Do a picture walk and have children predict what the book will be about.

- Read the book aloud. Have children track the print with their fingers as you read.

Kindergarten Reader 30

Phonics Consonant *Yy*

High-Frequency Words
red, yellow, blue

I am Ben.
Look at my mom.
Yes, we like blue water.
2

Look at Dot.
Dot is a big blue whale.
3

I am Pam.
Yes, I have big teeth.
4

What can we see?
Yes, it is a little whale.
5

One whale can hop in
the red and yellow sun.
6

Look at what two whales
can do!
7

Blue whale   Beluga whale

Humpback whale   Orca

Yes! We get wet!
8

Modeled Writing

Model Writing Asking Sentences

Model writing using sentences based on Kindergarten Reader 30 *Yes! We Get Wet!* For example: *Is Dot a big blue whale?*

As you write the sentence, model these strategies:

- Begin the sentence with a capital letter.
- Use a question mark at the end because it is an asking sentence.

Guided Writing

Ask children to read the sentence with you. Have them write a telling sentence that answers the question. Compare the two sentences with children.

ABC Wall

Have children find *red, blue,* and *yellow* on the ABC Wall. Ask them to name other color words, and model writing them correctly.

Day
3

Optional Resources

Phonics Sourcebook
pp. 84–85

Phonics Workbook
p. 148

High-Frequency
Word Cards

Full Day Options...

Independent Writing 🚶

Write Telling Sentences Invite children to draw a picture of themselves playing a sport. Have them write or dictate a telling sentence about their picture.

Phonics 🚶🚶

Make a *Y* Poster Help groups cut out a large capital *Y* from construction paper. Have them decorate the letter by writing words or drawing pictures with names that begin with /y/. They may also cut out and paste magazine pictures on their letter.

Character 🚶

Create a Character Invite children to draw a detailed picture of a character they would like to write a story about. Encourage them to be creative and provide details that tell what their character is like. Invite volunteers to introduce their characters to the class.

READING

Oral Language

Discuss Listening for Main Idea

Remind children that stories, rhymes, and songs all tell about something. Ask children how they can tell what a story, rhyme, or song is about.

Listen to Find Main Idea

As you reread pages 26–31 of *Franklin Plays the Game,* have children listen for what this part of the story is about. After reading, ask: *What were these pages about?* Work together to summarize the main idea. (Players can do more as a team than they can do alone.)

Read Aloud

Franklin
PLAYS THE GAME
Paulette Bourgeois • Brenda Clark

Trade Book

Comprehension

Identify Characters from Clues

Recall and list with children the characters in *Franklin Plays the Game.* (Franklin, Goose, Beaver, Rabbit, Coach, Franklin's father, Bear) Ask:

- **Which characters thought they would never score a goal?** (Franklin, Goose, Beaver)

- **Which character didn't mind losing?** (Coach)

- **Which character felt that trying your best and having fun was the most important thing?** (Franklin's father)

- **Which character tried to make Franklin feel better about losing by saying "nice try"?** (Bear)

Ongoing Assessment

Character

If... children have difficulty matching a character to a question,

then... reread the relevant part of the story and ask the question again.

Objectives

Children will

 recognize characters

 listen for main ideas

- use illustrations to reinforce information
- use prewriting strategies

Day 3

Name _____

Franklin Plays the Game

Draw.

Check children's drawings.

Directions: Draw a picture to show what Franklin, Goose, Beaver, or Rabbit used for their special skill.

Home Activity: Ask your child to talk about the picture and tell you how the characters used their skills.

192 Comprehension: Character

Character
Practice Book, p. 192
Teacher's Resource Book, p. 192

Reader Response

Learn Information from Pictures

Show the illustrations on pages 19 and 28–29 of *Franklin Plays the Game*. Ask children to use the illustrations to answer these questions:

- **Why are Franklin and his teammates in a heap? How do they feel about this?** (They went for the ball at the same time; They feel sad.)

- **What did Franklin's team do in the second game? How do they feel now?** (They work together and score a goal; They feel happy.)

Model Writing Sentences

Ask children to act out how the players on Franklin's team handled the ball in the first game and in the second game. Write a sentence on the board such as *How did Franklin pass the ball?* As you write the sentence, model these strategies:

- Begin the sentence with a capital letter.

- Listen to the sounds in words and write the letters that stand for those sounds.

- Notice that when a sentence asks about a person, place, animal, or thing, it is an asking sentence.

- Use a question mark at the end because it is an asking sentence.

Self-Selected Reading D.E.A.R. Drop Everything And Read

From your self-selected reading collection, have children choose their own books to read. Children may enjoy reading other books about Franklin, such as *Franklin Rides a Bike* by Paulette Bourgeois.

❄ Meeting Individual Needs
Other Ways to Learn

Verbal Invite children to think of other animals that could be on Franklin's soccer team and what the animals could do to help the team score a goal. Encourage children to describe how these new characters might act and what they might say during practice.

Day 3

Full Day Options...

Independent Writing 🧍

Use Question Words Write *who, what, where, when, why,* and *how* on the board and read them aloud. Explain that many questions begin with these words. Ask children to dictate or write a question that begins with one of the words.

Character 👥

Draw That Character Give each group a description of one of the characters in *Franklin Plays the Game*. Ask the group to draw the character that fits the description. Let children refer to the book if they need help recalling the characters.

Oral Language 🧍

Retell a Story Part Ask children to draw a picture that illustrates part of the story *Franklin Plays the Game*. Invite them to use their pictures to retell part of the story.

Handwriting 🧍

Write y/y/ Words Have children look for y/y/ words on the ABC Wall. Let them practice writing the y/y/ words on lined paper.

PHONICS

Objectives

Children will

- recognize initial /y/
- delete phonemes to make new words
- use high-frequency words
- write complete sentences

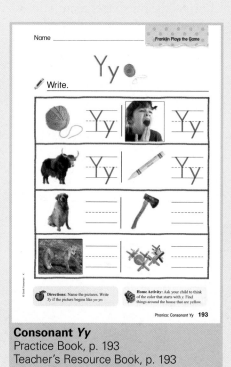

Consonant *Yy*
Practice Book, p. 193
Teacher's Resource Book, p. 193

Day 4

Daily Phonics Routine

Phonemic Awareness

Review Consonant x/ks/

Say: *I am going to say two words. Repeat the word that ends with /ks/.* Use these pairs of words: *hot/fox, mix/fit, ax/make, toy/box, wax/doll.*

Identify Initial /y/ or Final /ks/

Ask children to stand with their arms up and their legs together (like a Y) if they hear two words that begin with /y/ or to stand with their arms up and their legs apart (like an X) if they hear two words that end with /ks/. Have them practice both positions. Say these pairs of words: *yam/yellow, fox/box, mix/tax, yak/yell, six/wax, year/yes, young/you.*

Connect Sound to Letter

Identify Initial /y/ Words

Display picture cards for *yak, egg, yarn, x-ray, leg,* and *yellow.* Show the alphabet card for *Yy* and have children identify the picture and initial sound of its name. Hold the alphabet card above each picture. If the picture name starts with the same sound as *yo-yo,* children say *yes.* If the picture name has a different initial sound, they say *no* and a volunteer takes it down.

Ongoing Assessment

Connect Sound to Letter

If... children are having difficulty deciding if the name begins with y/y/,

then... repeat the name and ask: *Does it begin like* yo-yo?

Phonological Awareness

Delete Phonemes

Say the word *year.* Ask children what word they would make by taking away /y/: *Year without /y/ is ___.* (ear) Continue with *yam, sat, fit, bin.*

High-Frequency Words

Match Words to Colors

Ask children to draw and color a red, a yellow, and a blue square in any order on a large piece of paper. Give each child cards with the words *red, yellow,* and *blue* written on them. Have children match the word with the appropriate square. They can exchange papers and repeat.

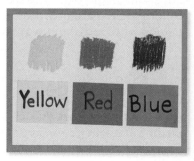

Interactive Writing

Review

Complete Sentences

Remind children that a complete sentence begins with a capital letter, ends with a punctuation mark, and tells a complete thought. Show page 5 of *Franklin Plays the Game.* Ask children to use a complete sentence to tell about the picture; for example, *Franklin kicks the ball.*

Write Complete Sentences

Write incomplete sentences on the board, such as *plays soccer, The team, The parents.* Read the phrases and ask children to tell if these are complete sentences and to explain why or why not. Have them suggest ways to complete the sentences by adding naming words (nouns) or action words (verbs). Ask volunteers to write what they can; help them with the rest. Read the sentences together.

> plays soccer
> The team
> The parents

Ongoing Assessment

Writing

If... children have trouble completing a sentence,

then... ask them to see if any of the phrases could go together to make a complete sentence: *The team / plays soccer.*

Meeting Individual Needs
Challenge

Display *Red and Blue Play Soccer* and ask volunteers to identify the title, the author, and the illustrator. As you read the book with children, encourage them to look for familiar words. You may wish to assign a consonant or vowel sound to children and have them search for words with the sound.

Independent Reader 30

Optional Resources

Phonics Sourcebook pp. 1–78, 84–85, 86–129

Phonics Workbook, p. 149

High-Frequency Word Cards

Day 4

Full Day Options...

Independent Writing

Use a Writing Journal Ask children to imagine they are sports superstars. Encourage them to write or dictate and illustrate a narrative sentence in their writing journals about their best imaginary play.

Phonics

Revisit Kindergarten Reader 30, *Yes! We Get Wet!* For more practice in high-frequency word recognition, have children reread *Yes! We Get Wet!* Let them take turns reading aloud the pages.

Kindergarten Reader 30

Phonics

Shared Poetry Help children reread "The Yak," one line at a time. After reading a line, ask children to hold up their fingers to indicate the number of words they read which began with *y.*

Phonics Songs and Rhymes Chart 30

 **READING**

Objectives

Children will

- ◎ recall and describe characters
- ◎ listen for the main idea of a poem

✻ Meeting Individual Needs

ESL

Have children act out how the characters felt at different points in the story. For example, say: *Show me how Buddy's parents felt when he didn't listen. Show me how Buddy felt when he thought the Scruffy Varmint was going to make soup out of him.*

Day 4

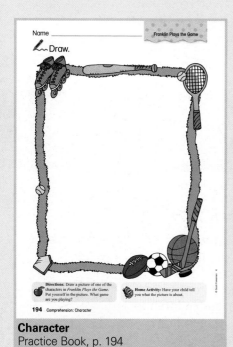

Name _____ Franklin Plays the Game

✎ Draw.

Directions: Draw a picture of one of the characters in *Franklin Plays the Game*. Put yourself in the picture. What game are you playing?

Home Activity: Have your child tell you what the picture is about.

194 Comprehension: Character

Character
Practice Book, p. 194
Teacher's Resource Book, p. 194

Comprehension

Activate Prior Knowledge

Display *Listen Buddy* from this unit. Ask:

> **Who are the characters in the story?** (Buddy, his parents, the Scruffy Varmint)

Reread *Listen Buddy.* After reading, ask:

> **What is Buddy's problem?** (He doesn't listen.)

Read Aloud

HELEN LESTER
Listen Buddy
Illustrated by
LYNN MUNSINGER

Trade Book

⊙ Assess Character

To assess children's understanding of character, ask children questions about the characters in *Listen Buddy:*

- **Whose big ears didn't help him listen?** (Buddy's)
- **Which characters felt puzzled and frustrated by Buddy?** (his parents, the Scruffy Varmint)
- **Who learned an important lesson?** (Buddy)

Ongoing Assessment

Character

If... children have difficulty with characters,	**then...** use the Character reteaching lesson on page AR21 of this Teacher's Edition.

Oral Language

Establish a Purpose for Listening

Remind children that every story, rhyme, or poem tells about something. Ask them to listen for what the poem is about as you read "The Playful Crickets."

Read Aloud

The Playful Crickets

A grasshopper once had a game of tag
With some crickets that lived near by,
When he stubbed his toe, and over he went
Too quick to see with your eye.

So off he went, though he wanted to stay,
For he was not hurt by the fall;
And the little crickets went on with their play,
And never missed him at all.

Ask volunteers to act out what happens in the first verse of the poem. Then ask: *What is this verse about?* (A grasshopper hurts himself playing a game of tag with his friends.)

Ask volunteers to act out what happens in the second verse of the poem. Ask: *What is this verse about?* (The grasshopper leaves and the crickets don't even miss him.)

Then help children combine their answers to tell what the whole poem is about. (A grasshopper hurts himself while playing tag and leaves, but the crickets he was playing with don't even notice he's gone.)

Ongoing Assessment

Listen for the Main Idea

If... children have trouble identifying the main idea of the rhyme,	**then...** ask them to retell the rhyme in their own words, two lines at a time, and help them use their retelling to tell what the entire poem is about.

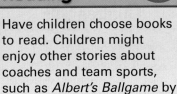

Self-Selected Reading

D.E.A.R. Drop Everything And Read

Have children choose books to read. Children might enjoy other stories about coaches and team sports, such as *Albert's Ballgame* by Leslie Tryon.

Optional Resources

Assessment Handbook

Full Day Options...

Character

Make Puppets Have each child make a finger or stick puppet of a favorite story character. Ask children to identify the character and use them to show what the character did in the story.

DRAMA CONNECTION Act 1

Oral Language

Recall Main Idea Display some of the trade books and big books children have read this year. Have children take turns choosing a book and retelling the story. When a child has finished retelling a story, the group decides the main idea, or what the story tells about.

Oral Language

Listen for Main Idea Review with children the book *Listen Buddy.* Talk about what happens in the story. Help children formulate the main idea. (It is important to listen carefully and follow directions.)

Independent Writing

Ask and Answer Questions One partner dictates or writes an asking sentence, and the other dictates or writes a telling sentence that answers the question. Then the partners reverse roles.

Day 4

PHONICS A-Z

Daily Phonics Routine

Prepare to Assess

Phonemic Awareness

/y/ /a/ /k/

Have Alphapotamus say /y/ /a/ /k/. Ask children to say the word by blending the sounds together: *yak.* Continue with /y/ /a/ /m/, /y/ /e/ /l/, /y/ /e/ /s/.

Assess y/y/

Connect Sound to Letter

Have children write *Y* and *y* on an index card. Tell them if they hear a word that begins with /y/, to hold up their card. Say: *yam, yo-yo, button, yellow, van, you, water, yarn.*

Ongoing Assessment

Phonics

If... children have difficulty identifying words that begin with /y/,	then... use the Consonant *Yy* reteaching activities on page AR20 of this Teacher's Edition.

Count the Syllables

Phonological Awareness

Model how to clap the syllables you hear in the words *year* and *Yoki.* Then have children clap the syllables they hear in the words *yard, yellow, yesterday, yell,* and *yummy.* Write the words and divide them so that children can see the number of syllables in each word.

High-Frequency Words

Assess

Ask children to draw or cut out pictures of red, yellow, and blue objects. Have them paste their pictures on a large sheet of paper and label each picture with the color word and the naming word, or noun. Let children share their pictures.

red apple

yellow duck

blue car

Independent Writing

Assess Writing Development

Remind children that in *Franklin Plays the Game* the characters play soccer. Tell children they are going to write a note to a friend about playing a sport or a game.

Think ALOUD

I'll write to my friend and ask if she likes baseball. I am going to write "Do you like to play baseball?"

Remind children that an asking sentence asks about a person, place, animal, or thing and begins with a capital letter and ends with a question mark.

Have children write a note to a friend. Encourage them to use both asking and telling sentences. Have them write their friend's name at the beginning and their name at the end. You may wish to assess each piece of work using the scoring guide.

Select Work for Portfolio

Invite children to select personal work to add to their portfolios.

Optional Resources

Phonics Sourcebook pp. 84–85

High-Frequency Word Cards

Phonics Workbook p. 150

Assessment Handbook

Shared Writing

Add to the Class Diary

Help children recall things they have done during the week. Ask questions about their activities and encourage detailed responses. Add the pages to the class diary.

Full Day Options...

Phonics 👥

Make /y/ Books Give children several sheets of paper and have them draw and label pictures of objects with names beginning with /y/ on each sheet. Add a construction paper cover, punch holes through all the sheets, and tie them together with ribbon or yarn to make a book.

Independent Writing 🧍

Write About Franklin Ask children to draw a picture of Franklin doing something else besides playing soccer. Have them write a narrative sentence telling what he is doing.

Reading 🧍

Read Aloud Ask children who have beginning reading skills to read *Red and Blue Play Soccer* aloud to you. Listen for evidence of sound blending and decoding strategies.

Independent Reader 30

Day **5**

Comprehension

Review
Author's Purpose

Remind children that authors write stories for different reasons. Say: *Sometimes the authors want to entertain us. Sometimes they want to give us information. Sometimes they want to teach a lesson.* Ask children to think about the author's purpose as you read the story "Why the Monkey and the Turtle Are Cold at Night." After reading, ask:

Read Aloud

TE Volume 5, p. AR9

- **Why do you think the author wrote "Why the Monkey and the Turtle Are Cold at Night"?** (to entertain; to teach a lesson)

- **What lesson do you think the author wanted to teach?** (why it is foolish to be lazy and put off doing things)

Ongoing Assessment

Author's Purpose

If... children cannot decide what the author's purpose for writing was,	**then...** prompt them with questions such as *Did the story make you laugh? What do you think the monkey and the turtle should have done? Did you learn a lesson?*

Draw a New Ending

Ask children to think about another way the story could have ended. Have children draw a new ending for the story. Let children take turns sharing their pictures and explaining the new ending.

Oral Language

Review
Speak Well

Remind children that it is important to speak clearly and not too loudly or too softly. Review other speaking rules such as: don't pause in the middle of sentences, don't repeat words, and don't use unnecessary words or sounds such as *umm* or *uh*.

My Little Book

Send home this unit's *My Little Book.*

My Little Book

This little book belongs to

Child's name

should go here

Directions: *Write your first and last name.*

Practice Book, p. 195–196
Teachers Resource Book, p. 195–196

Practice Speaking Well

Reread what the monkey and the turtle said to each other every night. Have pairs of children act out the conversation between the monkey and the turtle.

Remind children of the rules for speaking well. Encourage partners to keep the rules in mind as they practice the dialogue. Suggest that children use appropriate tones of voice, gestures, and expressions. Let pairs take turns performing before the whole class.

Self-Selected Reading

Help children look for books that they can read independently. One book you might suggest is *Bedtime for Frances* by Russell Hoban.

Full Day Options...

Phonics

Same Sound Sentences Give a volunteer a letter and the sound the letter stands for. The child makes up a sentence in which all or most of the words begin with that letter and sound. For example, for y/y/, a child might say: *A yellow yak yells yahoo!*

Author's Purpose

Decide Author's Purpose Review with children *Franklin Plays the Game.* Ask: *Why do you think the author wrote the story?* (to entertain; to teach a lesson) *What lesson did the author want to teach?* (If people work together as a team, they can achieve their goal.)

Oral Language

Practice Speaking Well Ask volunteers to speak to the class about a lesson they learned on their own, from another person, or from a book. Prompt children with questions such as these: *What have you learned about sharing? What have you learned about helping others? What have you learned about being a good friend?*

Reading

Reader Response: "Why the Monkey and the Turtle Are Cold at Night" Recall with children that when the turtle was warm during the day, he thought it was a waste of time to make himself a coat. Ask: *What would you have done if you were the monkey? If the monkey really wanted to make a coat, what could he have done?*

TE Volume 5, p. AR9

Day
5

Storytelling

Children Will

- listen responsively to stories that are told or read aloud
- examine and explore the point of view of the storyteller
- engage in creating and telling a variety of new story plots

Create an Adventure Story

An adventure is an exciting or unusual experience. Stories in which characters have exciting or unusual experiences are called adventure stories.

Listen Buddy

Discuss What It's Like to Have an Adventure

Encourage children to share exciting or unusual experiences they have had. Perhaps they have experienced a blizzard or a hurricane. Perhaps they have gone hiking or camping in a remote area. Ask: *How did you feel while you were having your adventure? How did you feel after the adventure was over?* Relate an adventure of your own and point out that you too felt excited and scared, then relieved and pleased.

Recall Buddy's and Other Adventures

Have children recall the adventure Buddy had in the story *Listen Buddy.* You may want to prompt children by asking questions such as these:

- **Did Buddy plan on having an adventure?** (No, it happened accidentally because he forgot which way he was supposed to go.)

- **How did Buddy feel while he was with the Scruffy Varmint?** (excited, eager to help, curious, then very scared)

- **Do you think Buddy enjoyed his adventure?** (no) **Do you think he will go looking for more adventures? Why or why not?** (No, he got into trouble on his adventure, so he may not want to have any more.)

Create "Further Adventures"

Explain that even though Buddy may not want to have any more adventures, they can happen unexpectedly—whether we want them to or not! Encourage children to use their imaginations. Have them use page 232 to draw a picture of another adventure that they think Buddy could have. Post the pictures on a bulletin board titled "The Further Adventures of Buddy."

From Another Point of View

A Storyteller's Decision

What if the Scruffy Varmint told the story? How do you think he would describe his adventure with Buddy? The skill of telling a story from a different point of view may be new to most children. Offer the following as a possible story beginning:

> Grrr, I'm the Scruffy Varmint, and I live in a cave in the woods. People say I have a nasty temper, but really I just like being on my own. And anyhow visitors can be so annoying! Why, just the other day this little bunny rabbit came to my cave. Right away he asked the silliest question about my soup pot.

As a group, retell the rest of the adventure from the Scruffy Varmint's point of view.

Students as Storytellers

Choose an activity for children to practice storytelling skills.

Animal Story

Help children create a story about an animal character by asking them to select a favorite animal and give this animal a name. Think about a possible adventure that animal might have. Encourage children to tell their stories to a partner or a small group.

"Oops" Stories

Buddy found himself in quite a tricky situation in this story because he went somewhere he should not have gone. Many clever and creative stories have been told about these kinds of tricky situations. Such stories might be called *"oops" stories.* Share with children a situation you once experienced that caused you to say *"oops."*

School-Home Connection

Have children ask family members to tell about a favorite adventure story. Suggest that children ask the narrators to choose the most exciting or unusual part of the story.

Name _____

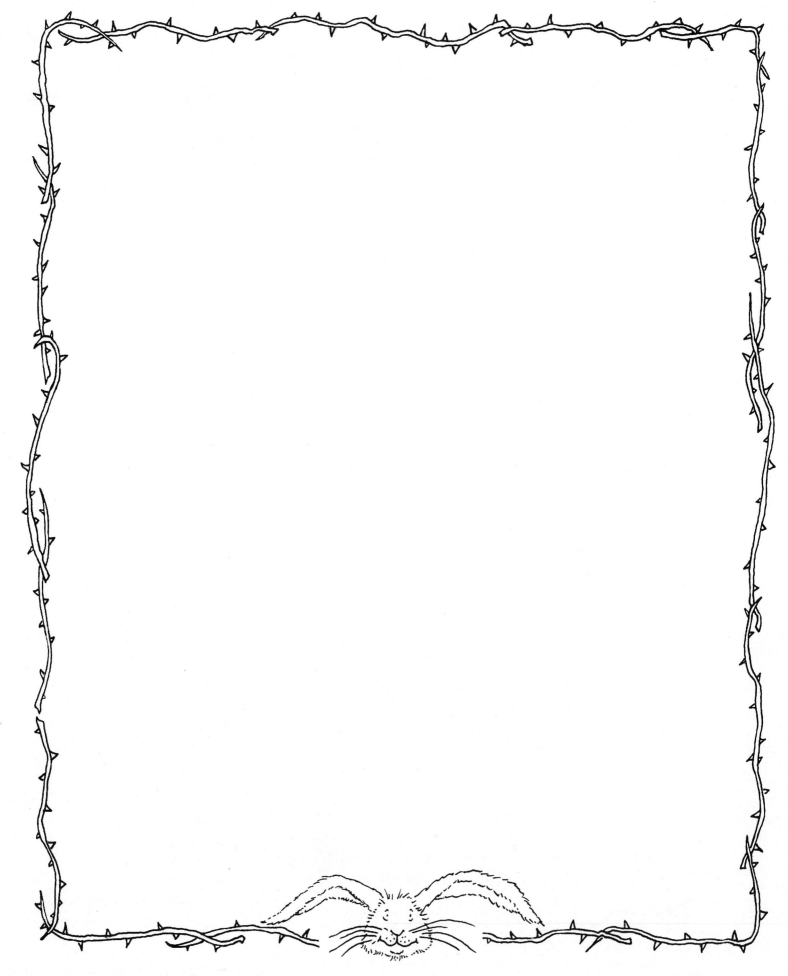

Additional Resources
Table of Contents

Objectives

Children will
- classify
- draw conclusions
- identify author's purpose
- identify sequence of events

Assess Reading Comprehension Development

Display the books read in this unit. Invite children to tell the sequence of events of each one and why the author wrote it. Have children find a variety of ways to classify and categorize the stories. Encourage them to make a general statement about each category.

Sequence Have children review the story *The Three Little Pigs* or some other familiar story. Have children tell what the story is about. Then have them act out the story, telling the events in order.

 Listen for children's ability to classify stories. Also assess children's ability to identify author's purpose and to draw conclusions.

Objectives

Children will
- name and identify letters
- identify letter-sound correspondences *j, v, qu, x, y*
- recognize short *e*, phonograms *-et, -en,* and rhyming words

Assess Phonics Development

Say the word *jet* and ask children to name the letter for the beginning sound. Have volunteers write the letter on the chalkboard. Continue with *yet, quit,* and *vet.*

Phonograms -et, -en Write *t_n* on the chalkboard and say the word *ten.* Have children read the words and write the letter for the vowel sound. Continue with *p_t, m_n, b_d,* and *l_g.* Then point to the word *ten* and have children name words that rhyme. As each word is named, have a volunteer write the word on the chalkboard. Continue with words that rhyme with *pet.*

 Listen for children's ability to identify the letter that stands for the beginning sound, to write the letter that stands for the sound, and to use phonograms to make rhyming words.

Objectives

Children will
- retell a message
- listen for rhyme
- speak well and with proper grammar
- listen for main idea

Assess Oral Language Development

Show a picture of some activity involving people. Give a brief message about the picture, including the main idea as well as some details. Ask what the picture is all about and help children state the main idea. Then ask children to tell if they think the people in the picture are having fun and if they would like to do the activity. Encourage discussion among group members.

 Observe children's ability to listen carefully, listen for main idea, and to retell the message using proper grammar.

Objectives

Children will
- add *-s* to verbs
- recognize past tense verbs
- identify asking and telling sentences
- orally distinguish complete and incomplete sentences
- recognize sentences in print

Assess Written Language Development

Have children fold a paper into two sections. Ask children to draw a simple picture showing what they did yesterday and will do tomorrow. Encourage children to dictate complete sentences about the pictures. Ask children to circle the capital letters that begin the sentences and the ending punctuation marks. Children should determine whether the sentences are asking or telling, complete or incomplete.

 Check children's ability to recognize and use verbs in sentences and identify the verb in the sentence they created.

Unit 5 Skill Development Checklist

Student Name	Matches spoken to printed words	Identifies a written sentence	Identifies some high-frequency words	Classifies	Draws conclusions	Identifies author's purpose	Identifies sequence of events
			Concepts of Print			Comprehension	
1							
2							
3							
4							
5							
6							
7							
8							
9							
10							
11							
12							
13							
14							
15							
16							
17							
18							
19							
20							
21							
22							
23							
24							
25							

Unit 5 Skill Development Checklist

	Phonics — Knows letter–sound correspondences:						Oral Language			Writing and Grammar	
j	v	qu	x	y	short e	Listens for rhyming and main idea	Retells a message	Speaks well and with proper grammar	Recognizes past tense	Identifies asking and telling sentences	Distinguishes complete and incomplete sentences

May be reproduced for classroom use.

The Lion and the Mouse (a fable)

Everyone knows that the lion is the king of the jungle. He is the most feared of all the jungle animals because of his power and his strength. That is why on this particular day, a young mouse did a very foolish thing. She ran right over the nose of a big, sleeping lion.

Now the lion had been sleeping peacefully out in the sun, so when the mouse ran over his nose he woke up. He smacked his huge paw right over the mouse. Then he roared a fearsome roar. He really did hate having someone wake him when he was taking a nap. He peeked under his paw at the mouse, who was trembling with fright. "Well, well," said the lion, "you will make a tasty snack for me now that I am awake."

The mouse in her bravest voice begged, "Oh, please, mighty lion, don't eat me. Spare my life, and some day I will do a kind deed for you."

"That's ridiculous," said the lion. "You're only a tiny mouse, and I, well, I am a mighty lion. What could you possibly do to help me?"

"I don't know," said the mouse, "but some day you may need my help. It couldn't hurt to have a little friend who is willing to help you."

The lion started to laugh. "I doubt if you could ever help me, but I think you are brave. I will let you go."

The lion lifted his mighty paw, and the grateful mouse scurried away. As she did, she called back to the lion, "I won't forget my promise."

A few days later, the mouse heard a terrible, sad roar. "That is the lion," she said. "Something must be wrong." She hurried toward the sound.

At last she found the lion. He was caught in a huge net that had been set out by hunters to trap lions.

When the lion saw the mouse, he said, "This is the end of me. The hunters will be back soon. When they come back, they will take me away from the jungle."

"Don't worry," said the mouse. "I know just what to do." She set to work gnawing on the ropes of the net with her sharp teeth. Soon she had chewed a hole in the net large enough for the lion to escape.

The lion was very grateful to the mouse. But the mouse just said, "I promised I would repay you, and I did, even though I am small." Then she said, "An act of kindness always comes back to you. If you help someone, some day you will be rewarded."

The Tortoise and the Hare

Once upon a time in a great field, there lived a hare and a tortoise. Tortoise was slow in everything he did. He sometimes ate breakfast so slowly that it was almost lunchtime before he had finished.

Hare, on the other hand, was quick in everything he did. He would be up in the morning, finished with breakfast, and out for a walk before Tortoise had gotten out of bed.

Tortoise spent his afternoons in the field painting pictures of the flowers, the trees, and the stream. He worked slowly, but his pictures were beautiful.

Hare thought painting a picture was boring. "That Tortoise is so dull," he would say. Hare enjoyed leaping around the field and rushing from house to house to visit his friends. Hare was a nice fellow, but he had one problem. He was sure he was the smartest, fastest, most handsome animal in all the land. And he would always tell his friends how wonderful he was.

Tortoise never bragged about himself. He knew that he was not particularly handsome and that he was very slow, but he did not mind. He was happy to spend his time working hard, painting his pictures at his own slow pace.

One day Hare met Tortoise in the field. "You are such a slowpoke, Tortoise. I could beat you at anything. Just name something, and I'll win it."

"All right," said Tortoise. "How about a race?"

"What an idea!" Hare thought to himself. He said, "Okay, Tortoise, you're on!"

On the day of the race, all the animals in the field gathered to watch. Tortoise and Hare stepped up to the starting line. Tortoise looked nervous, but Hare was smiling and waving at the crowd. He couldn't wait to show off for all of his friends.

Finally, the whistle blew and the race was on! Hare dashed across the starting line. He had disappeared over the first hill before Tortoise had gone three feet. But Tortoise kept going, slowly, slowly, up the very steep path.

Hare ran until he was sure he would win. "This is hardly a race!" he said to himself. "I can take a little rest and still have plenty of time to spare. There's no way that slowpoke will ever catch up to me!" So he lay down under a shady tree and soon fell fast asleep.

Suddenly, Hare awoke with a start. He could hear cheering. He leaped up and began running as fast as his long legs would carry him. But it was too late. Before Hare could get there, Tortoise had crossed the finish line and won the race!

The crowd cheered and cheered. They ran to the finish line to congratulate Tortoise. The wise old owl winked at Hare and said, "Slow and steady wins the race."

Sunshine Stories

Wind and Rain were arguing about who would tell a story. "Silence!" said Sunshine. "Today, I will tell a story!" And she spoke with glory and majesty.

"A beautiful swan flew over the sea. I shone on her feathers and they glittered like gold. One feather fell off and a young man on a ship found it. It became a pen and he wrote such wonderful stories that he became a wealthy merchant. I shone on his many riches."

"The swan flew over a green meadow where a little shepherd boy was asleep under a tree. The swan flew by and caused a leaf to fall into the boy's hand. The leaf turned into a book. The boy read this book and learned all about the wonders of the world. He spent his life reading and became a wise man. And I shone on him."

"The golden swan became tired and stopped to rest near a lake. A poor woman was gathering firewood nearby. She saw the swan fly away, leaving something glittering behind. It was an egg!"

"As the woman watched, the egg cracked open. There was a baby swan with four gold rings on its neck. The little swan soon flew away, leaving behind the rings. The woman took the rings home. She kissed the golden rings and gave them to her sons. I shone on this poor woman and her sons, and great things happened to them. The first boy took a lump of clay and shaped it into a wonderful statue. The second boy became a great painter. The third boy held his ring in his teeth and it made a song. He became a great composer of music."

"The fourth boy, who was the smallest, got a warm, sunny kiss from me. His body and mind were strengthened and he became a tremendous poet."

"I saw all this," said Sunshine.

"What a long, boring story!" said Wind.

"How tiresome!" said Rain.

"You may think so," said Sunshine. "But look at the lives that were changed because of the swan. They are not boring. They are full of excitement."

How Matti Almost Taught the Bear to Play the Fiddle

Once upon a time, there were two brothers. The older brother was called Toivo. He was hard working but gloomy. He never smiled or sang. While he fished or chopped down trees, he was silent.

The younger brother was called Matti. He was a good boy too, but he was full of fun. He loved to play jokes and tricks. Whenever Matti set to work, he sang a song. He laughed on his way to the river. When he played his fiddle, people would begin to dance.

One day Toivo went to the forest for some wood. He chose a pine tree and set to work. He chopped until sparks flew. The forest filled with the loud noise of chopping.

The noise woke a bear who was sleeping in his den nearby. "Who's that banging about and keeping me awake?" growled the bear. He crawled out of his den.

When Toivo saw the bear, he dropped his ax and fled like a scared rabbit. He came home with no ax and no wood.

It was cold and there was no wood for a fire. So Matti set off for the forest. He soon found the pine tree and ax. "This is where Toivo was chopping wood," thought Matti. "I will get to work, but first I will play my fiddle a bit."

The forest rang with cheerful sounds. The bear again awoke. He sprang up and began to dance. He danced and danced. He called out to Matti, "Young man, please teach me to play the fiddle too!"

Matti laughed, "Why not? Just try!"

The bear tried hard to play the fiddle, but he made an awful screeching noise.

Matti said, "Your fingers are too fat, bear. We must make them thinner."

He made a cut in the tree and held it open with a wedge. "Stick your paws in here," he said. The bear put his paws in and Matti pulled out the wedge. The cut closed up and pinched the bear's paws.

"Ouch! It hurts!" cried the bear.

Matti said, "I will let you out if you promise to stop frightening people and chasing them from the forest."

"Yes, I will! Please let me out!"

So Matti released the bear. The bear went back to his home in the forest and never frightened anyone again.

The Fox and the Crow

A crow sat on the top branch of a tree, holding a delicious piece of cheese in her beak. A fox came along and saw the crow. He was hungry and he wanted that piece of cheese. But foxes cannot fly to the tops of trees. The fox could not get it from her. So he had to think of a way to trick the crow into letting him have the cheese.

"Hello, beautiful crow," he called up to her. "You have the shiniest feathers I have ever seen. How lovely you are! And what sparkling eyes you have! You must have a wonderful voice that matches your beauty. If I can hear just one song from you, I will be able to tell all the other animals that you are truly the Queen of Birds."

The crow was far from being the most beautiful of all the birds. And many animals had told her that they did not like to hear her voice because she squawked. But she believed every word the fox said.

"He wants to hear my voice!" she thought. "The others say they don't like it, but he thinks it must be wonderful because I am so beautiful!"

With that, the crow opened her beak to sing—and the cheese fell from her mouth down to the fox.

"My dear," the fox said to her. "Don't believe everything you hear!"

Why the Monkey and the Turtle Are Cold at Night

One rainy night, deep in the rain forest, a monkey and a turtle were huddled beneath a tree, complaining about how cold they were.

"Brrrrrrr!" said the monkey. "I'm freeeeeezing."

"Me-e-e-e too-oo-oo," replied the turtle, shivering with cold.

Finally, they both agreed that the next day, as soon as the sun came up, they would chop down a tree and make themselves warm coats from its bark. But the next morning, when the sun came up, it warmed them both so nicely that the monkey climbed to the top of a tree and took a nap in the warm sunshine. The turtle found a spot on a log and sunned himself the entire afternoon.

The monkey woke up later that afternoon and climbed down from the tree to find his friend. He found the turtle still sunning himself in a clearing in the forest.

"Hey there, Turtle, how are you?" the monkey asked.

"Just fine! Excellent!" replied the turtle.

"What about the coats? Are we going to make them, like we said we would last night?" inquired the monkey.

The turtle looked up at the monkey and laughed. "That's a silly idea! What do we need coats for? We're warm enough, aren't we?"

The monkey agreed, so they continued to sun themselves the rest of the day. But unfortunately the day became night, and the moment the sun went down, it began raining and became very cold again. And just like they did the night before, the monkey and the turtle huddled beneath a tree and complained about the cold.

"Brrrrrrr!" said the monkey. "I'm freeeeeezing."

"Me-e-e-e too-oo-oo," replied the turtle, shivering with cold.

And, just like the night before, they both agreed that the next day, as soon as the sun came up, they would chop down a tree and make themselves warm coats from its bark. But once again, when the sun came up and warmed them both, they forgot all about making coats.

And so it went, day after day. And the lazy animals are still lazy to this very day. When it's cold and rainy at night, they huddle under a tree and complain about the cold and promise to make themselves warm coats the next day; and when the sun comes up and warms them both, they are lazy again and do nothing.

PHONICS A Z

Consonant Jj

Objectives

Children will

- identify the sound /j/
- know the sounds of the letters of the alphabet
- learn letter-sound correspondence: /j/ to *j*

Develop Phonemic Awareness

Identify /j/

Show the picture cards *jam* and *jet*. Exaggerate /j/ as you name each picture. Then say: *These words begin with* /j/. Have children say *jam* and *jet* with you, exaggerating /j/.

Picture Cards

Display picture cards *jacket, jacks, jar, jug, button, penguin, map, soccer, lollipop,* and *mask.* Let children find the pictures whose names begin with /j/ and exaggerate the /j/ as they say each name.

Say /j/

Show children how to say /j/ by rounding the lips and opening them slightly while pressing the tongue against the closed teeth. Air is forced out of the mouth, causing the teeth to part. With children, practice saying /j/ by asking them to repeat the silly sentence *June juggles jelly jars.*

Segment and Blend /j/ Words

Say: *Listen to the* /j/ *sound at the beginning of this word.*

- Segment *jet* by saying /j/ /et/ several times.
- Now blend the sounds together by saying *jet.* Ask children to identify the word.

Repeat the activity with *jug* and *jam.*

Connect Sound to Letter

Connect /j/ to *j*

Display *Animal ABCs* big book. Say: *Jellyfish,* /j/ *ellyfish, jellyfish.* The first sound in jellyfish is /j/. Point to *Jj.* Say: *This is the letter that show the sound* /j/: *j,* /j/, *jellyfish.*

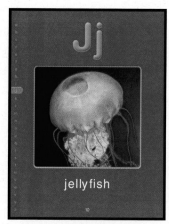
Big Book

Identify *j*

Display the word *jam* on the back of the *jam* picture card. Point to *j* and ask what letter is at the beginning of *jam.* Then write the names of children on the board whose first or last name begins with *j.* Add other names to the list, such as *Joe* and *Johnson,* and have volunteers circle the *j's.*

Classifying

Understand Classifying

Have available some new and some well used crayons. Have two green, two red, and two blue. Then say: *Let's sort these crayons in some way.* Ask:

• **How can we sort these so they're all alike in some way?** (by color, by new and old, by length)

Let volunteers sort the crayons according to the suggestions given. When they've been sorted, select one group and ask:

• **How are all these crayons alike?** (Possible answers: They are all blue. They are all short.)

Explain that putting things that are alike together in some way is called classifying.

Practice Classifying

Use the picture cards *cap, hat, jacket, necklace, ring, sock, vest.* Display the cards and have the pictures named. Ask:

• **How are these pictures all alike?** (They are all things to wear.)

Then say: *Let's classify, or sort, these things.* Write the headings *Clothes* and *Jewelry* on the board and read them. Then have children sort the pictures by telling in which group each picture should be placed. (Clothes: cap, hat, jacket, sock, vest; Jewelry: necklace, ring)

Apply Classifying to the Big Book

Display big book *Jump into the Jungle.* Draw two columns on the board. Then say: *Let's make a list of things we will read about in the book.* Write *Animals* and *Actions* as headings for the columns. Read the headings.

Big Book

Reread the book. Ask:

• **What animals did you hear about?** (insects, lions, frogs, cheetah, parrots)

• **What did they do?** (jump, buzz, roar, leap, bump, jump, sing, flap, stretch)

Write children's responses under the correct headings. Read the two lists with the class. Point out that they have classified, or sorted, information from the book *Jump into the Jungle.*

Objectives

Children will

 identify the sound /v/
- know the sounds of the letters of the alphabet
- learn letter-sound correspondence: /v/ to *v*

Consonant Vv

Develop Phonemic Awareness

Identify /v/

Show the picture cards *van* and *vest*. Name each picture as you hold up the picture card. Next point again to *van* and *vest,* saying /v/ several times before saying the name of the picture.

Now display *van* and *button*. Identify the new picture as *button*. Ask: *Which word starts with /v/,* button *or* van?

Repeat using *vest* and *duck*.

Say /v/

Show children how to say /v/ by placing the lower lip slightly under the upper teeth. Together repeat the silly sentence *View vegetable vines* a number of times. Children should be able to feel their lower lip vibrate as they say /v/.

Segment and Blend /v/ Words

Use three fingers to help children see the number of phonemes you are saying as well as hear them. Each finger will represent a phoneme in the word *van*.

- Segment *van* by saying /v/, /a/, /n/. Segment the word again and hold up a finger each time you say a sound until you have three fingers raised. Repeat this several times. Then ask children to segment, using their fingers as they do.

- Now blend the sounds. Lower all three fingers. Say *van*. As you do, quickly raise each finger one-by-one. Repeat this several times. Then let children blend.

Repeat the activity with other words that begin with *v*.

Connect Sound to Letter

Connect /v/ to *v*

Open the *Animal ABCs* big book to *Vv*. Say: *This bird is a vulture. The first sound in vulture is /v/. Listen for the /v/ as I say* vulture. Have children say *vulture*.

Point to the letters *Vv*. Say: *This is the letter that shows the /v/ sound*. Point to the letters, say /v/, then say *vulture*.

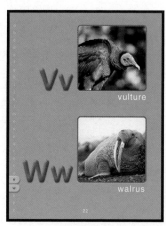

Vv
vulture

Ww
walrus

Big Book

Drawing Conclusions

Understand Drawing Conclusions

Use the following situations to help children draw conclusions. Say: *Listen to what I will read. Think about what is happening. Then listen to the question I will ask.*

- A cat is stuck in a tree. A man with a ladder walks by. What will the man do? (rescue the cat)

- Children and a teacher are on a field trip. They hear a lion roar. Where is the class? (at a zoo)

Explain: *You used information you already know to help you answer questions that the story doesn't answer for you. This is drawing conclusions.*

Practice Drawing Conclusions

Make a simple drawing on the board of a car with a flat tire. Ask:

Why will Mom have to wait to drive the car?
(because the tire is flat)

Explain to children that when they use information they already know to help them answer questions not answered in a picture or story, they are drawing conclusions.

Apply Drawing Conclusions to the Trade Book

Reread *Listen Buddy*. Ask:

What is Buddy's problem?
(He doesn't listen.)

Trade Book

Point out that it doesn't say anywhere in the story that Buddy doesn't listen. Help children see that they were able to draw that conclusion because of what they already know about listening and because of what Buddy does in the story.

Reteach

Objectives

Children will

- identify the sound /kw/
- know the sounds of the letters of the alphabet
- learn letter-sound correspondence: /kw/ to *qu*

Consonant Qq

Develop Phonemic Awareness

Identify /kw/
Show picture cards *queen* and *turkey*. Say the words as you point to the pictures. As you point to *queen*, say /qu/ several times. Then say *queen* and *turkey* again. Ask: *Which word starts with /qu/, queen* or *turkey?*

Picture Cards

Continue the activity with picture cards *quarter, sun; quilt, saw.*

Say /kw/
Explain that /kw/ is made up of two sounds that children already know, blended together. For /k/, press the back of the tongue against the back of the roof of the mouth. Round the lips. As the air moves forward, quickly pull the lips down and back for the /w/ part. Have children practice saying the sounds with the phrase *queen's quilts.*

Segment and Blend /kw/ Words
Give each child four math markers, two red, one yellow, and one blue. Explain that the markers will help children listen for the sounds in *quit.*

- Say *quit*, segmenting the word by saying /kw/, /i/, /t/. Segment the word again. This time, place the two red markers together on a table for /kw/, the yellow for /i/, and the blue for /t/. The two red markers should be close together. Have children repeat the activity.

- Now blend the sounds as you push the markers together and say *quit*. Have children do the same.

Connect Sound to Letter

Connect /kw/ to *qu*
Open the *Animal ABCs* big book to *Qq* and identify the bird as a quail. Explain that the first sound in *quail* is /kw/.

Point to *Qq* and say: *This is the first letter in* quail. On the board write *qu*. Explain that *q* always needs a friend—the *u.* Together they say /kw/.

Identify *qu*
Show picture card *queen* and have children identify it. Turn the card over so children see the word *queen.* Have a volunteer point to the letters that show the /kw/ sound. Repeat with *quarter* and *quilt.*

Sequence

Understand Sequence

Use the picture cards *cat, dog, fish,* and *rabbit* after you tell the following story:

> One day a family went to a pet parade. They saw many wonderful animals. First came a dog dressed like a clown. Next in the parade came a girl carrying a fish in a bowl. She had to be careful not to spill the water. After the fish came a rabbit in a wooden cage. The rabbit's nose wiggled. Last came a cat. It was being carried by its owner. The pet parade was lots of fun.

Show children the pictures and have them put the pictures in the order of their appearance in the pet parade. (dog, fish, rabbit, cat)

Tell children that putting things in order is remembering what happened first, next, and last.

Practice Sequence

Write the numbers 1 through 10 on index cards. Display the numbers in a pocket chart and have children help you put them in order.

Then distribute the cards to volunteers. Have volunteers put the numbers in sequence by standing in a row in front of the class.

Explain that putting things in order means showing what comes first, next, and last.

Apply Sequence to the Big Book

Reread pages 6–8. Then ask:

- **How many ducks go out?** (5)

- **How many come back?** (4)

Use the questions above, as you reread these pages: 10–12, 14–16, 18–20, 22–24.

Now reread pages 25–30.

Big Book

- **Who goes out alone?** (mother duck)

- **What happens when she quacks this time?** (Five little ducks come back.)

Have children count down from 5 to 1 and then count up from 1 to 5.

PHONICS A Z

Vowel Ee

Develop Phonemic Awareness

Identify /e/

Show and name picture cards *egg* and *olive*. Then say: *Listen as I say egg.* Repeat the word several times, emphasizing /e/. Show the pictures again and let a volunteer name them. Ask:

Picture Cards

> **Which word begins with /e/ — *egg* or *olive*?**

Next show the picture cards *jet* and *box*. Say: *Sometimes the /e/ sound does not come at the beginning.* Repeat *jet* several times, emphasizing the /e/. Then ask:

> **Which word has /e/ — *box* or *jet*?**

Say /e/

Explain how to say /e/ by opening the mouth and teeth slightly and relaxing the face muscles. Practice saying these rhyming words with /e/ together: *get, met, let, wet, jet, net.*

Segment and Blend /e/ Words

Draw three squares on the board. Use the squares to help children listen for /e/.

- Say *jet,* segmenting the word /j/, /e/, /t/. As you segment the word a second time, shade the middle square as you say /e/. Point out that the shaded square shows where the /e/ is heard. Let children segment.

- Blend sounds together by drawing an arc from one square to the next as you say *jet.* Have children repeat *jet.*

Continue the activity with the words *pen, let,* and *fed.*

Connect Sound to Letter

Connect /e/ to *e*

Display the *Animal ABCs* big book page for *Ee.* Have children identify the elephant. Say: *The first sound in elephant is /e/.* Point to the *Ee* and say: *This is the letter that shows the /e/ sound: e, /e/, elephant.*

Identify *e*

Focus attention on the *Ee* section of the ABC Wall. Let children point to the letter *E* or *e* in the words.

Have volunteers find words in other sections that have *e* in the middle. Let children point to the *e* as you read the word.

Big Book

Drawing Conclusions

Understand Drawing Conclusions

Use the following situations to help children draw conclusions:

• A present is placed in front of a girl who is having a birthday. What will the girl do? (open the present)

• An alarm rang and fire fighters jumped on a truck. The truck roared down the street. Where are the fire fighters going? (to a fire or accident)

• One winter morning children pulled on heavy coats, mittens, galoshes, hats, and scarves. Why did the children dress this way? (It was cold outside.)

Explain: *You used information you already know to help you answer questions that the stories didn't answer.*

Practice Drawing Conclusions

Show children these things: a piece of paper with a stain on it; some wrapping paper and a bow; a hammer, nail, and framed picture.

Use these questions to help children draw conclusions. Ask:

• **What happened to the paper?** (Someone spilled something on it.)

• **What will the paper and bow be used for?** (to wrap a present)

• **Why is a hammer needed?** (to pound the nail in the wall so the picture can be hung)

Explain to children that when they use information they already know to answer questions that aren't answered in a story, they are drawing conclusions.

Apply Drawing Conclusions to the Trade Book

Reread pages 3–6 of *Corduroy*. Ask:

• **Why is Corduroy sad?** (He wishes the girl had bought him.)

Trade Book

Reread pages 8–11. Ask:

• **Why does Corduroy think he might be climbing a mountain?** (because the escalator is going up high)

Reread pages 24–29. Then ask:

• **What does Corduroy conclude about the girl?** (She is a friend.)

Objectives

Children will

 identify the sound /ks/
- know the sounds of the letters of the alphabet
- learn letter-sound correspondence: /ks/ to *x*
- rhyme words

Consonant Xx

Develop Phonemic Awareness

Identify /ks/

Show picture card *x ray* and *fox*. Point to it and say /ks/ several times. Ask: *Where is /ks/ in fox?*

Explain that /ks/ sometimes comes at the beginning of words, but most of the time /ks/ comes at the end of words.

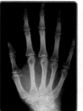 
Picture Cards

Say /ks/

Explain that /ks/ is made up of two sounds blended together and that children know both sounds. Say /k/ quickly followed by /s/. To help children practice saying the sounds, use the phrase *six foxes in six boxes.*

Segment and Blend /ks/ Words

Model how to segment and blend sounds.

- Segment *fox* several times by saying /f/, /o/, /ks/. Ask children to segment the sounds.

- Now blend the sounds together by saying *fox.*

- Finally separate the first two sounds from /ks/. Say: /fo/ /ks/. Ask children to identify the word. Have them make the sound heard at the end of the word.

Use the procedure in the final step above for the words *mix, fix, box,* and *six.*

Connect Sound to Letter

Connect /ks/ to *x*

Open the *Animal ABCs* big book to the *Xx* page and identify the picture of the X-ray fish. Ask a volunteer to say the sound heard at the beginning of *x ray*—/ks/.

Identify *x*

Point to the *Xx* on the page. Explain that the letter *x* stands for the /ks/ sound and that *x* is the sound heard at the beginning of *X-ray fish.*

Big Book

Display picture card *fox.* Ask: With what sound does and what letter does *fox* end? Then say: *Show me the x.* Have a volunteer turn over the *fox* card and point to the *x* in *fox.*

Author's Purpose

Understand Author's Purpose

Explain that authors write for many reasons. Sometimes they write to give information and sometimes they write to entertain people. Have children tell the reason they think each author is writing in these examples:

- **an author wants to explain how a house is built** (to inform)
- **an author wants to write a story about a teddy bear** (to entertain)
- **an author wants to write a book about a grandmother who likes to dance** (to entertain)
- **an author wants to write a book about what zookeepers feed zoo animals** (to inform)

Explain that when an author writes, he or she has a reason for writing, called a purpose. Sometimes an author's purpose is to give information and sometimes it is to tell a story and entertain the reader.

Practice Author's Purpose

Show children a number of books they have read recently, such as *Jump into the Jungle, Corduroy, Shoes Like Miss Alice's,* and *On the Go.*

Review each book by discussing the content with children and showing them some of the pictures. For each book, ask what the author's purpose was—to inform or to entertain. Have children explain why they chose the answer they did. (*Jump into the Jungle* and *On the Go* are meant to inform. *Corduroy* and *Shoes Like Miss Alice's* are meant to entertain.)

Remind children that an author has a purpose for writing. Sometimes an author's purpose is to give information; at other times, it is to entertain readers.

Apply Author's Purpose to the Big Book

Reread *I Need a Lunch Box.* Then have children put their heads down and close their eyes. Ask:

- **Who thinks the author wrote this book to entertain people? Raise your hand.**
- **Who thinks the author wrote this book to give information? Raise your hand.**

Discuss with children that the book was written to entertain. Ask why this is so. (The book tells a story about a make-believe boy and his family.) You may want to mention that by naming colors and days of the week, the author also wanted to give information to the reader.

PHONICS

Consonant Yy

Develop Phonemic Awareness

Identify /y/

Show picture cards *yellow* and *fork*. Say the words as you point to the pictures. As you point to *yellow*, say /y/ several times. Then say *yellow* and *fork* again. Ask:

Picture Cards

> **Which word starts with /y/, fork or yellow?**

Continue the activity with picture cards *yarn, jam; yo-yo, bat*.

Say /y/

Explain and demonstrate how to say /y/ by pressing the sides of the tongue against the upper teeth and stretching the lips from side to side. Together practice saying /y/ by repeating the silly sentence Yes, your yellow yak yells.

Segment and Blend /y/ Words

Use a yellow sheet of construction paper, a green sheet, and a red sheet. Each sheet will represent a phoneme—/y/, /e/, /s/—as you demonstrate segmenting and blending yes.

- Display the papers in a row. Point to each piece as you segment *yes* by saying /y/, /e/, /s/. Then have children segment the sounds as you point to each sheet of paper.

- Now blend the sounds together by sweeping your hand quickly over the papers as you say *yes*. Have children repeat yes as you sweep your hand again.

Connect Sound to Letter

Connect /y/ to y

Display the *Xy* page in the *Animal ABCs* big book. Say: *This shaggy animal is a yak. Yak begins with y.* Point to *Yy* and have children name the letter.

Now say: *The letter y says the /y/: y, /y/, yak.*

Big Book

Identify y

Stand near the *Yy* section of the ABC Wall. Ask children what letter they see at the top of the section. (y) Point to and read some of the words. Let volunteers come to the wall and point to the y in the words.

Make a word card for *yak*. Circle the y and place it on the wall.

READING A B C

Character

Objectives

Children will

 identify story characters
- use strategies to comprehend text

Understand Character

Use a drawing one of the children has created that includes people and possibly animals. Let the child who created the picture tell about it. Afterward, ask the class questions such as these:

- **Who are the people and animals?**

- **What are they doing?**

Let children use the people and animals in the picture to create a class story.

Remind children that the people and animals in a story are called the characters.

Practice Character

Read the following nursery rhyme:

Hey diddle diddle
The cat and the fiddle
The cow jumped over the moon.
The little dog laughed
To see such sport
And the dish ran away with the spoon.

Ask children to identify the characters—the animals and objects that were part of the rhyme. (cat, fiddle, cow, dog, dish, spoon)

Say: *The animals, people, and sometimes objects that appear in a story or rhyme are called the characters.*

Apply Character to the Trade Book

Read pages 4–17 and ask:

- **Who are some characters you met in this part of the book?** (Franklin, Goose, Beaver, Rabbit, Coach, Bear, Franklin's father)

Reread pages 22–32. Ask:

- **How does the team win the game?** (by working together as a team)

- **Who is the most important character in the book?** (Possible answer: Franklin)

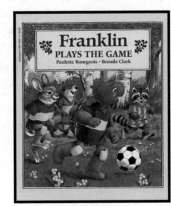

Trade Book

Providing children with reading materials they can and want to read is the first step toward developing fluent readers. A running record allows you to determine each child's instructional and independent reading level. Information on how to take a running record is provided on pp. AR24–AR25.

Instructional Reading Level

- Children reading at grade level should read regularly from the Kindergarten Readers with teacher support as suggested in the Teacher's Editions.

- Children reading below grade level can use the Wordless Stories.

- Children reading above grade level can use the Independent Readers, which provide more challenging text for children who enter kindergarten ready to read.

Independent Reading Level

Children should read regularly in independent-level material, text in which no more than approximately 1 in 20 words is difficult for the reader. Other factors that make a book easy to read include the student's interest in the topic, the amount of text on a page, how well illustrations support meaning, and the complexity and familiarity of the concepts. Suggested books for self-selected reading are provided with each lesson on pp. AR26–AR27 in this Teacher's Edition.

Guide children in learning how to self-select books at their independent reading level. As you talk about a book with children, discuss the challenging concepts in it, list new words children find in sampling the book, and ask children about their familiarity with the topic. A blackline master you can use to help children evaluate books for independent reading is provided on p. AR23.

Self Selected/Independent Reading

While oral reading allows you to assess children's reading level and fluency, independent reading is of crucial importance to children's futures as readers and learners. Children need to develop their ability to read independently for increasing amounts of time.

- Schedule a regular time for sustained independent reading in your classroom. During the year, gradually increase the amount of time devoted to silent reading.

- Help children track the amount of time they read independently and the number of pages they read in a given amount of time. Tracking will help motivate them to gradually increase their duration and speed. A blackline master for tracking independent reading is provided on p. AR23.

- More fluent readers may choose to read silently during independent-reading time. Other children might read to a partner, a stuffed animal, or to an adult volunteer.

Name _____

Choosing a Book to Read by Yourself

These questions can help children choose a book to read.

_____ **1.** Is this book about something that I like?

_____ **2.** This book may be about a real person, about facts, or a made-up story. Do I like reading this kind of book?

_____ **3.** Have I read other things by this author? Do I like the author?

If children say "yes" to question 1, 2, or 3, go on.

_____ **4.** Were there fewer than 5 hard words on the first page?

_____ **5.** Does the number of words on a page look about right to me?

If children say "yes," to questions 4 and 5, the book is right for them.

Silent Reading

Write the date, the title of the book, and the number of pages the child read.

Date	Title	Pages

Taking a Running Record

A running record is an assessment of a child's oral reading accuracy and oral reading fluency. Reading accuracy is based on the number of words read correctly. Reading fluency is based on the reading rate (the number of words read per minute) and the degree to which a child reads with a "natural flow."

How to Measure Reading Accuracy

1. Choose a grade-level text of about 80 to 120 words that is unfamiliar to the child.

2. Make a copy of the text for yourself. Make a copy for the child or have the child read aloud from a book.

3. Give the child the text and have the child read aloud. (You may wish to tape-record the child's reading for later evaluation.)

4. On your copy of the text, mark any miscues or errors the child makes while reading. See the running record sample on page 382, which shows how to identify and mark miscues.

5. Count the total number of words in the text and the total number of errors made by the child. Note: If a child makes the same error more than once, such as mispronouncing the same word multiple times, count it as one error. Self-corrections do not count as actual errors. Use the following formula to calculate the percentage score, or accuracy rate:

$$\frac{\text{Total Number of Word} - \text{Total Number of Errors}}{\text{Total Number of Words}} \times 100 = \text{percentage score}$$

Interpreting the Results

- A child who reads **95–100%** of the words correctly is reading at an **independent level** and may need more challenging text.

- A child who reads **90–94%** of the words correctly is reading at an **instructional level** and will likely benefit from guided instruction.

- A child who reads **89%** or less of the words correctly is reading at a **frustrational level** and may benefit most from targeted instruction with lower-level texts and intervention.

How to Measure Reading Rate

1. Follow Steps 1–3 above.

2. Note the exact times when the child begins and finishes reading.

3. Use the following formula to calculate the number of words per minute (wpm), or reading rate.

$$\frac{\text{Total Number of Words Read}}{\text{Total Number of Seconds}} \times 60 = \text{words per minute}$$

Interpreting the Results

An appropriate rate is roughly equal to the student's age x 10, plus or minus 10. For example, a 6-year-old child should read 50–70 words per minute.

Running Record Sample

"Take your _bath_, Fay." [H above bath]

"I'm May, said the baby."

"Oops!" said ᴧMother. [the inserted above, caret below]

"I'm Fay," said the baby.

"Oops!" said Mother.

One day Kay was not good. Off she went, under the fence. [/fensē/ above fence]

"Kay!" said Mother. "I told you (once) before! Don't go under the fence!" [once circled]

"But, Mother! I'm Fay!"

And the little pig cried.

Mother Pig had a plan. She turned _them_ around. And she curled their tails. [the pigs above them; sc circled above curled]

Fay's tail curled up. Kay's tail curled once. Then it curled once more. Kay's went round and round.

—From *Which is Which?*,
Leveled Reader 27A
Grade 1

Total Number of Words: **94**

Number of Errors: **5**

Accuracy Percentage Score: **95%**

Reading Time: **80 sec**

Reading Rate: **71 wpm**

Miscues

Hesitation
The student hesitates over a word, and the teacher provides the word. Wait several seconds before telling the student what the word is.

Insertion
The student inserts words or parts of words that are not in the text.

Mispronunciation/Misreading
The student pronounces or reads a word incorrectly.

Omission
The student omits words or word parts.

Substitution
The student substitutes words or parts of words for the words in the text.

Self-Correction
The student reads a word incorrectly but then corrects the error. Do not count self-corrections as actual errors. However, noting self-corrections will help you identify words the student finds difficult.

$$\frac{94 - 5}{94} = \frac{89}{94} = .946 = 95\%$$

$$\frac{94}{80} \times 60 = 70.5 = 71 \text{ words per minute}$$

Unit 5 Off We Go!

Easy	On-Level	Challenge

Jump Into the Jungle

Why Mosquitoes Buzz in People's Ears
by Verna Aardema (Dial, 1987) A pesky mosquito annoys the inhabitants of the jungle in this classic retelling of a West African tale.

Papagayo: The Mischief Maker
by Gerald McDermott (Harcourt Brace, 1992) Papagayo, a clever parrot, assists the nocturnal creatures of the jungle.

Greedy Zebra
by Mwenye Hadithi (Little, Brown, 1984) Learn how Zebra acquired his unique coloring because of his greedy actions.

Listen Buddy

Three Cheers for Tacky
by Helen Lester (Houghton Mifflin, 1994) Although clumsy Tacky is the weak link in the cheerleading competition, he comes through for the team just the same.

Top Banana
by Cari Best (Orchard, 1997) Benny the Parrot, an amazing reading bird, has everything a bird could want until he has to share his owner's attention.

The Wizard, the Fairy, and the Magic Chicken
by Helen Lester (Houghton Mifflin, 1988) The three main characters compete, each claiming to be the world's greatest!

Five Little Ducks

The Mitten
by Jan Brett (Scholastic, 1980) Nicki loses a mitten in the snow. Found by a growing menagerie of animals, the mitten is returned to Nicki.

The Princess and the Pea
by Hans Christian Andersen (Holiday House, 1989) Janet Stevens brings her fresh, energetic style to the classic tale of an extremely sensitive princess.

Little Red Ant and the Big Crumb: A Mexican Fable
by Shirley Climo (Clarion, 1995) A tiny ant finds a crumb in a field and goes off to find other animals to help her carry it.

Corduroy

McDuff Comes Home
by Rosemary Wells (Hyperion, 1997) While in hot pursuit of a rabbit, McDuff the terrier becomes lost and requires help in finding his way home.

Pooh Goes Visiting
by A. A. Milne (Dutton, 1993) This is the classic tale in which chubby Pooh gets stuck in Rabbit's doorway.

Where's My Teddy?
by Jez Alborough (Candlewick, 1992) A boy named Eddie looks for his teddy bear, Freddie, and meets up with a real bear who's looking for his teddy.

I Need a Lunch Box

Abuela
by Arthur Dorros (Dutton, 1995) Riding on a bus with her grandmother, a girl imagines that they are carried up into the sky to fly over the sights of New York.

Cat and Canary
by Michael Foreman (Dial, 1985) A city cat who lives out his fantasy of being able to fly finds out that staying on the ground is not so bad after all.

The Last Puppy
by Frank Asch (Simon & Schuster, 1989) The last born of nine puppies worries that he will be the last chosen as a pet for a new owner.

Franklin Plays the Game

Hooray for Snail!
by John Stadler (Crowell, 1984) Slow Snail hits the ball so far it flies to the moon and back. Will Snail have time to slide in for a home run?

Play Ball, Kate
by Sharon Gordon (Troll, 1988) Kate joins her team for a baseball game in the local park.

The Slumber Party
by Margaret Wild (Ticknor and Fields, 1993) A group of kids prepare for a friend's slumber party, play games, and attempt to settle down to sleep.

Read Aloud

One Little Monkey

by Stephanie Calmenson (Parents Magazine Press, 1982) One monkey, followed by various animals in groups of two to ten, swings through the jungle.

Read Aloud

Princess Penelope's Parrot

by Helen Lester (Whitman, 1989) Jealous of her invalid sister's royal treatment as she sits in a wheelchair, Patty tries out the conveyance and discovers that it's no fun at all.

Read Aloud

Little Red Hiding Hood

by Trina Schart Hyman (Holiday House, 1993) Exquisite paintings and a careful retelling mark this Caldecott Honor Book of the Grimm's fairy tale.

Read Aloud

I Lost My Bear!

by Jules Feiffer (Morrow, 2000) A little girl's family gives her suggestions for how to find her missing teddy bear, and finally the most unusual advice works.

Read Aloud

C.L.O.U.D.S.

by Pat Cummings (Lothrop, Lee, & Shepard, 1986) Chuku the angel is given the job of painting the skies of New York City, an assignment he approaches with reluctance but grows to love.

Read Aloud

American Indian Games

by Jay Miller (Children's Press, 1996) Color photographs and a longer text explain some modern-day games played by different Native American nations.

Suggestions for Self-Selected Reading

The rationale for self-selected reading is two-fold. It helps foster the idea of reading for enjoyment while it provides opportunities to practice reading and develop fluency. A common practice for self-selected reading is to begin with ten minutes per day and gradually increase that time. Your state or district may have guidelines in place for self-selected reading.

Reading aloud to children provides an opportunity to expose them to a range of literary genres and guide them in thinking about text. Reading aloud also provides children with a model of fluent reading and shows them how to read with expression. Books selected for reading aloud should appeal to children's interests, be appropriate to their developmental level, and engage their imaginations.

Use the following management suggestions to help maximize self-selected reading time in your classroom.

- Talk with children about their individual reading preferences, and their knowledge of genres, themes, and authors. Encourage them to choose books based on these preferences.

- If you set aside a day for children to share their books, encourage creative presentations. If more than one child is reading the same title, they may want to work together on a presentation.

Use the following activity suggestions to add variety to self-selected reading time.

- Children may have a favorite story, poem, or short passage. Provide time for students to share it with the class

- Children may want to encourage others to read their books. Suggest that they draw a picture for the book that will make others want to read it.

Unit 5 Theme-Related Titles

P. B. Bear's Treasure Hunt
Lee Davis
New York: DK Publishing, 1995

Eyewitness Readers
Time Traveler Angela Bull
New York: DK Publishing, 1999

See the 5-Day Planner for each lesson for daily suggestions for self-selected reading and read alouds.

Using a Computer

Objectives

Children will

- learn the important parts of a computer
- learn computer vocabulary
- learn about email
- send email

STEP 1 Allow children to show you what they know about the parts of a computer.
Tell students that the following parts are called a computer's **hardware**.

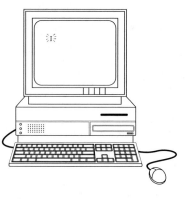

monitor a screen on which a computer shows words and pictures

cursor a flashing mark to show a position on the screen

hard drive a part of the computer where software programs and information are stored in memory

CD-ROM Drive a part of the computer that reads the CD-ROM discs

disc drive a part of the computer that needs "floppy" discs

keyboard a set of keys used to type letters and numbers

STEP 2 Ask children to look at the keyboard.
Have them notice the top row. Explain that they can type numbers using these keys. Then, have them look at the next three rows. Explain they can use these keys to type all the letters in the alphabet. Two other important keys are the space bar and the shift key. The space bar is used to add spaces between letters and words. The shift key is used to make capital letters. Demonstrate pressing shift and the key of a letter to make a capital.

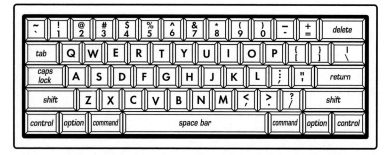

Extend Skills
Show students how they can copy, cut, and paste text.

STEP 3 Show children how to turn on, or boot up, the computer.
When the desktop appears, open up the hard drive by clicking on its icon. Explain these terms:

icon a small picture on the screen that can be selected with the cursor

email (electronic mail) a message sent between two computers

STEP 4 Launch your Internet browser or show children how to do so.
Then have them open their email program. Point out the icons similar to those on the right. Have children click on the icon for a new message.

Get Mail   New Mail

STEP 5 They should then see a window like the one below.
Help children fill in the email address where it says *To*. Then children can type what their message is about in the *subject* window. Children may wish to type a sentence to that person, or dictate one to be typed. Click on *send* to send their message. Show children how to properly shut down the computer when they have finished.

Address Book	Spell Check	Attachment	Detach	Send Mail

To: ▼   Subject:

Class Activity
As a class, launch the browser program and open the communications icon. Select *new message* and fill in the different parts (*To, subject,* and so on). Write an email message to another class or school.

NOTE: To complete this lesson, students should have access to one or more computers.

The goal of *Scott Foresman Reading* is the development and encouragement of fluent readers, articulate writers and speakers, and discerning listeners and viewers.

Reading Benchmarks

The Reading Benchmarks recognize that students do not progress at the same rate toward the goal of being mature, skilled communicators. Within the same classroom are students at varying stages in their journey toward that goal. The teacher can gauge their progress in general ways by comparing student behaviors against these benchmark guidelines.

Scope and Sequence

The major strands and individual learning expectations in the Scope and Sequence are supported by research on how children develop and learn and by expectations held for learners by national and state guidelines.

Reading

The goal of reading is that a reader construct the meaning of a text. This goal is achieved through the interaction of a reader's prior knowledge and the key features of the text. These features— graphophonic, syntactic, and semantic—offer clues that readers can use to help themselves understand what they read. Research has shown that children understand the role of word order (syntax) and meaning (semantics) in oral language, but to develop reading fluency, they need instruction in graphophonic features in written words and visual text. This instruction includes phonemic awareness (words are made of sounds), phonics (letters represent these sounds in words), and spelling (common spelling patterns can be found in words).

Proficient readers learn to interact with all three kinds of features so that they can "make sense" of their reading, recognize when they don't, and use strategies to get back on the meaning track.

Literature

Readers, listeners, and viewers who know the characteristics of different genre know what to expect of an author or playwright and therefore are better able to comprehend the writer's message. When readers can discern the techniques and literary devices authors use, they can better appreciate not only what the author is communicating but how the message is conveyed and how response is evoked.

Language and Communication
Research and Study Skills
Habits and Attitudes

While each language art is stressed more strongly at different times depending on the task, effective communication is often a meshing and interaction of them. *Scott Foresman Reading* encourages students to develop in their ability to communicate both orally and in writing. Skilled communicators do many kinds of writing. Informally, they write letters and notes and record their thoughts in journals and diaries. Formally, they formulate questions about which to communicate answers or ideas, research to find answers or support for their ideas, and present their ideas in an effective organization and a strong yet appealing manner. Success in school and the workplace requires that able communicators know how to locate and synthesize information and know how to present that information and its implications to an audience, whether orally, in writing, or visually. In our diverse world, communication best takes place when the communicator uses common and traditional rules of grammar, usage, spelling, capitalization, and punctuation.

Kindergarten

Novice

Novice indicates that the child is at an introductory level. Learners are at a Novice developmental level when they:

Reading Success Indicators for **Decoding and Word Recognition**	All students will develop the knowledge and skills necessary to begin to decode simple CVC words and recognize some high-frequency words.	• demonstrate book handling skills such as holding the book correctly and turning pages easily • identify own name in print and identify several high-frequency words • recognize some letters of the alphabet • demonstrate phonemic awareness by recognizing if two spoken words are the same or different and recognizing if two spoken words rhyme
Reading Success Indicators for **Strategies for Fluency and Understanding**	All students will develop the strategies, skills, and knowledge necessary to comprehend and respond to a range of materials.	• recall details when a story is read to them • retell parts of a story using illustrations • track print from top to bottom on a page • use pictures to "read" a story • follow the lead of others to chime in with patterned text read by an adult • respond to text read to them by drawing pictures • develop penmanship skills (stroke)
Reading Success Indicators for **Enhancing Understanding and Learning from Text**	All students will investigate important issues in-depth, being involved with a variety of genres, and demonstrate their understanding of issues and problems about the world they live in.	• participate in teacher-led discussions • discuss details when looking at pictures • demonstrate understanding of concepts and ideas through pictures • compare and contrast objects and pictures to find similarities and differences

Developing

Developing means that progress is being made toward achieving proficiency. Learners are at a Developing developmental level when they:

- demonstrate knowledge of concepts of print such as discriminating between letters and words
- identify at least 15 high-frequency words
- recognize the letters of the alphabet
- recognize that words are composed of sounds which are represented by letters
- demonstrate phonemic awareness by knowing rhyming words, hearing separate words in sentences, isolating and matching initial sounds, and blending sounds to make words

- comprehend details when a story is read to them
- retell a story using illustrations
- track print from left to right and from top to bottom on a page
- use pictures and some words to "read" a story
- chime in with patterned text read by an adult
- respond to text read to them by drawing pictures and attempting to write some words
- develop penmanship skills (grip, stroke, position)

- compare and contrast ideas related to one issue when presented orally and from teacher-led discussions
- discuss details when looking at pictures
- identify key concepts and ideas through pictures, transitional spelling, and some conventional spelling
- compare and contrast characters to find similarities and differences

Proficient

Proficient means that the child has achieved the advanced developmental level for that particular grade and is ready to move on to the next grade's success indicators. Learners are at a Proficient developmental level when they:

- demonstrate knowledge of concepts of print such as: that words are separated by space, that there is a one-to-one correspondence between speech and print, that print preserves meaning
- identify at least 36 high-frequency words and begin to spell them conventionally
- recognize the letters of the alphabet and the common sounds associated with them
- demonstrate phonemic awareness by suggesting rhyming words, recognizing word family patterns, hearing syllables, isolating and matching initial and ending sounds, blending sounds to make words, segmenting words into sounds
- apply picture clues and initial consonant sounds for decoding
- decode CVC words

- predict and comprehend details when a story is read to them
- locate the beginning and end of the text
- track speech to print, locate a place in text where someone left off reading, and locate particular words
- use words and some pictures to read a story
- predominately read orally with an adult or independently with familiar materials
- respond to text read to them by drawing pictures and writing some words
- develop penmanship skills (grip, stroke, position, letter formation)

- compare and contrast ideas related to one issue when presented orally from several texts and from teacher-led discussions
- discuss the most important detail when looking at pictures
- categorize key concepts and related ideas through pictures, transitional spelling, and some conventional spelling
- choose several characters across various texts, compare and contrast these characters to find similarities and differences

Novice

Novice indicates that the child is at an introductory level. Learners are at a Novice developmental level when they:

Reading Success Indicators for

Literature and Appreciation

All students will be involved with texts representing a wide range of literary genre for different purposes and will demonstrate their appreciation of literature through responses that indicate their ability to connect text to their world.

- respond to simple stories through drama and by oral retelling
- predict what will happen next in a situation read aloud
- participate in literature from a variety of cultures read aloud
- express feelings non-verbally about stories read aloud
- listen to both classic and contemporary literature
- participate in class activities based on selections read aloud

Success Indicators for

Application and Action

All students will apply what they have learned from texts to their lives and to the lives of others through the following themes:

- Getting to Know Us (Myself and Others)
- A World of Wonders (The World Around Us)
- So Much to Do! (Learning and Working)
- Every Day Is Special (Traditions)
- Off We Go! (Journeys in Time and Space)
- Open the Doors (Creativity)

- work in whole and small group situations on projects outlined by the teacher, participate in the generating of ideas, complete simple, one-step tasks in project
- begin to participate with others in groups and use a variety of materials and resources
- communicate ideas through pictures, follow a model to role-play, and use creative movement to express ideas

Developing

Developing means that progress is being made toward achieving proficiency. Learners are at a Developing developmental level when they:

- discuss basic plot of simple stories and respond through drama and by oral retelling
- predict what will happen next in the middle of a story read aloud
- talk about events in literature from a variety of cultures
- distinguish between real and imaginary
- verbally express feelings about stories read aloud
- actively listen to both classic and contemporary literature
- understand concepts of author and illustrator
- participate in class innovations based on selections read using patterned literature

- work in whole and small group situations on projects outlined by the teacher, brainstorm ideas as teacher takes dictation, complete simple multi-step tasks in a project, name steps in a project
- share materials and resources, respect others' space as they participate together in groups, use a variety of materials and resources
- communicate ideas through pictures and transitional spelling: role-play and use creative movement to express ideas

Proficient

Proficient means that the child has achieved the advanced developmental level for that particular grade and is ready to move on to the next grade's success indicators. Learners are at a Proficient developmental level when they:

- discuss basic plot, characters, and setting of simple stories and respond by drama and oral retelling
- predict what will happen next in a story read aloud
- discuss events in literature from a variety of cultures and relate them to their own experiences
- distinguish between real and imaginary
- express feelings and opinions about stories read aloud
- actively listen to and discuss both classic and contemporary literature
- can tell about the roles of author and illustrator
- write class innovations based on selections read using patterned literature

- work in whole and small group situations on projects, brainstorm ideas as teacher takes dictation, complete multi-step tasks in a project, name steps to complete a project
- share materials and resources, respect others' space as they participate together in groups, practice careful use of materials and resources
- communicate ideas through pictures, transitional spelling, and some conventional spelling: role-play and use creative movement to express ideas

Reading

Foundations of Literacy	K	1	2	3	4	5	6
Phonemic Awareness							
Identify and isolate initial and final sounds of spoken words	•C	•C					
Recognize and produce rhyming words	•C	•C					
Segment one-syllable words into initial, medial, and final sounds, and recombine sounds into words	•C	•C					
Identify, segment, and combine syllables in spoken words (e.g., by clapping syllables, moving manipulatives)	•C	•C					
Understand that spoken words are composed of sounds which are represented by alphabetic letters	•C	•C					
Print Knowledge and Concepts of Print							
Develop print awareness (concept of letter, word)	•C	•C					
Develop print awareness (concept of sentence, paragraph)	•	•C					
Track print: left to right on line, top to bottom on page, front to back of book	•C	•C					
Recognize that capitalization and punctuation are used for comprehension	•	•C					
Recognize environmental print	•	•					
Match spoken to printed words	•C	•C					
Develop awareness that print conveys and preserves meaning	•C	•C					
Emerging Reading/Writing Skills							
Show an interest in and respond to text read aloud	•	•					
Hold book right side up	•C	•C					
Identify parts of a book (cover, title page) and their functions	•C	•C					
Understand terms *author* and *illustrator* and distinguish their roles	•C	•C					
Describe how illustrations contribute to the text	•C	•C					
Know the order of the alphabet	•	•					
Know capital and lower case letter names and distinguish between the two	•C	•C					
Know letter/sound relationships	•C	•C					
Develop skill in gross and fine motor functioning and hand/eye coordination	•	•					
Gain increasing control of penmanship (e.g., holding pencil, paper position, stroke, posture)	•	•					
Write letters of the alphabet, both capitals and lower case	•	•					
Print own name	•	•					
Dictate messages/stories for others to write	•	•					
Write using pictures, some letters, transitional spelling if appropriate	•C	•					
Write labels, notes, and captions (e.g., for illustrations, charts, possessions)	•	•					
Use conventional spelling of familiar words in final drafts		•C					
Write messages that move left to right on a line, top to bottom on a page	•	•C					

Phonics, Word Analysis, Spelling, Vocabulary, and Fluency	K	1	2	3	4	5	6
Decoding strategy: Use phonics and structural analysis to decode words	•	•	•	•	•	•	•
Decoding strategy: Use semantic, syntactic, and graphophonic clues to identify words and their meanings	•	•	•	•	•	•	•
Vocabulary-in-context strategy: Use punctuation, explanatory phrases, and overall sense to gain and monitor word meanings		•	•	•	•	•	•
Process strategy: Know to ask and answer, What do I do when I come to a word I don't know?		•	•	•	•	•	•
Process strategy: Read fluently on development level with appropriate rate, stress, intonation, and style		•	•	•	•	•	•

Phonics and Decoding Skills

Phonics/Phonic Elements

	K	1	2	3	4	5	6
Letter/sound correspondence	•T	•T					
Blend sounds to make words	•C	•C	•	•			
Consonants	•T	•T	•T	•T	•	•	•

• = instructional opportunity   C = formal one-on-one teacher/child assessment conference   T = tested in standardized test format

Phonics, Word Analysis, Spelling, Vocabulary, and Fluency *Continued*	K	1	2	3	4	5	6
Consonant blends	•	•T	•T	•T	•		
Consonant digraphs		•T	•T	•T			
Short and long vowels	•	•T	•T	•T			
r-Controlled vowels (vowel + *r*)		•T	•T	•T	•	•	•
Vowel digraphs and diphthongs		•T	•T	•T	•	•	•
Phonograms (word families)	•T	•T	•T	•			
Common word patterns (CVC, CVCe, etc.)	•	•T	•	•	•	•	•
Schwa sound			•	•	•	•	•
Word Analysis							
Plurals and possessives	•	•T	•T	•T	•T	•T	•T
Contractions		•T	•T	•	•	•	•
Compound words		•T	•T	•T	•	•	•
Base words, endings, prefixes, and suffixes	•	•T	•T	•T	•T	•T	•T
Syllabication and common syllable patterns for word identification			•	•T	•T	•T	•T

Spelling

Sound and Letter Patterns

	K	1	2	3	4	5	6
Phonograms (word families)		•					
Vowels: short, long, *r*-controlled, digraphs, diphthongs, and unusual vowel spellings		•	•	•	•	•	•
Schwa sound				•	•	•	•
Consonants: single, double, blends, digraphs, silent, and unusual consonant spellings		•	•	•	•	•	•

Word Structure

	K	1	2	3	4	5	6
Endings on nouns and verbs		•	•	•	•	•	•
Irregular plurals						•	•
Syllable constructions			•	•	•		•
Affixes		•	•	•	•	•	•
Compound words		•		•	•	•	•
Apostrophes in contractions and possessives			•	•	•	•	•
Capital letters and abbreviations					•	•	
Greek and Latin word parts					•	•	•

Meaning Relationships

	K	1	2	3	4	5	6
Homophones				•	•	•	•
Easily confused words					•	•	•
Words related to each other					•	•	•
Words from other languages							•

Common Spelling Errors

	K	1	2	3	4	5	6
				•	•	•	•

Vocabulary and Fluency

Context Clues

	K	1	2	3	4	5	6
Picture clues	•	•	•				
Synonyms	•	•T	•T	•T	•T	•T	•T
Antonyms	•	•T	•T	•T	•T	•T	•T
Homonyms/homophones/homographs		•T	•T	•T	•T	•T	•T
Multiple-meaning words		•T	•T	•T	•T	•T	•T
Unfamiliar words		•T	•T	•T	•T	•T	•T
Specialized/technical/topical words				•	•	•	•

Vocabulary Building

	K	1	2	3	4	5	6
Classify words	•	•	•	•	•	•	•
Use graphic organizers to group, study, and retain vocabulary	•	•	•	•	•	•	•
Know abbreviations, acronyms, and shortened forms of words			•	•	•	•	•

• = instructional opportunity   T = tested in standardized test format

Phonics, Word Analysis, Spelling, Vocabulary, and Fluency *Continued*	K	1	2	3	4	5	6
Understand easily confused words and idioms			•	•	•	•	•
Understand connotation and denotation				•T	•T	•T	•T
Use etymologies for meaning (including Greek and Latin roots and affixes)					•	•	•
Develop vocabulary through listening and discussing	•	•	•	•	•	•	•
Develop vocabulary through meaningful and concrete experiences	•	•	•	•	•	•	•
Develop vocabulary through reading	•	•	•	•	•	•	•
Develop vocabulary through the use of grade-appropriate reference materials	•	•	•	•	•	•	•
Recognize words in the environment	•	•					
Recognize regular and irregular high-frequency words	•	•T	•T				
Understand selection vocabulary	•	•T	•T	•T	•T	•T	•T
Understand content-area vocabulary				•T	•T	•T	•T
Make analogies					•	•	•T

Comprehension	K	1	2	3	4	5	6
Comprehension strategy: Know and use the reading process: preview and activate prior knowledge, predict, read, self-monitor, use fix-up strategies, summarize, reflect and respond	•	•	•	•	•	•	•
Comprehension strategy: Construct meaning using all possible avenues: text, knowledge of selection and topic, illustrations, text features, other print and technological/software resources, resource people	•	•	•	•	•	•	•
Formal assessment strategy: Develop test-taking strategies and answer test-like questions (multiple choice, true/false, short answer)		•	•	•	•	•	•

Strategies and Skills

	K	1	2	3	4	5	6
Activate prior knowledge and preview	•	•	•	•	•	•	•
Self-question to assess overall understanding		•	•	•	•	•	•
Self-monitor and use fix-up strategies		•	•	•	•	•	•
Author's possible viewpoint/bias				•	•	•T	•T
Author's purpose (e.g., inform, entertain, persuade, express)	•	•T	•T	•T	•T	•T	•T
Cause and effect	•T	•T	•T	•T	•T	•T	•T
Classify/categorize	•T	•T	•T	•	•	•	•
Compare and contrast		•	•T	•T	•T	•T	•T
Context clues for understanding words, phrases, and word referents		•T	•T	•T	•T	•T	•T
Draw conclusions	•T	•T	•T	•T	•T	•T	•T
Fact and opinion			•T	•T	•T	•T	•T
Generalize	•	•	•	•T	•T	•T	•T
Graphic sources (e.g., charts, maps, lists, pictures, etc.)	•	•	•T	•T	•T	•T	•T
Make judgments about ideas and text			•T	•T	•T	•T	•T
Main idea or main idea with supporting details	•	•T	•T	•T	•T	•T	•T
Paraphrase					•T	•T	•T
Persuasive devices and propaganda						•	•T
Predict and verify or refine predictions	•T	•T	•T	•T	•T	•T	•T
Realism/fantasy or fact/nonfact/fantasy	•	•T	•T	•T	•		
Recall and retell	•T	•T	•	•	•	•	•
Sequence of events	•	•T	•T	•T	•T	•T	•T
Steps in a process			•T	•T	•T	•T	•T
Story elements							
Character	•T	•T	•T	•T	•T	•T	•T
Plot and plot structure	•	•T	•T	•T	•T	•T	•T
Setting	•	•T	•T	•T	•T	•T	•T
Theme	•	•T	•T	•T	•T	•T	•T
Summarize	•	•	•T	•T	•T	•T	•T
Text structure or method of presenting information				•T	•T	•T	•T
Visualize		•	•	•T	•T	•T	•T

• = instructional opportunity   T = tested in standardized test format

Comprehension *Continued*

	K	1	2	3	4	5	6
Critical Thinking							
Infer		•T	•T	•T	•T	•T	•T
Analyze		•T	•T	•T	•T	•T	•T
Organize ideas and information		•	•T	•T	•T	•T	•T
Make judgments		•	•T	•T	•T	•T	•T
Hypothesize		•	•	•	•	•	•T
Synthesize ideas within a text	•	•	•T	•T	•T	•T	•T
Synthesize ideas from different texts and media	•	•	•T	•T	•T	•T	•T
Compare and contrast across selections, genres, and cultures (intertextuality)	•	•	•T	•T	•T	•T	•T
Evaluate and critique ideas and text		•	•T	•T	•T	•T	•T
Make analogies		•	•		•	•	•T

Literature

Genres and Literary Craft

	K	1	2	3	4	5	6
Genres							
Fiction							
Animal fantasy	•	•	•	•	•	•	
Drama/play		•	•	•T	•T	•T	•T
Fantasy	•	•	•	•T	•T	•T	•T
Historical fiction			•	•T	•T	•T	•T
Humorous fiction	•		•	•	•	•	•
Mystery			•			•	
Picture book	•	•	•	•			
Realistic fiction	•	•	•	•T	•T	•T	•T
Science fiction				•			•T
Short story					•	•	•
Traditional stories: fable, fairy tale, folk tale, tall tale, legend, myth		•	•	•T	•T	•T	•T
Nonfiction							
Almanac entry				•	•	•	•
Biography/autobiography		•	•	•T	•T	•T	•T
Diary/journal						•	
Encyclopedia article (print or CD-ROM)				•	•	•	•
Expository article		•	•	•T	•T	•T	•T
How-to article		•		•	•	•	•
Internet article				•	•	•	•
Interview			•				
Magazine article				•	•	•	•
Narrative writing	•	•	•	•T	•T	•T	•T
Newsletter		•	•				
Newspaper article				•	•	•	•
Personal essay				•	•	•	•
Persuasive essay							•
Photo essay		•	•	•	•	•	•
Textbook				•	•	•	•
Poetry and Song	•	•	•	•	•	•	•

• = instructional opportunity   T = tested in standardized test format

	K	1	2	3	4	5	6
Literary Devices							
Allusion							•
Dialect					•	•	•
Dialogue and narration		•	•	•	•	•	•
Exaggeration/hyperbole				•	•	•	•T
Figurative language							
Simile			•	•T	•T	•T	•T
Metaphor	•	•	•	•T	•T	•T	•T
Idiom		•	•	•T	•T	•T	•T
Slang				•	•	•	•
Jargon				•	•	•	•
Invented words							•
Flashback					•	•	•T
Foreshadowing						•	•T
Humor					•	•	•
Imagery and sensory words					•T	•T	•T
Irony							•
Mood						•T	•T
Personification				•	•	•	•T
Point of view			•	•	•T	•T	•T
Puns and word play					•	•	•
Sound devices and poetic elements							
Rhyme	•	•	•	•	•	•	•
Rhythm and cadence	•	•	•	•	•	•	•
Repetition			•	•	•	•	•
Onomatopoeia			•	•	•	•	•
Alliteration				•	•	•	•
Line length						•	•
Symbolism					•	•	•T
Tone							•T
Understatement							•
Author's Craft/Style							
Recognize/analyze author's craft, style, language		•	•	•	•	•	•
Analyze the effect of author's perspective/viewpoint/bias on text and choice of genre			•	•	•	•	•
Illustrator's Craft/Style							
Recognize/analyze illustrator's craft or style		•	•	•	•	•	•
Analyze how art complements text					•	•	•
Analyze/appreciate fine art							•

Literary Response and Appreciation	K	1	2	3	4	5	6
Reflect on reading and respond in various ways	•	•T	•T	•T	•T	•T	•T
Recognize evocation—the thoughts and feelings aroused during reading or listening	•	•	•	•	•	•	•
Relate own experience and other literary experience to what is being read	•	•	•	•	•	•	•
Assume alternate points of view to explore a literary selection	•	•	•	•	•	•	•
Reflect upon the relevance of the literary experience to the reader's own life	•	•	•	•	•	•	•
Synthesize and extend the literary experience, e.g., through drawing, dramatizing, miming, storytelling, etc.	•	•	•	•	•	•	•
Evaluate the quality of the literary experience	•	•	•	•	•	•	•
Seek additional literary experience through varied voluntary reading	•	•	•	•	•	•	•
Make connections between literature and other curriculum areas	•	•	•	•	•	•	•

• = instructional opportunity   T = tested in standardized test format

Language and Communication

Grammar and Usage in Speaking and Writing	K	1	2	3	4	5	6
Parts of speech							
Verbs and verb tenses	•	•T	•T	•T	•T	•T	•T
Nouns	•	•T	•T	•T	•T	•T	•T
Pronouns		•T	•T	•T	•T	•T	•T
Adjectives	•	•T	•T	•T	•T	•T	•T
Adverbs			•T	•T	•T	•T	•T
Conjunctions				•T	•T	•T	•T
Prepositions				•T	•T	•T	•T
Interjections							•T
Phrases	•	•T			•	•	•
Sentences: kinds, types, parts, fragments, run-ons, complete, combining	•	•T	•T	•T	•T	•T	•T
Paragraphs			•T	•	•	•	•
Misplaced modifiers							•T

Writing Process, Strategies, and Skills	K	1	2	3	4	5	6
Engage in modeled, shared, interactive writing	•	•	•				
Use the five-step writing process		•	•	•	•	•	•
Prewrite using various strategies	•	•	•	•	•	•	•
Use published pieces as models for writing		•	•	•	•	•	•
Decide on audience, purpose, and kind of writing		•	•	•	•	•	•
Write based on a picture	•	•	•	•	•		
Write based on literature		•	•	•	•	•	•
Write about a TV show, movie, or play			•	•	•	•	•
Take notes during research			•	•	•	•	•
Organize ideas (graphic organizer, outline, etc.)	•	•	•	•	•	•	•
Evaluate research and raise new questions			•	•	•	•	•
Develop draft	•	•	•	•	•	•	•
Descriptive writing		•	•	•	•	•	•
Narrative writing		•	•	•	•	•	•
Expository writing		•	•	•	•	•	•
Persuasive writing		•	•	•	•	•	•
Write in a variety of appropriate forms (sentences, paragraphs, stories, letters, reports, sketches, etc.)	•	•	•	•	•	•	•
Revise drafts in various ways	•	•	•	•	•	•	•
Edit for correct spelling, grammar, usage, and mechanics		•	•	•	•	•	•
Publish	•	•	•	•	•	•	•
Take pride in neat and correct visual appearance	•	•	•	•	•	•	•
Use correct penmanship	•	•	•	•	•	•	•
Give multimedia presentation						•	•
Use technology in writing			•	•	•	•	•
Write for personal use (response logs, notes for comprehension, etc.)			•	•	•	•	•
Evaluate writing	•	•	•	•	•	•	•
Apply criteria for evaluation		•	•	•	•	•	•
Respond constructively to others' writing		•	•	•	•	•	•
Self-evaluate on whether own purposes were met		•	•	•	•	•	•
Review own collection of writing to monitor growth	•	•	•	•	•	•	•

Mechanics in Writing	K	1	2	3	4	5	6
Capitalization	•	•T	•T	•T	•T	•T	•T
Punctuation	•	•T	•T	•T	•T	•T	•T

• = instructional opportunity   T = tested in standardized test format

Listening and Speaking	K	1	2	3	4	5	6
Expand vocabulary by listening and speaking	•	•	•	•	•	•	•
Connect experiences, ideas, and cultural traditions with those of others through speaking and listening	•	•	•	•	•	•	•
Listen for various purposes	•	•	•	•	•	•	•
Listen carefully and critically to oral reading, discussions, and spoken messages	•	•	•	•	•	•	•
Use comprehension skills and strategies while listening to oral text and messages	•	•	•	•	•	•	•
Understand and retell text and messages heard	•	•	•	•	•	•	•
Understand the major ideas and supporting evidence in spoken messages					•	•	•
Identify and analyze a speaker's opinions and persuasive techniques					•	•	•
Self-monitor understanding of a spoken message and seek clarification as necessary					•	•	•
Respond appropriately to questions, directions, text read aloud, and oral presentations	•	•	•	•	•	•	•
Participate in rhymes and songs	•	•	•	•			
Participate in conversations and discussions	•	•	•	•	•	•	•
Speak for various purposes	•	•	•	•	•	•	•
Speak to a group or audience in appropriate ways and with appropriate delivery	•	•	•	•	•	•	•
Read orally with appropriate fluency (accuracy, expression, style, and attention to phrasing and punctuation)		•	•	•	•	•	•
Present dramatic interpretations of literature and literary experiences	•	•	•	•	•	•	•
Give precise directions, accurate information, and convincing ideas while speaking	•	•	•	•	•	•	•
Gain increasing control of conventional grammar and usage when speaking	•	•	•	•	•	•	•

Viewing	K	1	2	3	4	5	6
Develop awareness and understanding of the importance of the media	•	•	•	•	•	•	•
Interact with a variety of print and non-print media for a range of purposes (e.g., to learn, to receive information, to evaluate, to interpret, to appreciate)	•	•	•	•	•	•	•
Use comprehension skills and strategies to understand messages conveyed by the media	•	•	•	•	•	•	•
Use critical thinking to analyze and synthesize ideas and viewpoints in the media	•	•	•	•	•	•	•
Recognize bias, propaganda, and persuasive techniques in the media					•	•	•
Compare and contrast print, visual, and electronic media					•	•	•
Respond to the media (discussion, writing, multimedia presentations, etc.)	•	•	•	•	•	•	•

Research and Study Skills

Research Strategies and Skills	K	1	2	3	4	5	6
State the steps of the research process (set purpose, frame questions, choose sources, collect information, organize and present information)					•	•	•
Form and revise relevant questions for inquiry	•	•	•	•	•	•T	•T
Distinguish between and evaluate reference sources				•T	•T	•T	•T
Use specific study strategy (K-W-L, skim and scan, etc.) to find or learn information				•	•	•	•
Locate and collect information	•	•	•	•	•	•	•
Highlight				•	•	•	•
Take notes/record findings			•	•	•	•	•
Evaluate, interpret, and draw conclusions about key information				•	•	•	•T
Make outline					•T	•T	•T
Organize content systematically (e.g., sequentially or around main ideas)		•	•	•	•	•	•
Record knowledge, write report, or present orally		•	•	•	•	•	•
Credit primary and secondary reference sources					•	•	•
Select, organize, and incorporate visual aids				•	•	•	•
Know and use parts of a book	•	•T	•T	•T	•T	•T	•T
Use alphabetical order		•T	•T	•T	•T	•	
Follow directions	•	•	•	•	•	•	•

• = instructional opportunity   T = tested in standardized test format

Understanding and Using Reference Sources

Understanding and Using Reference Sources	K	1	2	3	4	5	6
Almanac				•	•	•T	•T
Atlas				•T	•T	•T	•T
Card catalog/library database				•	•T	•T	•T
Dictionary/glossary		•	•	•T	•T	•T	•T
Encyclopedia		•	•	•T	•T	•T	•T
Magazine/periodical				•	•T	•T	•T
Manual				•	•	•	•
Newsletter		•	•	•			
Newspaper	•			•T	•T	•T	•T
Readers' Guide to Periodical Literature						•	•T
Technology (non-computer electronic media–e.g., cassettes, TV, videotape, CD-ROM; computer programs and services; Internet)	•	•	•	•	•	•	•
Telephone directory				•	•	•T	•T
Textbook				•T	•T	•T	•T
Thesaurus		•	•	•	•	•	•
Trade book		•	•	•	•	•T	•T

Understanding and Using Graphic Sources

Understanding and Using Graphic Sources	K	1	2	3	4	5	6
Advertisement				•	•	•	•
Chart/table	•	•T	•T	•T	•T	•T	•T
Diagram/scale drawing			•	•	•	•	•T
Graph	•	•T	•T	•T	•T	•T	•T
Illustration (photograph or art) and/or caption	•	•	•	•	•	•	•
List	•	•	•	•			
Map	•	•T	•T	•T	•T	•T	•T
Order form					•T	•	•
Poster/announcement				•	•T	•T	•
Recipe						•	•
Schedule				•	•T	•T	•T
Sign		•		•	•		
Time line			•	•T	•T	•T	•T

Habits and Attitudes

	K	1	2	3	4	5	6
Derive pleasure from reading, listening, viewing	•	•	•	•	•	•	•
Value print as a means of gaining information	•	•	•	•	•	•	•
Value print as a means of assessing various opinions and points of view	•	•	•	•	•	•	•
Develop an appreciation of different genres and authors	•	•	•	•	•	•	•
Connect experiences and ideas with those from other perspectives, experiences, customs, and cultures	•	•	•	•	•	•	•
Develop attitudes and abilities to interact with members of other groups and cultures	•	•	•	•	•	•	•
Work cooperatively with others	•	•	•	•	•	•	•
Recognize that all peoples and cultures, native and immigrant, have made valuable contributions to the common culture of the United States	•	•	•	•	•	•	•
Recognize and study themes and connections that cross cultures and bind them together in their common humanness	•	•	•	•	•	•	•
Develop lifelong reading and writing habits	•	•	•	•	•	•	•
Read independently from a wide variety of genres (for enjoyment, to understand self and others, for information and utility, etc.)	•	•	•	•	•	•	•
Keep reading log/reading journal or have a list of favorite authors and works		•	•	•	•	•	•
Write and discuss independently (for enjoyment, to seek information, to understand, etc.)	•	•	•	•	•	•	•
Share reading and writing with others	•	•	•	•	•	•	•

• = instructional opportunity   T = tested in standardized test format

Program Themes

	Myself and Others	**The World Around Us**	**Learning and Working**
	We read about others to see ourselves and to discover the hopes, dreams, and concerns people share. We learn positive ways to work out differences.	We learn about living things in their environments. We gain respect for them so we can assume some responsibility for protecting them.	People learn and work together to accomplish things great and small. We read about these activities to value learning, to understand ways problems can be solved, and to respect the accomplishments of others.
K	**Getting to Know Us** **Look at Me Now!** Where do we grow from here? **Meet Family and Friends** Who are the people we love?	**A World of Wonders** **Claws, Paws, Sun, and Seeds** How do things grow? **Bears and Bunnies** What is your world like?	**So Much to Do!** **Finding Our Way** Where do I fit in? **In Our Big Backyard** What can we learn close to home?
1	**Good Times We Share** How are our families and friends special?	**Take a Closer Look** Look closely! *Now* what can we see?	**Let's Learn Together** What can we learn when we all work together?
2	**You + Me = Special** What makes us all special?	**Zoom In!** What can we learn from looking at the world around us?	**Side by Side** How can we learn and work well together?
3	**Finding My Place** How do friends and family help us grow?	**The Whole Wide World** How can we learn about and care for the world?	**Getting the Job Done** How can we learn from everything we do?
4	**Focus on Family** Who helps us find our talents, abilities, and dreams?	**A Wider View** What place do plants and animals have in the world around us?	**Keys to Success** How do learning and working lead to success?
5	**Relating to Others** What are the important things in life?	**My World and Yours** How do we show that we care about our surroundings?	**A Job Well Done** What do we learn from our experiences?
6	**Discovering Ourselves** How do our relationships with others help us learn about ourselves?	**The Living Earth** What can we learn from observing the world around us?	**Goals Great and Small** How do people accomplish their ambitions?

Traditions

We read about ways people are linked together and to the past. We grow in appreciation of who we are and what we value and in understanding others.

Every Day Is Special

All Together
Why is it better being together?

Let's Go
How did we get where we are?

Favorite Things Old and New
How do things get to be favorites?

Ties Through Time
What things do we do together in the same special way?

From Past to Present
How can our traditions and the traditions of others make our lives more interesting?

Timeless Stories
How do stories from the past help us live in the present?

Time and Time Again
What things are worth repeating over time?

The Way We Were– The Way We Are
How can understanding the past help us live in the present?

Journeys in Time and Space

We read about and learn to appreciate people and places in our world today and in the past. We speculate about the future.

Off We Go!

Let's Explore
How do we get from here to there?

Make a Wish
How do dreams keep us going?

Take Me There
Where will we go? How will we grow?

All Aboard!
What can we learn by traveling?

Are We There Yet?
How can visits to other times and other places make our lives better?

Other Times, Other Places
What can we learn from reading about times and places we've never been?

Traveling On
Where do people's journeys take them?

Into the Unknown
What can we learn from visiting real and imaginary times and places?

Creativity

We learn about ways people use their creativity to solve problems, make decisions, create works of art, and express new ideas.

Open the Doors

Anything Is Possible
How do we think in new ways?

Imagine That!
How do we use our thinking caps?

Surprise Me!
How do we get all those great ideas?

Just Imagine!
How do we use our imaginations to do things?

Imagination.kids
How many ways can we use our imaginations?

Express Yourself!
How many forms can creativity take?

Think of It!
How do we find a new way?

I've Got It!
How many ways can people be creative?

Position for Writing

Left-handed and right-handed writers slant their papers differently from one another, but they sit and hold their pencils the same way.

Body Position

- Children should sit tall, with both feet flat on the floor and arms relaxed on a table or desk.
- Children should hold their papers at the top with their non-writing hand.

Paper Slant

- Paper should be positioned at a slant that is approximately parallel to the writing arm.
- For left-handed children, the paper should slant from the right at the top to the left at the bottom.
- Right-handed children should slant the paper from the left at the top to the right at the bottom.

Pencil Grip

- Children should grasp the pencil lightly between the thumb and index finger, usually about an inch above the pencil point.
- For a child who grasps the pencil too close to the point, a simple remedy is to wrap a rubber band around the pencil about an inch above the point. Have the child hold the pencil above the rubber band.

Legibility

Legibility should be the goal of handwriting instruction. Children should be praised for writing legibly, even though their writing may deviate from a perfect model. Legibility is based on flexible but standard criteria for letter form, size, and slant, and for letter and word spacing.

Letter Form

- Standards for letter form enable each letter to be distinguished clearly from other letters.
- In the letter *a*, for example, the round part of the letter must be open, and the letter must be closed at the top. The letter *a* must not be confused with *u*, *d*, or *o*.
- The letters *t* and manuscript *f* must be crossed; the letters *i* and *j* dotted.

Letter Size

- Small letters sit on the bottom line and touch the middle line.
- Tall letters sit on the bottom line and touch the top line.
- Letters with descenders have tails that go down under the bottom line and touch the line below.

Letter Slant

- Letters slant should be consistent.
- All letters may slant to the right, to the left, or be straight up and down.

Letter and Word Spacing

- Letters in a word should be evenly spaced. They should not be written too close together or too far apart.
- There should be more space between words in a sentence than between letters in a word. This allows each word to stand out.

D'Nealian™ Alphabet

a b c d e f g h i

j k l m n o p q r s t

u v w x y z

A B C D E F G

H I J K L M N O

P Q R S T U V

W X Y Z . , ' ?

1 2 3 4 5 6

7 8 9 10

Manuscript Alphabet

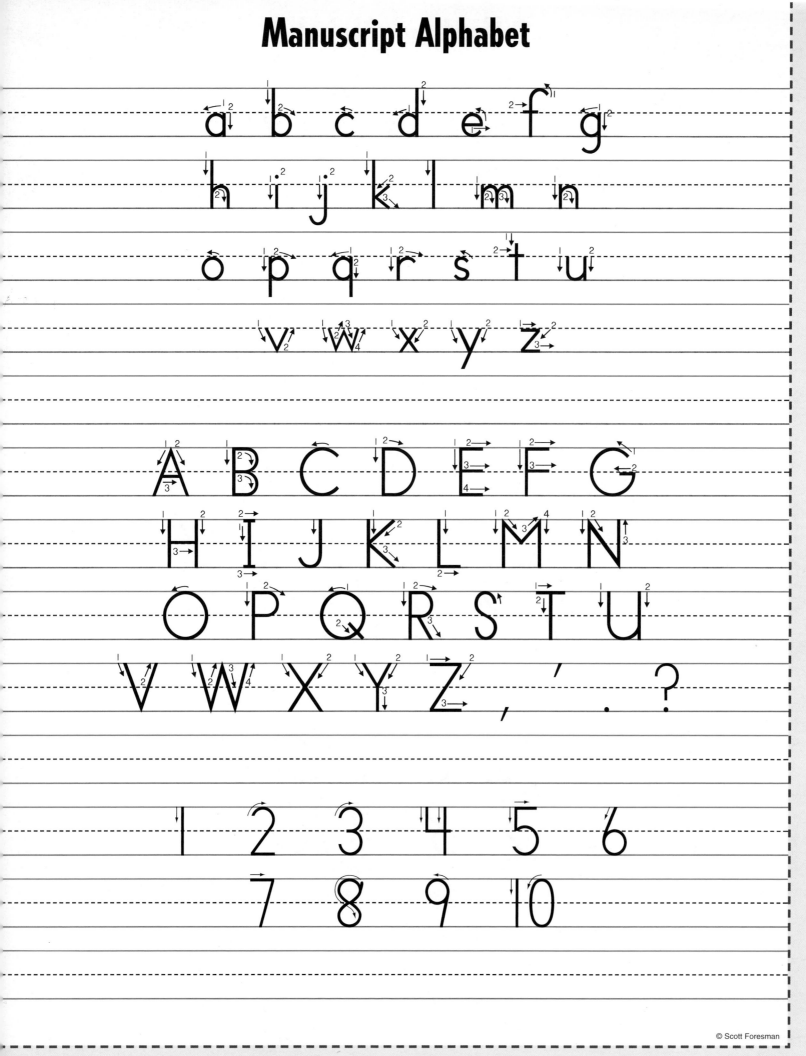

Word List

**High-Frequency/
Tested Words**

Unit 2 **A World of** **Wonders**	a the can at I am
Unit 3 **So Much to Do!**	like is big in it but
Unit 4 **Every Day Is** **Special**	look see my we little have
Unit 5 **Off We Go!**	not red do yellow what blue one two three
Unit 6 **Open the Doors**	here you to that up go get and where

Awards

Unit 1 **From Head to Toe**
by Eric Carle
Author awards: ALA Notable Book and ALA Best Book of the 1980s List

Mice Squeak, We Speak
by Arnold L. Shapiro and illustrated by Tomie dePaola
Illustrator awards: School Library Journal Best Books list, 1974 and 1977

Unit 2 **Mouse Mess**
by Linnea Riley
Book award: School Library Journal Best Books list, 1997

Miss Bindergarten Gets Ready for Kindergarten
by Joseph Slate
Author awards: New York Public Library citation, Library of Congress citation, and the Blue Hen Award, 1997

Growing Vegetable Soup
by Lois Ehlert
Author awards: American Library Association Notable Children's Book and *Boston Globe-Horn Book* Honor Award

Dinner at the Panda Palace
by Stephanie Calmenson and illustrated by Nadine Bernard Westcott
Author awards: Children's Choices Lists, 1995 and 1998
Illustrator awards: Children's Choices Lists, 1989 and 1990

Bunny Cakes
by Rosemary Wells
Book awards: School Library Best Books list and Children's Choices list, 1998

Unit 3 **Lilly's Purple Plastic Purse**
by Kevin Henkes
Book awards: Children's list and ALA Notable Books for Children list, 1997

No, No, Titus!
by Claire Masurel and illustrated by Shari Halpern
Illustrator award: Children's Choice List, 1997

Ginger
by Charlotte Voake
Book award: ALA Notable Book for Children, 1998

Mrs. McNosh Hangs Up Her Wash
by Sarah Weeks and illustrated by Nadine Bernard Westcott
Illustrator awards: Children's Choice lists, 1989 and 1990

Raccoons and Ripe Corn
by Jim Arnosky
Author awards: Outstanding Science Trade Books for Children list, 1988–1989, 1992, and 1995–1998, and Children's Choice list, 1989

Unit 4 **Looking for Crabs**
by Bruce Whatley
Author awards: Children's Book Council of Australia Notable Book, 1993, Children's Picture Book of the Year, 1998, and Australian Book of the Year, 1998

In the Rain with Baby Duck
by Amy Hest
Author awards: ALA Notable Books for Children list, 1986, and *Boston Globe-Horn Book* Award, 1996

On the Go
by Ann Morris
Author awards: Notable Children's Trade Books in the Field of Social Studies list, 1990, 1995, 1997

Three Little Kittens
by Paul Galdone
Author awards: Caldecott Honor Books, 1957 and 1958, and Newbery Honor Award, 1953

Shoes Like Miss Alice's
by Angela Johnson
Author awards: School Library Journal Best Books list, 1989, and Coretta Scott King Award, 1994

Unit 5 **Listen Buddy**
by Helen Lester
Author awards: California Young Reader Medal, 1991, and Children's Choice list, 1995

Corduroy
by Don Freeman
Author award: Caldecott Honor Book, 1958

I Need a Lunch Box
by Jeanette Caines and illustrated by Pat Cummings
Author awards: *Boston Globe-Horn Book* Award, 1992, and ALA Notable Books for Children list, 1996

Unit 6 **Zoom! Zoom! Zoom! I'm Off to the Moon**
by Dan Yaccarino
Author award: Children's Choices list, 1997

Hush! a Thai Lullaby
by Minfong Ho
Book awards: Caldecott Honor Book, 1997, and ALA Notable Books for Children list, 1996

Flower Garden
by Eve Bunting
Author awards: Caldecott Medal, 1995, ALA Notable Books for Children, 1990, 1991, 1992, 1995, and 1997

The Wolf's Chicken Stew
by Keiko Kasza
Book award: ALA Notable Books for Children list, 1988

Machines at Work
by Byron Barton
Book award: Notable Children's Trade Books in the Field of Social Studies list, 1987
Author award: ALA Notable Books for Children list, 1989

A House Is a House for Me
by Mary Ann Hoberman
Book award: American Book Award, 1993

Index

H

M

Skills in Context lessons and After Reading lessons.

N

O

P

R

idioms, **K.2** 176, **K.3** 58, 138, 208, **K.4** 132

multiple-meaning words, **K.2** 137, 138, **K.6** 186, 191

synonyms, **K.4** 96

unfamiliar words, **K.1** 202, **K.2** 59, 138, 174, **K.3** 24, 61, 99, 135, 173, 209, **K.4** 22, 60, 169, **K.5** 22, 62, 133, 169, 206, **K.6** 61, 95, 173, 182, 186, 190–191, 210

W

Webbing. *See* **Graphic organizers.**

Word attack skill. *See* **Phonics, Structural analysis, Vocabulary strategies.**

Word choice. *See* **Author's purpose.**

Word identification. *See* **Structural analysis, Vocabulary strategies.**

Wordless stories. *See* **Bibliographies.**

Word structure. *See* **Structural analysis.**

Word study. *See* **Phonics, Structural analysis.**

Word wall. *See* **ABC wall.**

Work stations. *See* **Cross-curricular work stations.**

Working with words. *See* **Vocabulary building, Vocabulary strategies.**

Writing assessment. *See* **Assessment,** scoring guide (rubric).

Writing forms/products
  ad, **K.2** 159
  book, **K.3** 193, **K.6** 193
  class diary, **K.1** 41, 75, 111, 149, 185, 221, **K.2** 43, 81, 119, 159, 195, 231, **K.3** 43, 81, 117, 157, 193, 229, **K.4** 43, 79, 115, 153, 189, 225, **K.5** 43, 81, 117, 155, 191, 227, **K.6** 45, 81, 117, 155, 193, 233
  description, **K.4** 67, 111, 149, 177, **K.6** 41, 229
  facts, **K.6** 221, 233
  fantasy, **K.6** 45
  labels/captions, **K.1** 33, 67, 103, 141, 177, 185, 209, 213, **K.2** 31, 35, 69, 73, 111, 153, 195, **K.3** 37, 187, **K.4** 103, 141, 153, 189, **K.5** 73
  letter/note/card, **K.4** 115, 225, **K.5** 31, 75, 227
  list, **K.1** 41, 207, **K.2** 69, 119, **K.4** 177, **K.5** 43, **K.6** 69, 181
  message, **K.2** 43, **K.6** 75
  multimedia presentation, **K.1** 15, 83, 157, 193, **K.2** 15, **K.3** 51, **K.5** 127, **K.6** 15, 127, 163

  name, **K.1** 41, 63, 71, 75, 107, 144, **K.2** 181, **K.4** 39, **K.5** 227
  news story, **K.3** 117, **K.5** 117
  personal experience, **K.2** 81, **K.4** 43, 79, **K.5** 39, 179, **K.6** 69, 117, 143, 193
  poem/rhyme, **K.2** 217, **K.5** 177
  poster, **K.2** 159
  sentence, **K.1** 209, 213, 221, **K.2** 39, 191, **K.3** 31, 35, 43, 105, 109, 111, **K.4** 39, **K.5** 105, 109, 117, 143, 147, 155, 223, **K.6** 117, 189, 221, 225, 233
  story, **K.2** 231, **K.3** 43, **K.4** 43, 79, **K.5** 81, 191, **K.6** 45, 193
  story extension, **K.5** 105, **K.6** 81
  summary, **K.6** 155

Writing, interactive, K.1 37, 71, 107, 145, 181, 217, **K.2** 39, 77, 118, 155, 191, 227, **K.3** 39, 77, 113, 153, 189, 225, **K.4** 39, 75, 111, 149, 185, 221, **K.5** 39, 77, 113, 151, 187, 223, **K.6** 41, 77, 113, 151, 193, 229

Writing modes
  descriptive, **K.4** 43, 189, **K.6** 233
  expository, **K.2** 43, 81, 119, 195, **K.3** 81, 117, 157, 193, 229, **K.4** 153, 225, **K.5** 43, 227
  narrative, **K.2** 231, **K.3** 43, **K.4** 79, 115, **K.5** 81, 117, 191, **K.6** 45, 81, 155
  persuasive, **K.2** 159

Writing process
  prewriting, **K.2** 35, 73, 109, 149, 185, 221, **K.3** 35, 73, 109, 149, 185, 221, **K.4** 35, 71, 107, 145, 181, 217, **K.5** 35, 73, 109, 147, 183, 219, **K.6** 37, 73, 109, 147, 185, 225
  publishing, **K.1** 41, 75, 111, 149, 185, 221, **K.2** 43, 81, 119, 159, 195, 231, **K.3** 43, 81, 117, 157, 193, 229, **K.4** 43, 79, 115, 153, 189, 225, **K.5** 43, 81, 117, 155, 191, 227, **K.6** 45, 81, 117, 155, 193, 233
  revising/editing, **K.1** 41, 75, 111, 149, 185, 221, **K.2** 43, 81, 119, 159, 195, 231, **K.3** 43, 81, 117, 157, 193, 229, **K.4** 43, 79, 115, 153, 189, 225, **K.5** 43, 81, 117, 155, 191, 227, **K.6** 45, 81, 117, 155, 193, 233

Writing strategies. *See* **Assessment,** scoring guide (rubric); **Writing process.**

Writing, with technology, K.1 15, 83, 157, 193, **K.2** 15, 51, **K.3** 51, 127, **K.4** 51, **K.5** 51, 127, **K.6** 15, 127, 163, 201

Acknowledgments

Text

K-W-L Strategy: The K-W-L Interactive Reading Strategy was developed and is used by permission of Donna Ogle, National-Louis University, Evanston, Illinois, coauthor of *Reading Today and Tomorrow,* Holt, Rinehart & Winston Publishers, 1988. (See also *The Reading Teacher,* February 1986, pp. 564–570.)

The Know Zone™: The Know Zone™ is a registered trademark of Addison Wesley Longman, Inc.

Scott Foresman Phonics System™: Scott Foresman Phonics System™ is a registered trademark of Addison-Wesley Educational Publishers, Inc.

Page 19: "Eletelephony" from *Tirra Lirra* by Laura E. Richards. Copyright © 1935 by Laura E. Richards. Reprinted by permission.

Page 55: "The Swing." Public domain.

Page 93: "Quack, Quack!" from *Oh Say Can You Say?* by Dr. Seuss™ and copyright © 1979 by Dr. Seuss Enterprises, L.P. 1979. Used by permission of Random House Children's Books, a division of Random House, Inc.

Page 131: "My Teddy Bear" from *Farther Than Far* by Margaret Hillert. Used by permission of the author who controls all rights.

Page 167: "Yesterday's Paper" by Mabel Watts. Reprinted by permission of Mabel Watts.

Page 203: "Rope Rhyme" from *Honey, I Love* by Eloise Greenfield. Text copyright © 1978 by Eloise Greenfield. Used by permission of HarperCollins Publishers.

Artists

Cynthia Fisher: pages 16a, 17b, 52b, 53b, 90a, 91a, 128a, 129a, 164a, 165b, 200a, 201a
Laura Freeman-Hines: page 89c
John Steven Gurney: page 198c
Lyn Martin: pages i, ii, 21, 57
Deborah Melman: pages 126c, 162c
Warner McGee: page 88a
Laura Ovresat: page 15c
Jennifer Schneider: pages 51b, 51c
Paul Sharp: pages 14c, 50c

Photographs

Unless otherwise credited, all photographs are the property of Scott Foresman, a division of Pearson Education. Page abbreviations are as follows: (T) top, (C) center, (B) bottom, (L) left, (R) right.
Page 93: PhotoDisc
Page 167 (T): PhotoDisc

Notes

Notes